D1028862

SOUTHWEST INDIAN
CRAFT ARTS

SOUTHWEST INDIAN CRAFT ARTS

Clara Lee Tanner

UNIVERSITY OF ARIZONA PRESS · TUCSON

About the author . . .

CLARA LEE TANNER is the author of *Southwest Indian Painting, Prehistoric Southwestern Craft Arts,* and *Apache Indian Baskets,* as well as of many articles on Indian arts, crafts, and religion. A member of the Anthropology Department of the University of Arizona since 1928, she has traveled extensively among the Indians of the Southwest and has frequently served as a jury member for Indian craft and painting shows.

Sketches by	*Photography by*
John Hannah	Douglas Lindsey
Frances Angleman	E. Tad Nichols

Sixth printing 1982

THE UNIVERSITY OF ARIZONA PRESS

Copyright © 1968
The Arizona Board of Regents
All Rights Reserved

This book was set in 10/12 Linotype Times Roman
Manufactured in the U.S.A.

I.S.B.N.-0-8165-0083-5
L.C. No. 66-24299

TO JOHN

A Word From the Author

DEEPLY GRATEFUL am I to all who contributed, in large ways and small, to the production of this book. Whatever virtue there may be in a published volume, the author whose name it bears can claim but a small part thereof, for the information comes from many sources, inspiration from numerous directions, and the tedium of commas and colons and their ilk must be shared with others. To one and all my thanks.

Time is of the essence in writing: To The University of Arizona and its Department of Anthropology my deepest appreciation for a sabbatical year in which to pursue the unbroken chain of thought essential to the first writing of a book. My gratitude also goes unstintingly to the publishers, The University of Arizona Press, and most particularly to Mr. Marshall Townsend and Miss Kit Scheifele who converted chores into pleasures through their happy cooperation. Most grateful am I to Mr. Raymond Carlson, editor of the ever beautiful *Arizona Highways,* for his cooperation in arranging use of the color sections from that magazine.

During more than twenty-five years of research in the field of the craft arts, I visited and worked in more museums, art galleries, shops, and other storehouses of craft treasures than could be listed here. A generous thank you to each and every one of them. Most particularly should be mentioned the Arizona State Museum, The University of Arizona, Tucson; not only have their collections been made available by the directors, Drs. Emil W. Haury and Raymond Thompson, and Edwin N. Ferdon, Associate Director, but also the majority of black and white photos in this book were made possible through their courtesy — my deep appreciation to them and to Wilma Kaemlein, Curator of Collections, and Douglas Lindsey, photographer, of their staff. E. T. Nichols, Tucson, took the remaining black and white pictures. Frances Angleman and John W. Hanna are responsible for the drawings. Special thanks too, to the following directors and their respective museums for full cooperation extended to me to use their collections for study purposes: Dr. Edward B. Danson, Museum of Northern Arizona, Flagstaff, Arizona; Dr. Carl S. Dentzel, Southwest Museum, Los Angeles; Mr. H. Thomas Cain, Heard Museum, Phoenix, Arizona; Dr. Charles C. DiPeso, Amerind Foundation, Dragoon, Arizona; Dr. Bertha Dutton, Museum of New Mexico, Santa Fe.

Other museums or other collections which have been of value for study through the years include: The Laboratory of Anthropology, Santa Fe, New Mexico; Indian Arts Fund Collection, Santa Fe; Denver Art Museum, Denver, Colorado.

Many Indian traders in the Southwest have been most gracious to let me study their collections. Among others I should like to acknowledge the following: Clay Lockett, Tom Bahti, and John F. Tanner in Tucson; Dave Newman and the late Frank Patania, Santa Fe, New Mexico; M. L. Woodard, Tobe Turpin, and The Gallup Indian Trading Company, Gallup, New Mexico; and Tony Reyna, Taos, New Mexico. Very helpful also were the collections of the Navajo Arts and Crafts Guild, at the time of study under the direction of Russell Lindgren, and the Hopi Silver Craft Guild, directed by Fred Kabotie. Elizabeth Estrada of Tucson collected baskets from the Papago Indians and sold them for the tribe; she generously put them at my disposal for study.

Without fail there are individuals who wittingly or unwittingly contribute information to one's files. Again there are far too many to mention; the following but head the long list of names which I shall always remember: Florence Hawley Ellis, who answered many bothersome questions which arose after the first writing of the book; Kenneth Chapman, Santa Fe, who has always shared generously of his wealth of knowledge in this field; George and Mahala Rummage, whose years with the Indians have enriched my store of knowledge; Dorothy and Kendall Cumming who shared their firsthand information about the Jicarillas; and Read Mullan of Phoenix whose superb collections are an inspiration. Ethel Chambers and Troy McDonald volunteered their time and talents for the onerous — but not thankless — task of manuscript reading.

This book was written with several thoughts in mind. Perhaps the greatest motivation was the fact that there existed no single volume covering all the craft arts of the Indians of the Southwestern United States. Obviously, one book cannot be all things to all people. The writer is aware of gaps in each chapter. However, an effort has been made, first, to cover all the major and the more important minor crafts of these Indians, and second, to give certain pertinent facts relative to these in their recent and current developments. There are inequalities in the treatment of each craft, sometimes intentional, to avoid boring repetition, sometimes because emphasis on certain aspects was decidedly more significant.

With pride the writer points out that the majority of the black-and-white pictures were taken from the collections of the Arizona State Museum, with a few from the John F. Tanner collection. Individual credit is given on the several remaining photos. Negatives of the photographs of the specimens from the Arizona State Museum have been deposited in their files.

To paraphrase a former acknowledgment, I should like to say that my words cannot equal the beauty of the Southwest Indian craft pieces. Indian art objects have been the inspiration through the years for the build-up of knowledge on this subject. To their creators go my deepest appreciation and thanks for their works of a beauty which words and pictures can but fleetingly capture and pass on to others.

Clara Lee Tanner

Tucson, Arizona

Contents

Culture Molds the Craft Arts   *Chapter I*

THE AMERICAN SOUTHWEST is an area whose geographic boundaries have changed as white men have viewed it from different viewpoints. The core of the area, however, in terms of the approach to this survey of the craft arts of the Southwest Indians, consists of the states of Arizona and New Mexico, and small sections of Colorado and Utah.

Prehistorically, the Southwest was occupied by populations which ranged from the first sparsely distributed hunting and gathering groups to later settled agriculturalists. There were two manifestations of the former, the more easterly Big Game Hunters, and a western Desert Culture which concentrated on small game and the collection of plant foods. The two cultures met in the Southwest. Large projectile points, sometimes associated with the bones of mammoth or other big game, testify to the presence of the first group. Less spectacular, but equally significant to this story, are the remains of the small-game hunters and gatherers — smaller stone tools and weapons, bits of basketry, and fragments of crude textiles.

Perhaps it was the food gatherer who, because of his knowledge of plant life, became the first cultivator. Transition to settled village life was slow at best: the first Big Game Hunters date back some ten or twelve thousand years and the Desert culture was, perhaps, a little later, while the earliest farmers made their debut well within the first millenium B.C.

Although certain qualities were basic to many expressions of all aboriginal settled Southwesterners, within the area as a whole there were sufficient differences between groups to warrant the archaeologists' designation of Hohokam, Anasazi, and Mogollon cultures (Fig. 1.1). The Hohokam occupied southern Arizona, developed a high stone-age culture based on irrigation farming, and distinguished themselves in the making of fine red-on-buff pottery, excellent shell and small stone carving, and, very probably, outstanding textiles. Anasazi folk of northern Arizona and New Mexico and southern Colorado and Utah excelled in the building of pueblos (multiple-unit houses), in the precise decoration of black-on-white pottery, in basketry, and in shell and turquoise mosaics. The Mogollon of southwestern New Mexico very possibly were an important link between the Southwest and Mexico, transmitting significant traits to the other two groups.

The consensus is that the Mogollon people — as a distinct culture — disappeared from the Southwestern scene before the arrival of the Spanish in 1540; possibly some few of them migrated into the Rio Grande area. The Hohokam were the probable ancestors of the historic Pimas and Papagos, while the Anasazi were the ancestors of the pueblo folk. Ties seem not to have been too strong between the Hohokam and their presumed descendants, for the latter did not pursue the advanced irrigation agriculture nor produce the fine ceramics so typical of their ancestors.

Quite a different story can be told for the Anasazi and their connections with the historic puebloans. Archaeologists have divided the total Anasazi culture history into Basket Maker and Pueblo periods, the first so named because of high sophistication in the basketry craft, and the second for the most unusual type of architecture developed in the entire Southwest — the pueblo. To be sure, there are other important culture traits which characterize each phase of each period, these leading to divisions into Basket Maker II and III, and Pueblo I, II, III, IV, and V (the last the historic period).

A pueblo is a large unit of joined houses; there may be one or several such "apartments" in a village. The historic peoples who continue to live in this unusual type of village are called "puebloans." Continuity of culture from Anasazi times to the present can be seen in pueblo traits today: the puebloans have remained basically a stone-age people, following in the ways of their ancestors in their rituals, government, social order, and mores, and further carrying on their craft traditions.

Until quite recently those things which Europeans brought to the native Southwesterner were

1

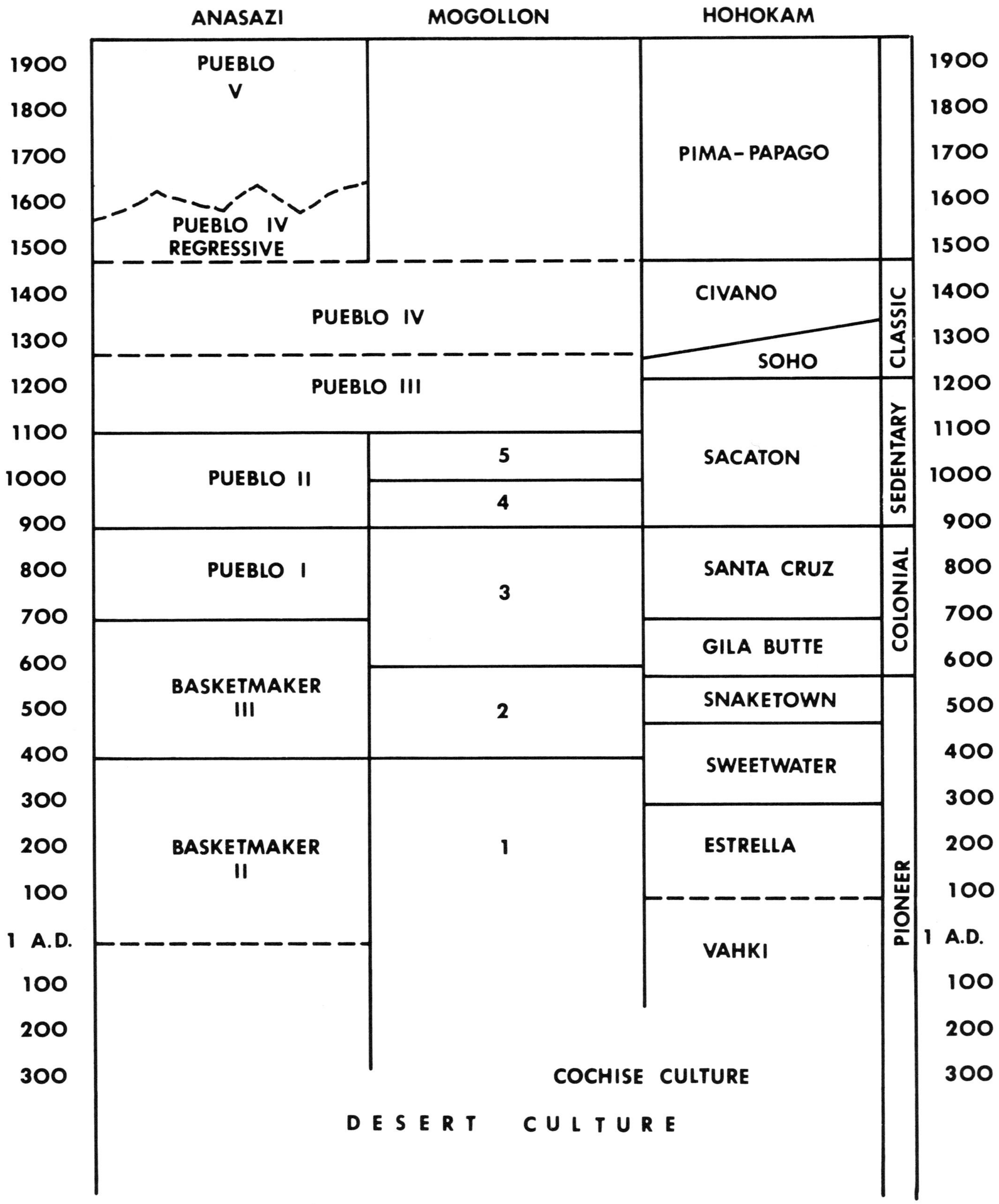

ANASAZI | MOGOLLON | HOHOKAM

Year	ANASAZI	MOGOLLON	HOHOKAM		Year
1900	PUEBLO V				1900
1800			PIMA – PAPAGO		1800
1700					1700
1600	PUEBLO IV REGRESSIVE				1600
1500					1500
1400	PUEBLO IV		CIVANO	CLASSIC	1400
1300			SOHO		1300
1200	PUEBLO III				1200
1100	PUEBLO II	5	SACATON	SEDENTARY	1100
1000		4			1000
900					900
800	PUEBLO I	3	SANTA CRUZ	COLONIAL	800
700			GILA BUTTE		700
600	BASKETMAKER III		SNAKETOWN		600
500		2			500
400			SWEETWATER		400
300					300
200	BASKETMAKER II	1	ESTRELLA	PIONEER	200
100					100
1 A.D.			VAHKI		1 A.D.
100					100
200					200
300			COCHISE CULTURE		300

DESERT CULTURE

FIGURE 1.1 Sequence of Southwest culture periods.

superimposed on the stone-age base of the aborigines' culture. Many of these culture traits have been accepted superficially; some have penetrated more deeply. Up until World War II, some of these people were still living a life which reflected that of their ancestors more than it did their historical contacts. But that situation has changed rapidly in the years since the war.

Today, the pueblo people include the Hopi Indians of northeastern Arizona, the Zuñis of western New Mexico, and the numerous villagers of the Rio Grande Valley (Fig. 1.2).

Hopis, who speak a Shoshonean language, occupy three mesas in northeastern Arizona (Fig. 1.3). In addition to their two tribal villages of Walpi and Sichomovi on First Mesa — to the east — there is a third pueblo, Hano, which was established about 1700 by Tewa-speaking people from the Rio Grande. At the foot of this mesa is a more recently established village, Polacca. Twelve miles away is Second Mesa; the three Hopi villages here are Mishongnovi, Shipaulovi, and Shungopovi; at the base of the mesa is Toreva. Another ten miles to the west is Third Mesa on which are the villages of Old Oraibi, Hotevilla, and Bacabi. New Oraibi is at the foot of this mesa. Moenkopi, another Hopi village, is forty miles to the west of Third Mesa.

Zuñi Indians speak a language quite different from all other puebloans and it has been named "Zuñian." Most of the Zuñis live in the main pueblo of the same name as the tribe, although some live in three smaller, outlying villages, Ojo Caliente, Pescado, and Nutria.

The Rio Grande villagers speak either a Keresan or a Tanoan language, the latter including the Tiwa, Tewa, and Towa subdivisions. Towas occupy the village of Jémez, while the Tiwas live in Taos, Pícuris, Isleta, and Sandía. Tewas inhabit the villages of Santa Clara, San Ildefonso, San Juan, Tesuque, and Nambé, and the Keresan-speaking people live in Acoma, Laguna, Cochití, Santo Domingo, Zía, Santa Ana, and San Felipe. Members of a language group often share closer affiliations in other traits than they do with members of another language group. This is true in some measure with the craft arts.

Other Southwest Indian tribes include the previously mentioned Pimas and Papagos of southern Arizona (Fig. 1.2), the former living along the Gila River, and the latter on the desert to the south. These two tribes are language brothers, both speaking the Piman tongue. Members of the Yuman language group are widely dispersed in Arizona — Yumas and Cocopas in the extreme southwestern section, Mohaves about half way up the Colorado River on the western edge, Havasupais in a canyon of the same name just west of the Grand Canyon, and Walapais on the high plateau to the west of this last tribe. Two other members of the Yuman group live in the interior of Arizona, the Yavapais around Prescott, and the Maricopas near Phoenix. Some Yavapais-mixed-with-Apaches also live on the fringes of Phoenix.

The Athabascan-speaking Navajos and Apaches were the last tribes to arrive in the Southwest (Fig. 1.2). It is quite likely that they preceded the Spanish by several centuries; they came from the far north, possibly by way of the Plains. Some Navajos have remained in northwest New Mexico, but in time many others have spread into north-central and northeastern Arizona. Apaches, on the other hand, have settled largely in the south, the Mescaleros now living in south-central New Mexico, and several bands each on the San Carlos and Fort Apache reservations in east-central Arizona. The Jicarillas are located in extreme northern New Mexico.

It is believed that the Apaches and Navajos borrowed many culture traits from the settled populations of the Southwest. Quite significant are the puebloan influences on the Navajos. Many of these seem to date back to the years following the Pueblo Revolt of 1680 against the Spanish, as the result of which some puebloans left the Rio Grande and lived with the Navajos in the Governador country of northern New Mexico.

A background knowledge of these tribes as a whole is helpful in understanding their craft arts. No two groups are exactly alike, yet all have inherited broadly comparable patterns of culture traits. Historic contacts have affected these groups differently, for they have varied: some have been direct and intensive, as in the Rio Grande Valley, while others have been indirect and sparse, as in the case of the Hopis. Some of these people have taken on white man's religion; puebloans in the Rio Grande, for example, have become Catholics, and yet at the same time they have preserved their own rituals. The Pimas, on the other hand, gave up their native religion when they were Christianized. Preservation of aboriginal patterns in religion has been a factor in the perpetuation of many aspects of native culture, crafts no less than other traits.

All of the Southwest Indians lived in villages or small settlements. Some farmed more extensively than others; all hunted to some degree. Before the arrival of Europeans (and in varying amounts thereafter), they supplied their own meager household equipment, largely vessels of clay or basketry. They wove their own clothing of cotton, supplementing or supplanting this with animal skins in some instances. They were nature worshippers, some developing elaborate religious rituals. At most,

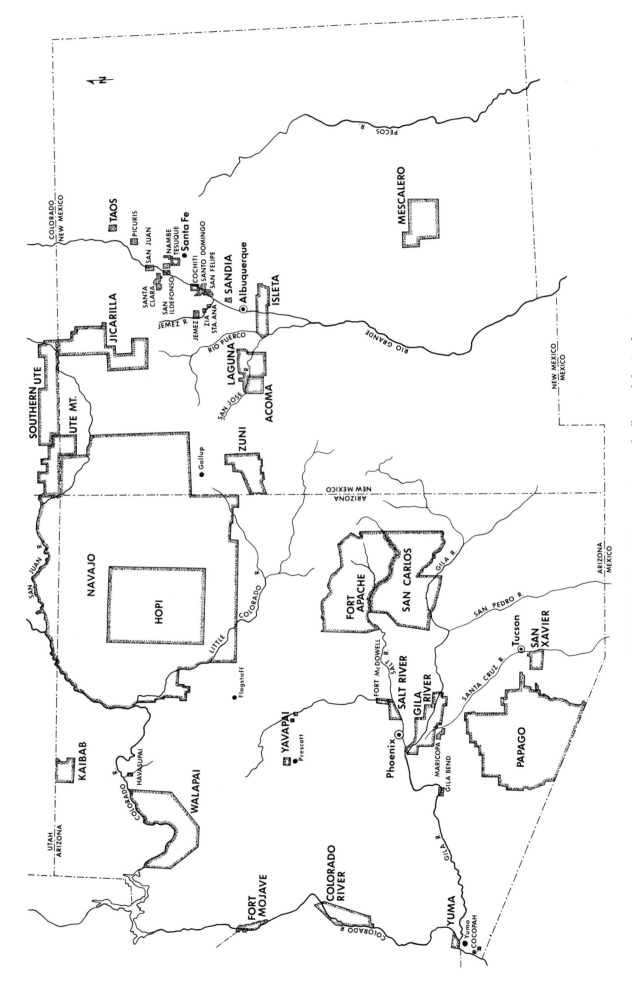

FIGURE 1.2 Map of the reservations and villages of the Southwest.

the native tribes had village chiefs or leaders; none had a leader over all the tribe.

Natively there was a high integration of the social, political, and religious elements which led to unity of thinking and purpose. Where these ideas have prevailed, they have tended to aid in the perpetuation of the Indians' craft arts. With their breakdown, some of the crafts are disappearing.

The native and highly integrated social order is giving way to a white-introduced tribal council. The latter is a separate and distinct entity, and it tends to function as a matter-of-fact unit divested of any connections with other aspects of native life. The council is more concerned with the economic aspects of life than with the religious; it is more interested in formal education than in the "old ways." Since the tribal council is not directly concerned with the enactment of age-old rites nor the perpetuation of the traditional ways of life, it seems to have created the first great dichotomy in the lives of many of these native populations.

And what has this to do with the native crafts? Possibly a great deal. Just a few years ago the Navajo Tribal Council was about to abolish the Navajos' own Arts and Crafts Guild, for it was not an economic success as was uranium. It is quite possible that, with no financial support from the tribe, the efforts of many fine crafts workers would have come to an end, for the guild has been an assured outlet for the best in rugs, silver, and other Navajo arts. The guild was saved by an understanding Navajo on the council — a man who is also a fine craftsman.

Perhaps one of the most important aspects of the changing or disappearing craft arts is the economic. With increased populations and means of transportation, the Indian is becoming more and more a part of the white man's world. He is coming to realize that he must get on the economic bandwagon of the whites, and that one of the first and most important ways to get along in his expanding world is to better his economic status. The old patterns of reciprocal relationships between the Indian and the universe, wherein the native danced for the gods and the gods brought the rain in return, are fast disappearing with the acquisition of a cash economy which brings in its wake scientific knowledge and machinery. Thus will disappear the kilt adorned with the cloud-rain prayer. Sifter baskets will no longer be needed when the village winnowing machine can do the job faster and more effectively. Native needs for native crafts will be wiped out by a changing economy, by the loss of native religion, through education, and through the acquisition of substitute materials.

Thus, several avenues of change may be approached, or the crafts will disappear completely.

White men may perpetuate the old forms by demanding them, as they were formerly made for and used by the Indians. Some basket types, such as certain Hopi styles, have been perpetuated in this manner. Or the craft may be changed in some ways to suit the tastes of the non-Indian — pottery, for example, has decreased in size, and new shapes have been added in response to demands of the buying public. Or completely new developments may take place, such as the weaving of rugs in place of wearing-blankets by the Navajo Indians, or the making of silver chokers for sale to the white man in place of the "squash blossom" necklace.

But this is the story of any craft art in any part of the world. Change is inevitable. The only unpredictable qualities are the manner and degree of change. Circumstances peculiar to the Southwest have directed the nature of this change. The Spanish brought the first new religion, sheep, horses, new ideas pertaining to dress, household furnishings, and politics. Mexicans gave the natives new design ideas, further trade items such as cloth and metal objects, and new styles in textile fabrics. Then came the Anglo-American with a never-ending variety of new ideas and material objects; reservations, education, religion, tribal councils, and changing philosophies of a way of life have all affected each tribe in varying degrees. The first Anglo traders of the early nineteenth century brought beads and cloth, the railroads of the 1880's brought endless bolts of materials, blankets, household utensils and furnishings, and in time, the farm equipment which would revolutionize the economy of the natives.

World War II was to be one of the most vital factors in the Indian's changing way of life. First, it took many of the natives into another world. Young men came to know the value of education, they came to realize the importance of scientific knowledge in agriculture and in other areas of economic interest, they had their first real taste of another way of life. The simplicity of aboriginal life could not withstand the experiences of the young people in World War II and postwar years.

The Navajo hogan and the Apache wickiup have been exchanged in many cases for a stone or timber house like that of the white man. The digging stick has been replaced by the tractor. Business suits and crew cuts are more commonly seen among Navajos than ever before. Public schools are quickly replacing the old federal Indian schools and attendance is not only greater but also more regular. The new education, which is no longer of a special and limited variety for the Indian alone, is better preparing the native for his inevitable competition with the whites. Many young people are going on to college.

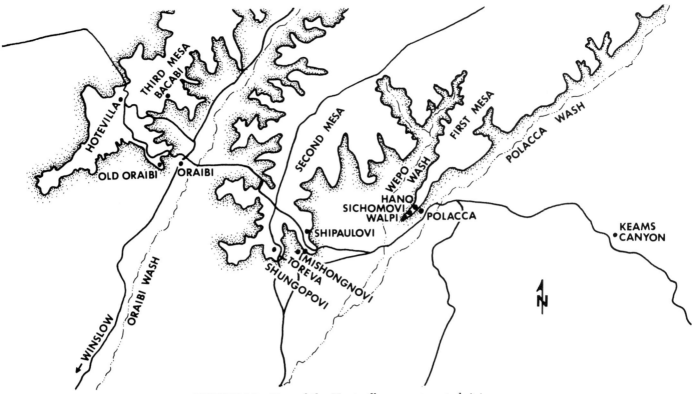

FIGURE 1.3 Map of the Hopi villages, east-central Arizona

Again, all of these trends are affecting the native crafts of the Indian, tending to wipe out many of them. Higher education is directing some of the young Indians into the realm of the fine arts and completely away from the crafts. What will come of this trend is unpredictable; too, it is not a part of this book which is concerned solely with the Southwest Indians' native expressions, their craft arts.

Baskets  *Chapter II*

BASKETMAKING is the oldest utensil-producing craft in the New World. It was formerly thought that this art was introduced from the Old World; more recently, however, archaeologists have found evidences which possibly indicate a native origin for basketry, particularly for the twined variety. Several of these finds "permit a suggestion that simple basketry and probably other weaving techniques . . . were widely practiced in western North America before textile work was known in the Eurasiatic Neolithic."[1] The date for this earliest work is before 7,000 B.C., while additional evidences of twined and coiled basketry, cordage, netting, and matting have been found in various Desert Culture sites dating from 6,000 to 1,000 B.C. Although direct connections cannot be made, this long ancestry may explain the marked degree of sophistication of this craft in Basket Maker II times.

Basketmaking is a technique for constructing utensils and occasional other objects from natural elements such as rushes, willow, or grasses. Various plants limited to certain locales are also important, such as yucca, squawbush, devil's claw, and beargrass in the Southwest. Elements derived from these plants are sufficiently rigid to allow the weaver to produce the basket without benefit of any artificial device, in other words, solely by hand manipulation of the materials. Most of the materials used by native historic basket weavers were also exploited by the prehistoric folk.

Prehistoric Background

The basic techniques in use historically were established in pre-Columbian times. The three most important techniques — coiling, wicker, and plaiting — were highly developed in prehistoric years. Designs in all three were likewise of high artistic quality.

Coiling is a technique in which a flexible element (weft) is wrapped or sewed about a foundation (warp) which is more or less rigid (Fig. 2.1). Sewing elements may be narrow or broad, carefully prepared or irregular, vertical or slanting in rela-tion to the horizontal foundation. The weaver may manipulate the coil in a clockwise or counterclockwise motion. Foundations may consist of a single rod (rare), three rods, two rods and a bundle (a mass of shredded material), a bundle, or multiple rods or slats. Arrangements of foundations may vary from tribe to tribe. Sewing is accomplished by piercing the previous coil with an awl and inserting through the resulting hole the moving element; the latter also encloses the coil. Coils may be spaced apart (open coil) or touching (close coil).

Although prehistoric coiled basketry was elaborately developed, it was also widely standardized. In spite of variety in the types of foundations and the arrangement thereof, common combinations persisted, such as two rods and bundle, three rods, or a single rod. Stitching was usually close. Much Basket Maker sewing was fine, counting five to seven coils and nine to twelve stitches to the inch. A great deal of the later prehistoric Pueblo basketry had the same coil count, but some of the sewing was finer, with as many as twenty stitches to the inch. Rare instances of extremely coarse coiling did appear, with examples of one or two coils per inch and stitches more than an inch apart.

There are two major types of rim finish in coiled basketry: a self rim, which is one finished in the regular sewing stitch of the basket, and a false braid or herringbone stitch (Fig. 2.1). Morris and Burgh note that about 75 percent of the Anasazi rims were finished off in the latter manner, either in the tip alone, which was standard for this type, or occasionally around the entire circuit of the basket.[2]

Basketry design is important in relation to the craft arts in general. Prehistorically, Anasazi basketry designs influenced patterns in pottery, textiles, and possibly in many lesser arts. Form and design were closely connected in the ancient baskets. Plain or more complex encircling bands were featured on open trays (Fig. 2.2); so, too, were simple and complex vertical or spiraling bands. Decorative fields on this form were often divided into thirds, fourths,

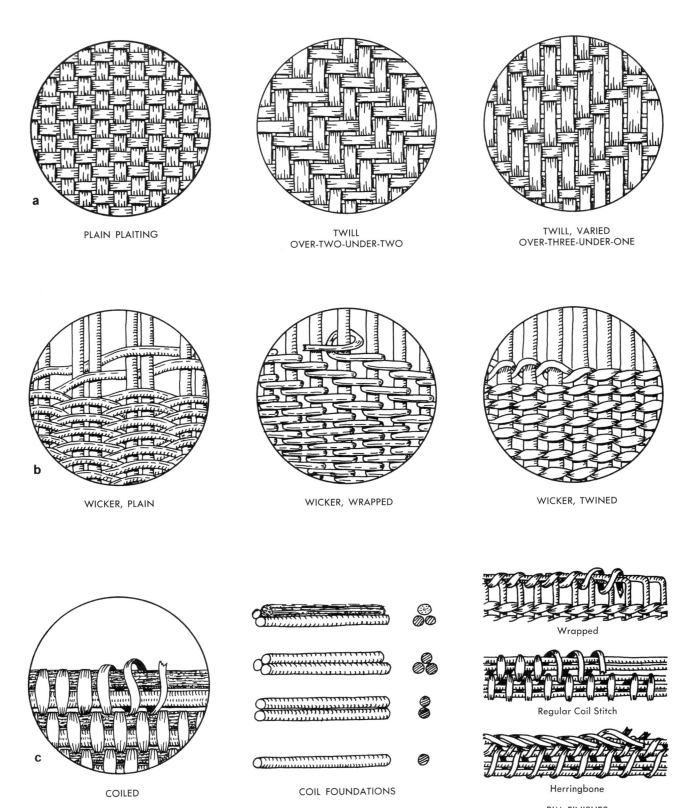

PLAIN PLAITING

TWILL
OVER-TWO-UNDER-TWO

TWILL, VARIED
OVER-THREE-UNDER-ONE

WICKER, PLAIN

WICKER, WRAPPED

WICKER, TWINED

COILED

COIL FOUNDATIONS

Wrapped

Regular Coil Stitch

Herringbone

RIM FINISHES

FIGURE 2.1 Techniques for making baskets. (a). Plaiting. Plain plaiting is a simple alternation of elements over and under each other in a simple one-one-one-one rhythm. When the rhythm changes to over-two-under-two or over-three-under-one or some other variation, it is called twilled. It is in twill plaiting that all designing is done in this weave. (b). Wicker weave may be plain: a single element (the weft) woven over and under the stationary "spokes" (warps). Designing is possible when wefts are dyed. The weft can be wrapped around the warp, or double wefts can be alternated in passing over and under the warps and twined about each other. (c). Coiled weave is the most productive of design; it is simply sewing wefts about the warps. The foundation in this weave can be varied: a bundle, two rods and a bundle, or one, two, or three rods. Over the bundle is sewed the weft which may be wider or narrower and the color of which can be changed at any point. *Rims* vary in basketry: they may be simply wrapped, or sewed in the regular coiled stitch, or finished off in a more elaborate herringbone stitch.

or in half (Fig. 2.2). Basket Maker tray patterns were more complex than the later Puebloan; the latter also had a tendency to be more spotty in the placement of designs, with clusters of three or four units commonly used.

Burden or carrying baskets, which were deep forms often expanding from a small base to a very wide mouth, featured banded decoration (Fig. 2.2). Single or double bands of decoration were typical; in the Basket Maker period they were more complex in variety and number of elements used, while in Pueblo III times they tended to be simpler in the same features. Bowls presented the simplest decoration of these three shapes. Prominent designs on bowls were plain repeated bands, radiating patterns, and spotty designs, all of equally elemental nature (Fig. 2.2). All in all, prehistoric basketry displayed excellent adaptation of design to specific forms.

Designs on prehistoric baskets were angular, for, then as now, they were controlled by technique — the crossing of relatively wide elements at right angles, or nearly so, dictated this angularity. Earlier designs were executed in black, later ones in black and red. Later, too, the weavers increased the number of design elements, balanced motifs in both form and color, used framing lines, and increased the mass of pattern in relation to total space. The still-later Classic Puebloan again used black alone; framing lines were seldom employed and the amount of pattern in relation to total area was greatly decreased. When red was used, there was simple, opposed balance in color and design. It is quite likely that increased interest in ceramic decoration accounted for decreased artistry in basketry.

Basket decoration was predominantly in dyed splints used against natural colored ones. Bird quills and turquoise mosaic occurred on rare pieces of prehistoric basketry.

Elements of design in coiled basketry were more numerous and occurred in more complex forms than in the other two types of weaving. Common elements included lines, bands, steps, zigzags, triangles, squares, rhomboids (which result from loose coiling), diamonds, and highly geometric life forms such as birds and mountain sheep (Fig. 2.3). A single design usually incorporated several of these elements.

The simplest of basketry techniques is plain wicker: it is the weaving over and under of relatively stiff twigs or elements. It can become more complex, for, in addition to plain wicker, there are twined and double wicker. This weave was much more limited than coiling in its use prehistorically, and very limited in distribution. Underhill reports its first use by the ancestors of the Hopi Indians between 1200 and 1300[3] (Fig. 2.1).

In all prehistoric wicker work, design was simple and limited. Patterns were usually in horizontal bands, with an occasional diagonal slant to them. Elements included small triangles, zigzags, wavy lines, cogwheels, and straight lines.

In the Anasazi area, plaited basketry was not quite as old as the coiled style. Although similar to the general weaving process of wicker, plaiting is done with more flexible elements, usually with wider splints, and with sharp right-angle relationships of warps and wefts. In wicker, the warps are usually whole rods while the weft is whole or split; in plaiting, both elements are equal in size, shape, and flexibility. In wicker, the warps are vertical, the wefts horizontal, while in plaiting there is no distinction and therefore no consistent direction for either element (Fig. 2.1).

Plain plaiting, which was rare in the prehistoric Southwest, involves a simple over-one-under-one rhythm of weaving. Twilled plaiting, which was more popular, is over-two-under-two, or over-three-under-three, although there may be occasional other alternations of elements. In all rhythms except plain plaiting this technique produces a design in the weave itself. In prehistoric times some splints were dyed black; in this manner the design was emphasized against the natural-colored elements.

Designs in ancient plaited basketry were large in size, angular and geometric, usually allover, and almost always balanced and symmetrical. Design elements were simple and included frets, lines (particularly in the meander style), diamonds, zigzags, chevrons, and squares. Simpler or more complex arrangements of one or several of these elements formed the design. Parallel zigzags, diamonds within diamonds, or other comparable dispositions of the basic forms were employed. The most common form of plaited basket was the shallow bowl, characteristically with a wooden ring enclosed by the plaiting at the rim. This "ring basket" has persisted from the Basket Maker III period down to the present.

The above is but the briefest summary of prehistoric basketry. Nonetheless, it demonstrates the pre-Columbian existence of all the basic techniques of basket weaving, and of the traditional forms, elements, and designs. This was the inheritance of the historic Southwest Indian.

Historic Background

To what degree this inheritance was carried on is unknown to ethnologists (except for the Hopis) since the historic record is incomplete. Again with the exception of the Hopis, the trend has been in the direction of the gradual elimination of basket-making among the puebloans as well as among some of the other tribes. Commercialization has

FIGURE 2.2 Layouts, or methods for arranging design, for decorating baskets. *Top row:* all banded, with a continuous layout, a spotted one, the band quartered, and an organizationally banded style — no drawn lines but the pattern occupying a definite band. *Second row:* radiate static and dynamic, allover, and centered. *Bottom row:* repeated, circling continuous, irregular — pendent from the rim, and composite — this one centered and banded.

FIGURE 2.3 Design elements in prehistoric coiled basketry. There were a few life forms — birds and mountain sheep — but geometrics were much more common. Many of the latter have carried over into historic years.

played a part in perpetuating the craft among the Hopis and Papagos.

Women are the basket weavers among the contemporary Southwest Indian tribes except for Rio Grande Puebloans. Ellis says that basketry in the Rio Grande was a man's job except for the "old style twilled baskets of yucca made by their own women."[4] Formerly, some Hopi men produced a limited amount of basketry,[5] but today they no longer weave. No basket weavers were known to have given all their time to this craft, for this was always a part-time or pick-up chore. One interesting and late historic trend has been for individual women to develop reputations as outstanding weavers. However, no names have become as famous in basket weaving as in other crafts.

Plaited Basketry

Plaiting survived into the modern period among the Jémez, San Felipe, and other Rio Grande Puebloans, and the Hopis, Pimas, and Papagos. Quite recently some of these tribes have given up the craft. There is no evidence that Navajos, Apaches, Paiutes, or Yumans made this type of basketry. Today, Hopi and Jémez women are the chief producers of plaited work.

Jémez

For a number of years Jémez puebloans have produced a ring-bowl basket which measures from about 11 to 15 inches in diameter; larger ones were woven for wood baskets. All of these baskets are characteristically shallow but deeper than the same style made by Hopis. The material is yucca. To form the rim, a square slightly larger than the rim of the basket is plaited and pushed into a heavy ring made of a sumac rod; the edges of the square are then pulled over the outside of the basket. With twined stitching the outer portion is secured to the wall of the basket, and the uneven outer edge is then cut, leaving a fringe more than an inch in length all the way around; the Jémez fringe tends to be longer than that on the Hopi basket. According to Douglas, this is the only plaited shape at Jémez (Fig. 2.4). He says also that "the only design produced shows concentric diamonds."[6] Today

there is slight elaboration of the diamond motif and some use of zigzags.

Papago and Pima

Papago and Pima plaited basketry reflected greater variety in both shapes and designs. Moreover, these tribes used different materials, the Papagos favoring leaves of the sotol (a native long-leafed plant), and the Pimas using stems of a native cane. Although an over-three-under-three technique was used by both tribes, a few other variations occurred, such as over-two-under-two in old Pima mats and in later Papago pieces.

Papagos scraped the spines off the sotol leaves, split them lengthwise, and dried them in the sun. To make the elements flexible when the weaver was ready to use them, they were formerly buried in damp sand, and more recently sprinkled and wrapped in a towel.

Kissel reported that the Pimas formerly produced only mats in the plaited weave and in the river cane, since the cane which they used in this technique was too stiff for the production of other forms.[7] She reported no plaiting among the Pimas at the time of her research in 1910–11. On the other hand, the Papagos produced a variety of objects in this weave in later years. Kissel reported sleeping mats, headrings, burden-basket (kiaha) mats and headbands, and medicine and trinket baskets. To this list Shreve added strainers.[8]

Historically, there have been interesting changes in the use of plaited items made by the Papagos. Between 1915 and 1925, beds were distributed

FIGURE 2.4 Jemez plaited basket. Three elements are used as one, following a basic alternation of over-three-under-three to create concentric diamonds. A heavy withe in the top accounts for the term "ring basket."

among these Indians, and sleeping and sitting mats disappeared. With canvas and oilcloth available, the mat used for drying grains and vegetables was no longer necessary. In fact, the mat survived in later years solely for bedside use,[9] or — rarely — was made for sale. Headbands and backmats for the "kiaha" disappeared when this burden basket became obsolete some years ago (Fig. 2.5). On the other hand, some native forms found slight favor as commercial items, for example, the cylindrical, round-topped and square-based plaited trinket basket (Fig. 2.6). The headring (Fig. 4.32), used for supporting pottery and baskets on the floor or on the heads of women, was quickly replaced by a bundle of old rags, and is made today only as a novelty piece. A very large one was observed in 1963 which was made by twilling a cylinder and folding it three times.

The usual decoration for the square-based, round-topped basket was a series of concentric squares on the bottom and zigzags on the sides. Rims varied: a double style was produced by turning elements back and interweaving them for a short distance, while a second type was plain plaited to the edge. Strainers were made like these baskets but were not quite as deep and were of more open plaiting. The latter have remained popular for use in straining a sahuaro fruit preparation for the making of wine or jam by the Papago. These baskets may or may not have lids (Fig. 2.6).

One of the most interesting of the Papago plaited forms is the medicine man's basket (Fig. 2.7). In all specimens of this piece which were examined, the common design was a series of zigzags, usually in bands. This style was most suitable to the longer dimensions of the piece: one example measured 10 inches long and 2½ inches wide, while a second was 18 inches by about 5 inches. Both had lids of slightly larger dimensions.

Hopi

The most versatile plaited basketry, in form and design, is that of the Hopi Indians. Produced through the years and today found on all three mesas and in all villages, basketry of this technique is made for both native utility and for sale. Although the ring basket like that from Jémez is the main form, other shapes have been or still are woven, including mats, hoods for baby cradles, pottery rests, forehead straps, the wide belt used with the waist loom, and bottles. Part of the very important "piki" tray (used with paper-thin piki bread) is plaited, while the rest is woven in the wicker technique. A few oval, square, and rectangular ring baskets have been made in recent years. All of these except the piki tray are made of yucca leaves.

From the standpoint of design, the Hopi ring basket shows the greatest versatility, with a range from simple checkerwork to elaborate twilled patterns (Fig. 2.8). Formerly most of the designing was accomplished in the weave alone; in more recent years there has been a tendency to emphasize the woven pattern by using white, green, or yellow yucca leaves, or sometimes by adding dyed black elements. White leaves are from the core of the yucca plant, green comes from the outer leaves, and the yellow color is obtained from partial bleaching in the sun.[10] In the past few years, an unpleasant aniline orange has also been used.

Diamonds or squares are favored in Hopi plaited designing. They may appear as single large themes, as a concentric series working outward from a smaller to a larger one, as a row or series of rows, or in an allover arrangement. Solid diamonds or squares may be used, or an outline form which is plain or has a dot or a simple element in the center. There may be a cluster of diamonds forming a square, with parallel straight lines bordering its

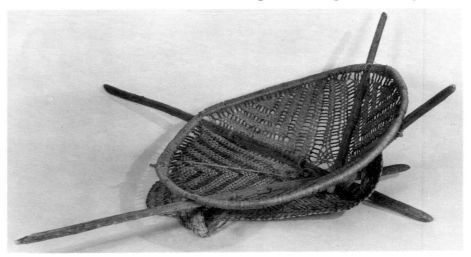

FIGURE 2.5 Plaited headband and backmat on the Papago kiaha (burden basket). The plaiting is simple. The kiaha is lace-like in weave but a sturdy burden basket.

FIGURE 2.6 Papago plaited utility basket, square base, round top. Allover zigzags decorate the piece. The basket complete with lid has been made in recent years. The round rim and inside of the basket are also shown.

edges, or rows of them with zigzags in between. The zigzag is another popular motif; it is used alone or in combination with other elements. Series of parallel zigzags may cross and fill the entire field of decoration. Crosses, lines, and frets are also used to add to the variety of Hopi plaited design, but it is in the size, number, and endless arrangement of diamonds that the greatest versatility of this basketry design is attained.

Today the Hopi ring basket measures from 12

to 16 inches in diameter in most pieces; some few larger specimens may be woven, particularly for native use. The common rhythm in the weave is three-three, but quite a few baskets are made in the two-two alternation.

When Mason made his comprehensive survey of American Indian basketry at the turn of the century, he offered this comment about Hopi plaiting: "The modern twilled basketry is as rough as it can be. The same is true of the flat mats used about their dwellings; in fact, the mat and the basket are identical in weaving."[11] This situation has changed greatly, particularly since the organization in 1930 by the Museum of Northern Arizona, Flagstaff, of the Hopi Craftsman show. This exhibit has continued annually to the present, and has influenced for the better the quality and design of plaited baskets, as well as other crafts and arts. Currently there is as much or more basketry of this type made for combined native uses and commercial purposes as has ever been recorded. Much of the contemporary work is of excellent craftsmanship and is well designed.

Wicker Basketry

Wicker is a basketry technique which has been rather widely used by Southwest Indians for utility objects, including everything from trays to water bottles. Not only is there variety in the nature of objects produced, but also there are variations of the basic technique.

Depending upon the desired use of the wicker basket, elements were coarser or finer, more tightly or more loosely woven. Utility also influenced the exact nature of wicker weave to some degree, determining whether there should be single or multiple wefts and warps, or whether the moving elements should be simply woven over and under or securely twined about the stationary rods. Artistry played a part too, for variation in weave could add a note of interest. Furthermore, the latter could add strength at vital spots: the Apaches added several rows of multiple twining at points of strain to otherwise simple wicker-weave pieces.

Paiute

In the past, Paiute Indians made several types of baskets in wicker weave (Fig. 2.9). One was a very artistic twine-woven water bottle made some years ago. Curving from a pointed or almost-pointed bottom to a mid-point of greatest diameter, the form then repeated its graceful lines to a tiny neck. This water bottle, with variations, fulfilled artistic demands in form alone; occasionally it carried an additional bit of decoration in variety of weave or color. Another Paiute water bottle is the opposite of this one: it is flat bottomed, full, and rather gross bodied with a fairly wide mouth. Often

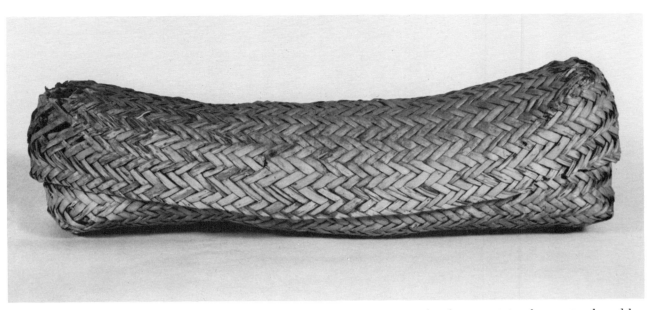

FIGURE 2.7 Papago medicine man's plaited basket. One of the most interesting of such pieces, it is a long rectangle and has a lid. A simple alternation of over-three-under-three creates zigzags over the entire surface.

carelessly coiled (now substituted for twining), it offers nothing in the way of artistry. This water bottle is still made by the Paiutes of southern Utah and by Navajos. The Paiute Indians of the northwestern corner of Arizona no longer do any weaving.[12]

Other varieties of wicker weaving have been produced by the Paiutes. One piece occasionally seen today is a winnowing tray in open weave. It is fan shaped, with elements splayed out from a narrow handle and twined into place at wide intervals. Euler reports that a piece comparable to this one, a seed beater, was formerly made by the Arizona Paiutes. However, the last woman who wove these beaters died sometime before 1960.[13]

Walapai

Several of the Yuman tribes practiced wicker weave in the past and continue to use it to the present. Walapai basketry is made of squawberry and is woven in diagonal-twined technique. Formerly, the Walapais made a large, openwork wood basket. They also produced conical burden baskets, ornamenting them in a few simple bands of brown or black, or with a few rows of three-ply twine.

Trays of wicker were usually undecorated, although there may have been a few with some three-strand twining in rows. Two types of water bottles were made, one with a conical and the other a flat bottom. Surfaces were first covered with red paint, then the entire bottle was pitched with piñon gum to make it waterproof.

The modern commercial basket of the Walapais is a bowl with straight or slightly rounded sides (Fig. 2.10); however, in place of the more subtle types of decoration employed in earlier pieces, red

and green aniline dyes are used today for the design splints (Fig. 2.11). Common motifs include vertical zigzags, diagonal stripes, fringed lines, and rows of chevrons, all arranged in bands. An older version of this same shape was often larger in size and lacked the bright commercial dye in its decoration.

Havasupai

More varied than the above are the materials used by the Havasupai weaver. Although acacia is common, cottonwood and willow are also used, and the outer covering of the devil's claw (martynia) pod adds decorative black. Forms include a conical burden basket (some with an odd, nipple-like base) (Fig. 2.12), a shallow tray, and a water bottle. Although a few of the large burden baskets were made shortly after 1946, this attractive piece is no longer woven. However, small copies of it are made today in limited numbers.[14] Plain or diagonal twining was used quite generally in the burden basket, often with lines or rows of three-strand wefts against a two-strand background. The workmanship in these baskets varied from coarse to even and fine. Decoration in black or reddish-brown appeared in plain stripes, or bands of cogwheels, triangles, or zigzag patterns, or in lines with short diagonals on one or both of its sides.

Havasupai trays were woven in the same techniques and decorated in the same styles as the burden baskets. Water bottles show some variety in shape; they too are decorated in variations in weave. A pointed-bottomed, full-bodied, and small-necked type lacks the grace of the Paiute bottle. A second form is flat-bottomed and full-bodied, while a third is hourglass shaped. All three bottles

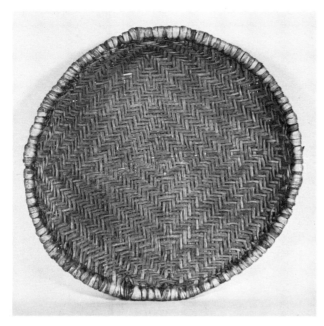

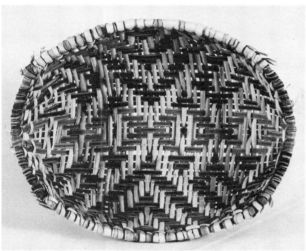

FIGURE 2.8 Hopi ring baskets and sketches of additional designs in this type. The round basket is well woven; it has a simple pattern in weave alone, while the oval form has color added to stress the pattern. The sketches show the variety of design made from a few basic elements. Other ring-basket designs are also given in the sketches.

have a first coating of yucca or soapweed paste, then the usual outer covering of piñon pitch. To-day, the first two bottle shapes are made mostly in

small sizes.[15] Euler reported that in 1963 there was a Havasupai woman married to a Walapai man, living at Peach Springs, Arizona, who made a few of the flat-bottomed water bottles for sale.[16]

Apache

Better known than the Havasupai work are the twined products of the Apache Indians. New Mexico Mescaleros produced a carrying basket in this technique, while the Arizona Apaches twined both burden baskets and water jars. The water jar is called a "tus."

Generally, all Apache tribes used similar materials and methods in the production of the burden basket; however, the wefts used by the San Carlos division were often wider than those used by the other Apache tribes. Around 1918, only the finest of burden baskets were woven of mulberry by the White Mountain Apaches,[17] while earlier and later the common materials were willow or cottonwood, sometimes sumac. Squawberry or sumac were the materials used in water bottles (the tus).

Very few burden baskets and water bottles are made today. The whole twig forms the warp, but the weaver slits it three ways, with teeth and fingernails, for the wefts. Plain or twill twining or three-strand twining are the techniques used (Fig. 2.1). Although there is variety in the quality of the weaving in both products, quite generally the tus is more coarsely woven.

In form, the Arizona Apache burden basket is predominantly bucket-shaped, with a wide mouth,

FIGURE 2.9 Paiute wicker water bottle. The small neck is characteristic, as is the full body. Some of these baskets have more pointed bottoms. Simple bands are created in natural on a dark reddish-brown background.

more or less sloping sides, and a rounded or concave bottom (Fig. 2.13). The latter feature is often concealed by the placement on the basket bottom of a buckskin or leather patch which insures longer wear. A second form is smaller-based. Fairly wide mouths characterize the water bottle, while the body shape may be one of three types: a rounded body with a fairly rounded bottom; a flat-shouldered type, generally with a concave base; and a flat- or slightly round-bottomed hourglass shape (Fig. 2.13). Roberts remarks about the poor weave in the San Carlos bottle.[18] Actually, the weave in all varieties of the tus is concealed be-

neath heavy coatings of ground leaves and piñon pitch, so perhaps the Indian considered it expedient to produce the bottle as quickly as possible, wasting no time on fine weaving.

For the most part, the Apache water bottle has no decoration. Ground juniper leaves and red ochre are rubbed into the surface, the latter imparting some color even after the application of the water-repellent pitch. Occasionally a simple black line or other limited geometric design will be painted on the shoulder of the tus; this is done in soot, often with the finger. Arizona Apache women swab the melted pitch onto the surface with a rag on the end

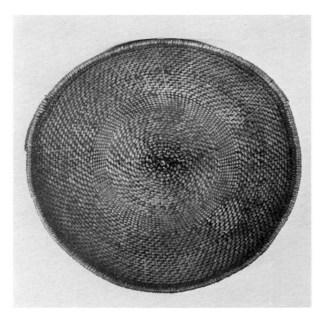

FIGURE 2.10 Walapai wicker baskets. The flat plain tray (top left) is no longer made. In the jar form, also no longer made, designing is done in both color and variety of stitching (top right). The two bowls are the common forms today: one (bottom left) has no decoration; the other has several colored bands and a row of double twine for decoration.

FIGURE 2.11 Walapai wicker bowls. These examples show some of the aniline dye coloring used today. Red and green are the favored colors; the simple bowl is the main form. (*Photo by R. H. Peebles*)

of a stick, then pour more of the stuff inside and turn the basket around and around so that the bottle interior is also covered.

When the pitch is too heavily or irregularly applied, it may conceal the diagonal nature of the allover weaving which is typical of Arizona Apache water bottles. Pitch also often hides the variation in stitching which occurs rather commonly at points of stress. On one tus there are several rows of three-ply twine on either side of a plain black band close to the outer edge of the flat shoulder; here the variation in weave is decorative. Reinforcement at points of stress, usually at the curves and in three-ply twine, is found occasionally on the San Carlos tus.[19]

The rim of the water bottle is finished rather poorly in many instances, particularly in the San Carlos basket. Sometimes jars lack a specific finishing, and warps are simply close-cropped at the top;

in such cases the pitch serves to stabilize the rim. Otherwise, there may be a double coiled rim; in one such case, for example, the first coil is simply overcast while the edge coil is finished in a crude false braid. Roberts reports a common early use of false braid on the rim of the San Carlos tus basket, although she found none at the time of her study.[20] A third rim finish is a plain coil, often not too well done.

Burden baskets reveal more variety in twining than do water jars. For example, sometimes they are woven entirely in plain twining or in twill twining, while at other times the two methods are combined in a single basket; three-strand twining is less commonly used. Workmanship varies from crude to almost perfect; the latter seems to reflect the pride of individual weavers in the production of an item which they use both daily and for special occasions. San Carlos burden baskets are extremely well made. They have more conical bases, the finer mulberry specimens lack the four heavy strengthening ribs common to other types, and often there is a diagonal slant to the weave.

A few Apache women still use the burden basket, supporting it by means of a strap across the forehead. Formerly it was the chief means of conveying miscellaneous objects. Through the years it has been used at the puberty rite of the Apache girl; double rows of the lovely baskets are filled with cigarettes, fruits and other edibles which are passed out to all who attend the ritual.

Generally, the decorative bands in burden baskets appear above center. Twill-twined stripes interspersed between wider areas of plain twining may be left undecorated or they may be colored. Color alone is a more popular type of decoration, either of native or aniline dye or in the natural colors of the weft materials. Black and red or reddish brown are the most common colors, although more variety, albeit less esthetic effect, is attained by using commercial reds, greens, and blues. Splints are sometimes dyed and woven in, while at other times the paint is applied after the weaving is completed. In either case, designs are usually restricted to narrow positive or negative bands which incorporate simple geometric elements, such as vertical or diagonal and short lines, checkers, bands, triangles, zigzags, and paired or multiple-grouped short lines usually arranged in horizontal or diagonal units. Opposition, alternation, and balance in the use of several colors add variety to these simple elements. Occasionally more elaborate treatment appears, such as the addition of pendant triangles from lines or diamonds between bands of simple units.

Many other small details may be resorted to for decorating the Apache burden basket. The four heavy vertical ribs often incorporated with the lighter elements are covered on the outside by wide buckskin bands. At intervals up and down the bands and around the rim, buckskin thongs are attached, usually in clusters. To the ends of the thongs may be added small tin cones or tinklers. These make a delightful sound as the women move along with the baskets on their backs. Sometimes beads are strung on the thongs. Scraps of red cloth may also be added to give further decorative effect, particularly around the buckskin patch on the base. In some instances, hand-tanned buckskin thongs have been replaced in recent years by chamois.

Rims of burden baskets, like those of water bottles, are either poorly or beautifully finished. Two heavy coils at the edge are common, one utilizing the warp twigs from the body of the basket for the coil, or these plus an additional and heavy wooden ring or hoop. The second coil often incorporates a heavy metal wire, either alone or as part of a bundle of native material. The first rim coil is poorly sewed; the edge coil is generally of a little better workmanship. One interesting example shows the first coil wrapped in the sumac of the basket while the edge coil is more carefully wound in buckskin thongs.

Both burden baskets and water bottles often have two loops on their outer walls for suspension. Typically, these are of buckskin or leather on the former and of the same materials or horsehair on the latter. However, in some cases there are three loops on the water bottle, each formed of a native rod of heavy nature; these are carefully pitched along with the rest of the basket bottle.

Quite naturally there is some variation in size of both the burden basket and tus. The former averages about 12 to 15 inches high. Tus heights are apt to vary more, as native use might dictate that a smaller one be made for a "canteen" and a larger one for storage of water or other liquids. Opler say that "jars for tiswin [a native drink] are usually larger than those for carrying or holding water."[21] Many of the storage jars are 18 inches in height. Smaller versions of both water bottles and burden baskets have been made in recent years for sale; generally they are not as well made as the utility pieces.

Hopi

True wicker (the use of a single weft element or several elements manipulated as one) is characteristic of much Hopi basketry. This tribe has devel-

FIGURE 2.12 Havasupai burden basket of twined wicker weave. The conical form is typical. Simple geometric designs are in black. The cone-shaped end is usually wrapped in buckskin, and the rim is completed by sewing two coils about the top.

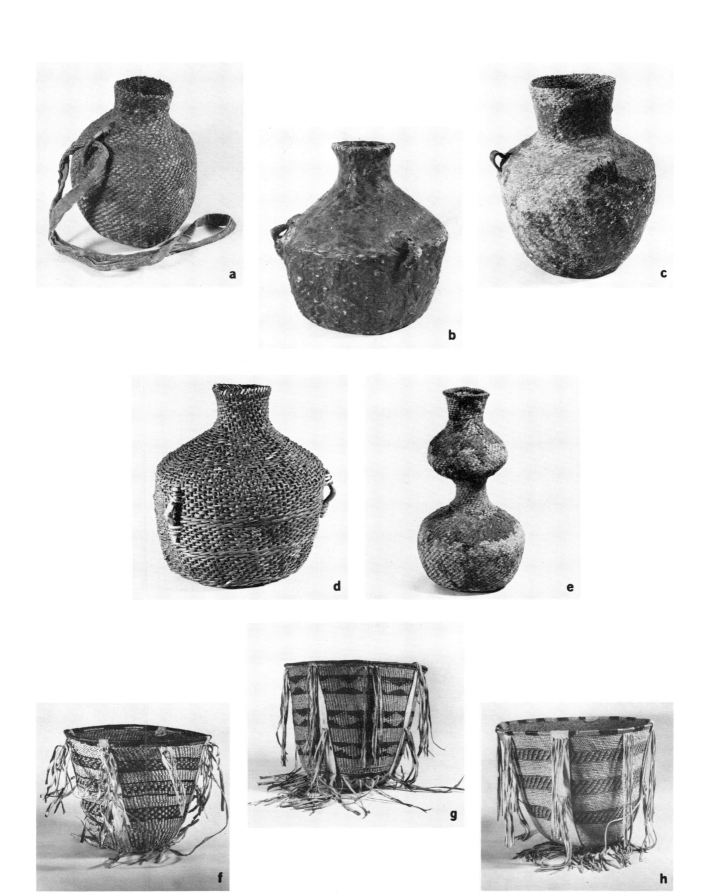

FIGURE 2.13 Western Apache twined woven water bottles and burden baskets. The three main forms of the water bottle, or tus, are represented here: the rounded body (a), the shouldered type (b, c, and d), and the hourglass style. The nature of the weave is indicated in the unpitched examples (a and d), with one (d) showing a combination of weaves for simple patterning. Better weaving is seen in the burden baskets (f, g, and h); also, banded pattering is executed in black or black and red. The usual fringes appear on all three forms.

oped the elaboration of design in wicker technique to the highest point of any tribe in the United States. A great variety of pleasing colors adds further to the high artistry of Hopi wicker baskets. Both warps and wefts are stiff, for the Hopi uses the whole twig of the sumac or wild currant as the warp and the full stem of one of several varieties of rabbit brush for the weft. Wicker is a technique followed on Third Mesa only, except for the "piki" tray border and peach baskets, cradleboard hoods, and a few other utility items. Although the wicker piece is often called the "Oraibi basket," it is woven in the other Third Mesa villages of Hotevilla and Bacabi, and in Moenkopi, the village to the west.

Woven and used by Hopi men in earlier years, the peach basket was produced in a coarse weave (Fig. 2.14). Sumac twigs plus two heavy U-shaped wooden rods served as a foundation, the heavier elements imparting a squarish or oblong shape to the basket. Usually sumac served as the weft. Edges were crudely overcast, with the tips of the four wooden rods sticking up beyond the finished rim. A heavy buckskin band served to support the basket over the forehead; it was looped through the loose weaving, then caught under one or several of the warp strands. Zuñis, and possibly other puebloans, made comparable baskets in the past. One oblong peach basket measured 27½ inches in length and 8 inches in width at the top, had smaller base dimensions, and was 17 inches high. All other peach baskets examined were about the same size or smaller.

Other wicker items include a baby cradle which is woven on First and Third Mesas, and windbreaks, which are often set up in Hopi fields. In some of the Hopi houses, the supports for chimney hoods were made in the same way.[22]

Women in all Hopi villages make piki trays (Fig. 2.15), for these are requisite in certain ritual situations. The tray is often piled high with rolls of the wafer-thin bread of various colors — red, blue, and others — all made from a watery mixture of native corn meal. The tray is flat or nearly flat. Split sumac elements are used for plaiting the center, while whole rods of the same material serve for the wicker border. Often warps and wefts are manipulated in groups of four. The split elements are so used that the outer dark color of the splints forms a pattern against the white inner portion. The border, an inch and a half to several inches wide, is generally a plain dark band around a patterned center. This center decoration is usually built up of triangles, chevrons, diamonds, or diagonal bands. One tray examined was decorated with diagonal rows of diamonds; another had nests of chevrons arranged at sides and ends, with their

FIGURE 2.14 Hopi peach basket. Oblong in shape, these deep baskets are woven of heavy elements which combine brown for the background with natural for the design. Two heavy ribs which are crossed in the bottom of the basket show at the four corners.

tips at the edges and apexes pointing to the center of the piece. One piki tray measured 25½ inches by 22½ inches. Others were about the same size or a little smaller.

In Third Mesa wicker basketry, there are three basic shapes. Two of these, a plaque and a bowl (Fig. 2.16), are native; the latter is called a feather bowl. The third is a popular commercial piece and can best be described as a wastebasket. Actually, it is often no more than a deepened bowl. The round plaque has a hump in the center of the top surface and the edges may turn up a bit. Bowls are basically round, although a few oval ones have been made in recent years; their sides are gently sloping, and bases are flat, or nearly so, except for the hump in the very center. This convexity is also found on the inside bottom of the wastebasket.

In the majority of these wicker baskets made by the Hopis, three or four wrapped bundles are crossed at right angles by the same number of other wrapped bundles for the beginning of the piece. This is, of course, what creates the hump. Individual warps are splayed out from the multiple bundles in spoke-like fashion and the actual wicker work begins with them. Whenever necessary, additional warps are inserted to accommodate the increasing diameter of the basket. Radial ridges, which are created by the wefts, increase in size from center to edge, this resulting from the expanding diameter of the piece. Walls of bowls and wastebaskets tend to have ribs of more equal size from the turn of the bottom to the rim, for there is little or no expansion in size. Rims in all pieces are invariably overcast and rather poorly done; yucca is the sewing material. Quite naturally, all of the warp elements could not be used in this rim, so excess warps are clipped off just below it; if not carefully done, these are all too obvious. A good rim is a mark of a well-made wicker basket.

Colors are used in greater variety and abundance in Hopi wicker pieces than in any other type of Southwestern Indian basketry (Fig. 2.17). Some of the colors are of mineral origin, some vegetal, and before and shortly after the turn of the century many were commercial dyes. Native dyes were revived about 1904 and have been used extensively since that date. Indigo has been used over a long period of time.

Some sources of Hopi wicker basketry colors include the following: white is bleached rabbit brush washed with kaolin clay, while a pale green is the

FIGURE 2.15 Hopi wicker and plaited piki trays. The centers of the trays are plaited and the edges are in wicker weave. The wide center of the wicker tray (top) has diagonal patterning created by an over-two-under-two weave. A wide wicker border surrounds the plaited center with chevron designs (bottom).

natural color of the shoots of the same plant. Other shades of green may be a dye derived from flowers of the rabbit brush or this dye plus indigo. The source of one dark blue is a cultivated black navy bean; both purple and carmine are obtained from purple maize; and yellows are extracted from rabbit brush flowers.[23] Larkspur provides a light shade of blue; cockscomb may give either lavender or carmine; and reds may be obtained from cockscomb, sumac, or alder. Red-browns are produced from several native grasses. In addition to all of these color sources, Underhill also mentions mineral colors, such as soot or coal for black, iron ochres for reds, browns, and yellows, and copper carbonate for some greens.[24] Mineral paints are rubbed on the twigs, but for the vegetal colorant the twigs are dipped in the dye bath. Colors are set by smoking the twigs over burning wool.

In the Hopi wicker plaque, the entire surface is viewed as a decorative unit; this has been no small factor in the development of one of the most dynamic of basketry designs. In asymmetric patterns, whether a simple crescent style pendant from the rim or some more elaborate theme, there is terrific flow of line. Plaques are also decorated with symmetrical designs, usually repeated motifs radiating from the center, or encircling band-like arrangements. On the other hand, on bowls and deeper forms, side walls are the main decorative areas. As in so many instances of this nature, only a part of the design is seen at one time; therefore, simpler and repetitive banded layouts are more common. Geometric elements are used on wastebaskets and bowls, with lines and bands, varied arrangements of squares and rectangles, cog wheels, checkers, circles, wedge-shaped figures, almost-triangles, and almost-diamonds appearing on these forms. The wide foundation does not allow for much in the way of oblique lines. Occasional realistic themes, such as kachina masks, are used.

There are geometric themes on plaques, but far more interesting are life designs. Some of the latter are so highly conventionalized that they are hardly recognizable as such, while others are quite realistic. Among the life themes are birds or parts of birds, full kachinas or kachina masks, butterflies, Hopi girls with the traditional "whorl" hair-do, and a few other subjects. Life forms such as kachinas and butterflies are centered in plaques and balanced left and right, or there may be a slight break in balance — such as a bird's head on one side — but the body, tail, and out-spread wings are balanced. Mirrored symmetry, as in whirlwinds or double volutes, also occurs.

In a sense, most wicker plaque designs, even the life forms, are banded, for the edge of the colored central circle combines with the rim to create such an area. Geometric styles may be simply banded or have successive encircling units, or they may be more complex in layout — rayed or starred, or with simple or complex pendant volutes.

As a whole, wicker basketry has much balance and rhythm in color as well as in design. Generally, design is allover, or nearly so. A single basket may utilize only a few colors, such as a black-and-white bird with the barest touches of green and orange on wing and tail tips; another piece may use many colors and have a banded decoration of various combinations of green, black, red, gray, orange, and white. In the clean and often brilliant shades of the natural dyes, juxtaposition of certain of these colors is intentional and effective.

Balance may occur in design and be broken in color — one-half of the background color may be green and the other half red-brown. Varied repetitions occur in design and/or color, with identical repeated (a-a-a-a), alternated (a-b-a-b), or complex repeated (a-a-b-a-a-b) designs. Variety is the essence of Hopi wicker basketry.

Rio Grande Pueblos

Willow rods are used for the weaving of baskets of openwork wicker at Santo Domingo (Fig. 2.18), San Felipe, and at one of the Laguna villages. Recently made at a number of other pueblos, this style is either of native origin or Mexican-influenced. An example from Santo Domingo is illustrative of the style. It is 12 inches in diameter at the rim, 7 at the base, and about 4 inches deep. Sides slope straight and outwards from base to rim. A combination of peeled and unpeeled rods is used to give a more decorative effect in the play of white and brown. Bottom and lower side walls are more solid, while upper walls are in openwork lacing with two white and three brown elements carried along as units. The top edge is scalloped.

Coiled Basketry

By a wide margin, coiled basketry has been and still is the most popular technique among the natives of the Southwest (Fig. 2.1). The technique itself produces a closer weave; therefore, it has many utility advantages over plaiting and wicker, and its potential in design is far greater than in the other methods. Even after the introduction of pottery, which discouraged basketry as a vessel-producing industry, some tribes continued to use baskets by preference for certain special purposes or for obvious uses, such as sieves. Apaches and Navajos never developed pottery to any degree, and as they became more nomadic through historic times, they found the unbreakable basket more desirable as an all-purpose utensil than the fragile clay pot. Tradition played its part in relation to

basketry also: among some Indians it was requisite that certain pieces of basketry be used for specific ritual occasions, such as the Hopi wedding plaque or the Papago wine-ceremony bowl basket.

At any rate, basketry, particularly the coiled variety, survived into historic times among many of the Southwest tribes. Coiled pieces also held the greatest appeal for the white man; this fact has helped to perpetuate the technique up to the

FIGURE 2.16 Hopi wicker plaque (top) and bowl (bottom). Life forms are popular in this flat plaque form; they are done in a single color on natural or in a great variety of colors. The bird is a readily adaptable design to this basically left-right symmetry. Bowls, or this deeper form which may be called a waste basket, are decorated in a comparable manner; here a smaller bird is placed between two more colorful bands. Note that narrow rim bands are similar in both forms.

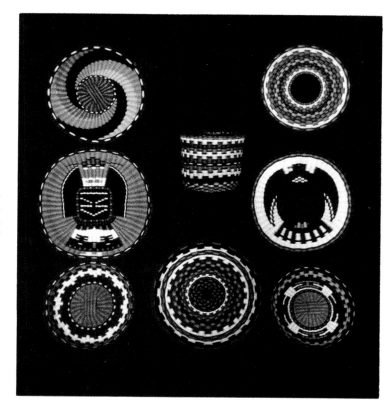

FIGURE 2.17 Hopi wicker baskets. Note the variety of colors — reds, greens, yellows, black, brown, tan, and others. There is variety in design, too, from static bands to dynamic whirls to life themes. (*Photo by J. H. McGibbeny*)

present. Some tribes have, to all intents and purposes, completely abandoned this type of basketmaking, while a few tribes have only a very limited number of weavers who do coiling. Hopis and Papagos are the only ones who produce any quantity of this work today.

Very little coiled basketry is made today among the Yuman tribes. The Yavapais, some of whom have been associated with the Apaches for a long time, still make a few such pieces. As of 1963, Havasupais were represented by about a half-dozen weavers who still made coiled baskets, most of them of smaller size and for sale.[25] The rest of the Yuman tribes no longer produce this type of basketry; the recency of production by some of them, however, warrants brief comment.

Cocopa, Mohave, Maricopa

No record of Cocopa coiled work exists except statements such as this one by Douglas: "The Yuma and Cocopa made very large, extremely coarse storage baskets having the general appearance of a bird's nest."[26] This bird's-nest coiling involved a bundle of coarse material, sometimes with small leaves attached, sewed at wide intervals with another very coarse material. Douglas also says that the Yumas proper made other coiled bowls, "apparently like those of the Pima-Papago group, except that two rods in a vertical position were used in the foundations."[27]

There seems to be some disagreement regarding the Mohaves. The statement by Douglas, "The Mohave made a few bowls of openwork coiling,"[28] leaves much to be said for the accomplishment of this tribe. Other authors mention no basketry at all for the Mohaves or only the crudest of open "wrapped weaving."[29] Needless to say, none of these three tribes — the Mohaves, Cocopas, or Yumas — has produced any in recent times.

Spier gives a fairly complete picture of a Maricopa true coiled basket. One type the Maricopas made was a burden basket, wide-mouthed and with sides gently sloping to a flat base. A split cattail bundle foundation was wrapped with martynia for the base and with willow for the walls. Decoration on the latter was in martynia also, and consisted of two encircling bands of designs like those on some Pima baskets.[30] The Maricopas also made a storage basket of large wheat-straw coils with open and wide-spaced willow sewing. It would seem that the idea of the latter coiled piece was borrowed from the Pimas and that the burden basket was an older type. A coiled tray basket made by the Pimas was used by all Maricopa women.[31]

Walapai, Yavapai, Havasupai

In earlier years, the Walapais, Yavapais, and Havasupais used a three-rod foundation coil, with the rods arranged in triangular formation. Whole willow twigs served as the most common foundation material, although cottonwood or squawbush was occasionally substituted. Split willow was the usual sewing material; however, some substitutions may have been made. Decoration was in black martynia, with occasional red touches on Yavapai baskets; source of the red was the inner bark of the yucca root. Tray bowls and flat plaques were the most common Yavapai forms although deep jars were produced occasionally.

Although all three of these Yuman-speaking tribes — the Walapais, Yavapais, and Havasupais — favored relatively simple and concentric circles in the design of their coiled baskets, there was some variation from one group to another. For example, Walapai baskets tended to have the simplest design of all, utilizing a few geometric elements in concentric circles. Designs were often more solid or heavier-lined and were less Apache-like than the Yavapai patterns.

Often Havasupai designs are allover, yet they preserve the feeling of being banded (Fig. 2.19). There are banded layouts too; these sometimes have enclosing lines. Still other Havasupai arrangements are radiating, with dynamic themes swirling outward from a smaller or larger central black circle. Design elements include stars, triangles, squares, diamonds, heavy crosses, lines, zigzags, and chevrons. Stepped patterns, outlines of solids, and lines with pendant elements are typical. Touches of yellow are added — rarely — to the black and white combination. Braided rims are fairly abundant.

Quite different are many of the Yavapai designs, particularly those created by the members of this tribe who have been in long association with the Apache Indians (Fig. 2.19). Their baskets have the most dynamic patterns of all the Yuman types, and also have the addition of life subjects such as men, deer, dogs and other quadrupeds, birds, and a few patterns which may be plant-life themes. Geometric elements in Yavapai designs are apt to be smaller

FIGURE 2.19 Havasupai (top) and Yavapai (bottom) coiled baskets. The small coil in the Havasupai tray is complemented by fine sewing. Typical are banded patterns in black, here with small touches of red outlining the upper parts of the joined outline diamonds. The flat-bottomed Yavapai bowl is also quite finely woven; its gently sloping walls are decorated in black with a repeated motif.

in size also — another reflection, perhaps, of the long contact period with the Apaches. Design, coupled with comparable small and round coils, makes some Yavapai baskets look more Apache than anything else; without specific knowledge of the origin of some of these, it would be difficult to determine the source. Perhaps Yavapai-Apache is the most accurate name to apply to these pieces, just as it is applied to some of their makers.

Today the Walapais make no coiled baskets; the Havasupais produce very few and these are small ones made for sale; and the Yavapais continue

FIGURE 2.18 Santo Domingo open wicker bowl basket. This flare-rimmed, scallop-edged form is rare in the Southwest. Heavy, dark brown multiple elements are woven diagonally and in an open fashion to create this style.

limited production in this line. Women from the latter tribe occasionally demonstrate the craft of weaving for special events, such as the Arizona State Fair or at art conferences. Living in the Phoenix area as some of these women do, the chances for sales are far greater than for the other two tribes. Visitors rarely go into Cataract Canyon and thus the Havasupais have little incentive to commercialize their craft. And even though Walapais live close to, or on, transcontinental Highway 66, from the standpoint of sales they too have little inspiration to develop their craft commercially.

Navajo

One of the best known of Southwestern Indian baskets is the so-called Navajo "wedding basket" (Fig. 2.20). Today it is woven largely by Paiute Indians of southeastern Utah, but it has been and is used in several Navajo rituals in addition to marriages. This basket has had an interesting history: it has been made by Apaches,[32] by Utes of southwestern Colorado, and by the Navajos themselves, as well as by the Paiutes. Ellis is of the opinion that this basket may have been made also by several pueblo groups of the Rio Grande.[33] Hester maintains that the shift from Navajo-made to Paiute-made wedding baskets occurred in the nineteenth century.[34]

The Navajo demands certain things of those who weave this basket: the rim must be finished off in herringbone or false braid; the traditional design must be woven into the piece; the tray-bowl form must be followed; and the end of the rim coil must be opposite an opening in the pattern.

The foundation of the basket when made by the Navajos is two rods and a bundle; the Utes, Apaches, and Paiutes use three rods. Adams suggests that the Navajos terminate the rim more abruptly, while other weavers produce a sloping ending to the rim coil.[35]

Adams, who worked for a year as a trader on the Navajo Reservation during the mid-1950's, said that during this period of time approximately 500 Navajo wedding baskets came into and went out of the post, all for Indian use. This does not mean that 500 baskets were woven during this period; rather it points up the extensive use of the piece for ceremonial purposes among the Navajos. Many baskets were "repeats," that is, the same basket was in and out a number of times. Adams was of the opinion that perhaps one out of every twenty or thirty baskets was new.[36]

Navajo baskets are made of sumac (*Rhus trilobata*) generally, with a few woven of willow. Yucca (*baccata* preferred, some *glauca*) is used for the foundation.[37] Dyed elements are used in creating the design. For many years there has been a standard pattern with some variation as to size of elements, width of bands, and elaboration of the basic themes. The pattern has a red center, usually in the form of a plain and straight-sided band, and a stepped black band on either side of the red one. There is considerable variety in size and complexity of the two black bands. A continuous open space through all three units of this design is significant in ceremonial orientation when the basket is in use. The termination of the rim directly opposite the opening in the design is helpful to the ceremonialist

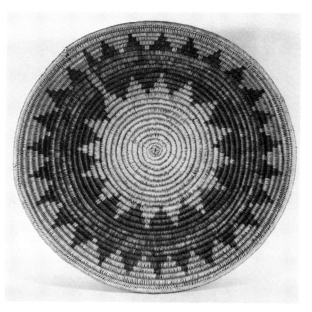

FIGURE 2.20 Navajo "wedding basket" trays. Both examples have the requisite braided rim and traditional pattern, the latter composed of black, stepped, outer and inner portions, a red center — a plain band. It is likely that the top basket was made by a Paiute, while the bottom one was woven by a Navajo.

in establishing direction when the basket is full of sacred meal.

In earlier years, Navajos wove a variety of designs in this same tray-basket type (Fig. 2.21). A favorite consisted of three, four, or more solid red crosses outlined in black with tiny black squares at the outer corners of each arm of the cross. These were usually arranged in a single row, but sometimes in double and overlapping rows. Other themes included simple lines of steps arranged diagonally or in chevrons, curving and radiating stepped elements, squares, arrow points, triangles stacked in various ways, and numerous odd geometric forms. The most common color distribution was a black outline around a red motif, but solid black or solid red was also used. These design motifs were generally spotted in a band-like area around the basket. In some early baskets there was also a band or zigzag pattern, sometimes with a broad red center outlined in black. The "ceremonial break" (an open space in an encircling line) was present. This last style may well have anticipated the later wedding-basket design.

An analysis of a number of Navajo baskets in the Southwest Museum, Los Angeles, revealed the following traits: counterclockwise weaving; stitches generally ten to twelve and coils three to five per inch; the red and black always dyed and usually aniline; and always a false braid rim. Sewing was close and even. Most of the baskets were 12 to 14 inches in diameter and about 4 inches deep. Many of the baskets made today have fewer coils and stitches to the inch (some have two coils per inch!),

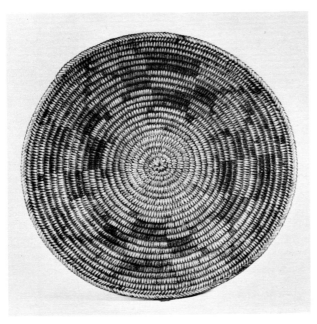

FIGURE 2.21 Jicarilla Apache coiled basket-tray. Although made by the Jicarillas, this tray exemplifies the old-style Navajo basket design and colors — black and red.

and the sewing is often coarse and uneven. On the other hand, a collection of eleven very fine baskets at the Navajo Arts and Crafts Guild, Window Rock, Arizona, revealed excellent workmanship. These were woven in 1963 by three Navajo women. One basket measured 9 inches in diameter and had four coils and twelve stitches to the inch. The smallest was 2½ inches in diameter; it was beautifully made, counting twenty-six stitches and ten coils to the inch.

Jicarilla Apache

Jicarilla Apache coiled basketry is sometimes of the three-rod type; most unusual in Southwestern Indian basketry as a whole is their use of five rods. Whether three or five, the foundation elements are arranged in a mass which results in a large coil. Rod material is willow, while the characteristic sewing materials are sumac, willow, and squawberry. In earlier years a simple design in natural brown was common; later, red and green were added; today they use aniline dyes of red, green, black, brown, blue, yellow, and turquoise. One recent example combined a brown design with turquoise. Designs have become more complex also. Although simplicity and massiveness may be said to have characterized the typical Jicarilla basket patterns for some years, a recent revival has featured smaller design elements and designs[38] (Fig. 2.22).

Baskets of the Jicarillas include two forms: quite deep tray-bowls which in more recent pieces have handles, and deep, straight-sided, flat-bottomed baskets which often have lids. In most Southwestern baskets, lids are a late innovation. Shallow round trays are popular today; they are 12 to 20 inches in diameter. Fish creels were also made by this tribe. Decoration of the first two forms includes simple zigzag lines made up of stepped squares, single or multiple star patterns, terraced diamonds, crosses with little blocks at the corners, and large conventional animals. For the most part, these elements are arranged in bands of joined or isolated units.

This basketry almost died out for a while; when revived in the 1960's it incorporated the many aniline colors listed above and a wider variety of designs, including deer, horses, floral themes, and conventionalized birds.[39]

Mescalero Apache

Mescalero Apaches manipulate the foundation elements in their baskets in an unusual manner: whether two-rod-and-bundle, three-rod-and-bundle, or a wide-slat-and-bundle, all are arranged in vertical fashion. This results in a wide and flexible coil which is quite distinctive of this group. As a result of the arrangement, there are usually no more than two or three coils to the inch. Colors are in definite contrast to those used by the Jicarillas, for the Mescaleros use yucca sewing elements which are white, yellow, or green, and the root of the narrow-leafed yucca which is a deep red-brown. These natural colors are softer and more appealing than the garish aniline colors used by the Jicarillas. In the Mescalero basket, large simple patterns predominate: stars used alone or in combination with stepped triangles pendant from the rim, and terraced pyramids, diamonds, or squares in bands or spotted arrangements (Fig. 2.23). Often the pattern is in solid green or yellow and outlined in the reddish brown. Massive simplicity characterizes the designs of Mescalero Apache basketry.

Western Apache

Arizona Apache baskets are far more complex and much more elaborate than the products of either of the two New Mexico Apache groups. In the past, both the San Carlos and the White Mountain Apaches were great basket weavers; today there is a rare woman here and there who has the talent of her ancestors and expresses it. The three-rod foundation is made of slender twigs of willow, cottonwood, or sumac; characteristically, the coil is small and round, giving a corrugated surface to the finished basket and a rigidity which adds to its wearing qualities. The typically fine and regular stitching is of narrow and even sewing splints of the same material as the foundation, rarely of other materials. The black of the design is derived from the devil's claw, while rare touches of red are from the inner bark of the root of yucca. In a few of the many specimens examined, the weaver used aniline dye for the red color.

The dominant shapes in Arizona Apache baskets are open trays and storage jars (Fig. 2.24). Most tray diameters vary from 11 to 15 inches, although some are smaller and some larger in size. In an analysis of forms of San Carlos bowls (trays), Roberts illustrates sixteen variations of the older style and seventeen of the newer types.[40] Within the demands of utility and tribal tradition, the weaver expresses herself as an individual in these matters, a fact which explains the great differences in both form and design in many basketry types. Depths range from 2 to 4 inches, again with some variations. In a sample of more than 250 baskets, the majority counted four to five coils and thirteen to fifteen stitches per inch. There is not as much consistency in stitch count within one basket as there is in Hopi baskets.

Jar sizes are diverse, but the majority range from about 18 to 22 inches in height. The mouth diameters range from large to small; in a few cases this diameter is greater than the jar height. There are several interesting Apache jar or olla shapes.

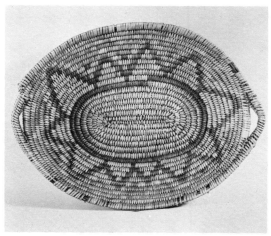

FIGURE 2.22 Jicarilla Apache coiled baskets. The deep tray at the top has a braided rim and a banded repeated design in reddish brown. The oval tray (center) has a combination reddish-brown and black design; handles were common on these baskets in earlier years. The contemporary Jicarilla basket (bottom) has a more elaborate pattern and a greater variety of colors woven into the pattern: from the inside to the outside of the star design there are red, blue, orange, and black, with additional touches of blue and red near the rim.

One has a flaring or straight and fairly high neck, rounded body, and flat bottom. A second has a straight or gently inward-sloping neck, wide mouth, sharp or sloping shoulder, and flat bottom. The third form is constricted in the middle and has a small neck. This is a broad categorization of Arizona Apache jar-basket shapes, for there is considerable individual variation within each class.

Designs in Arizona Apache coiled baskets throughout the twentieth century have been dynamic, varied, and quite complex (Fig. 2.24). Both

FIGURE 2.23 Mescalero Apache coiled baskets. The wide, thin, and flat coil of this basket is unusual. Patterns are massive but simple; the large star (top) is in the favored color combination, dark red and a pale greenish shade. The other basket uses larger quantities of the latter for the main floral theme, then outlines in red. These baskets are very flexible and shallow. The top one, for example, is 14″ in diameter and about 3 1/2″ deep.

geometric styles and angular life forms have been used; the latter, perhaps, are more common in Western Apache work than in any other coiled basketry in the Southwest.

A few general design traits should be mentioned. Characteristically, they are allover; sometimes they are more confined to bands, while at others they are interwoven. A solid black central circle or star is the normal take-off point for most of the designs; the outer edge of the circle and the rim of the basket often combine to create a banded area. Designs usually go to the rim. Small blocks, squares, or rectangles make up the vertical, zigzag, diagonal, or other arrangements, with life forms or small geometric elements spotted in at various points. The latter have a tendency to relieve the tension created by the great animation of the allover designs. Geometric elements include the above blocks, plus crosses, diamonds, chevrons, terraced figures, ladder-like affairs, triangles, lines straight or wavy and long or short, swastikas, and arrows. Some of these elements, of course, are combined into various units or motifs. A variety of life forms appears, including generalized quadrupeds and birds, or definite creatures such as dogs, horses, deer, cattle, men, women, men on horseback, and a few others.

Layouts in tray baskets may be classed as divided and undivided. The divided layout is banded; in the undivided style there are four basic layouts — repeated, centered, circling-continuous, and radiating. In the first of these layouts, large elements are repeated within the area between the central motif and the rim. The centered style is created by exaggeration of size of the central motif. The circling-continuous layout is formed by motifs such as frets completely encircling the decorative area. Radiating designs take off from the central black circle and go to or almost to the rim. This layout can be divided into a static and a dynamic style: in the former, the elements of design move straight out from the central circle to the edge, while in the latter they emanate as zigzags, spirals, or other more moving patterns. Several of these layouts are combined in some baskets to form composite styles.

Stars are very common in Western Apache baskets. They may have three, four, five, six, seven, or eight points. Rarely are they more complex. Rows of stars or star points may be repeated several times, generally overlapping in such a way as to create a complex style. Each point of a star may be dark or light, and may be plain or have single or multiple elements within its outline.

Apache coiled jar designs vary to some degree. All jars examined had decorated bottoms; in some instances these were independent, while in others they united with the wall design. In all samples examined, composite layouts appear. Several lay-

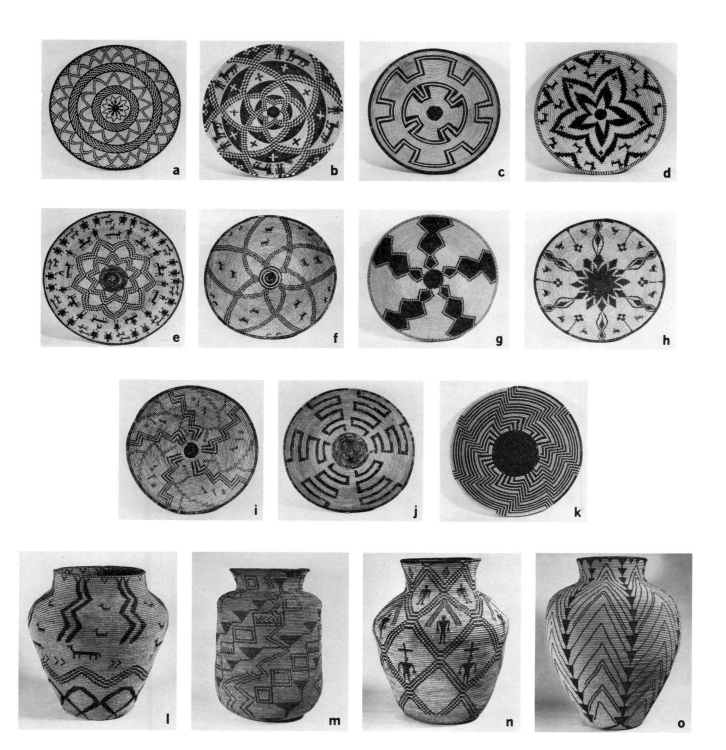

FIGURE 2.24 Typical Western Apache tray bowls and jar baskets. Representative of the typical trays made by this tribe, and also illustrating the major layouts and designs, are baskets (a) through (k). Baskets (a) and (b) show banded layouts, the first a simple one with alternate repeated elements, while (b) is much more complex, with units from band to band merging in such a way as to give quite a different character to the overall feeling of design. Examples (c), (d), (e), and (f) show circling continuous patterns, three of them a combination of geometrics and life forms. Radiate patterns are represented in the remaining basket trays, with (g) and (h) more static and the others quite dynamic. These examples mostly range from 15" to 17" in diameter and are of excellent workmanship. The four jars show the typical wide mouths, some slight variation in neck and layout styles, and the variety of elements which appear on this form. Many of these jars are graceful in gross shape, such as the high-shouldered (l), (n), and (o). In design arrangement, (l) combines vertical and encircling styles, (m) is allover diagonal, (n) is allover net-like, and (o) combines a vertical and encircling layout. Weaving is good in all. The jars are from 20 1/2" to 24" tall.

out styles of jar walls include allover, spotted, and vertical arrangements. The first is made up of horizontal or oblique zigzags, or an allover network. The vertical style is static. Multiple zigzag lines are common, and they sometimes have spotted life elements between them. Spotted layouts often have larger geometric and smaller life themes repeated all over the body and neck of the vessel. Vertical arrangements utilize lighter and/or heavier geometric bands reaching from base to rim, with or without scattered life designs between them. The network style is composed of large crisscrossed bands forming diamond-like areas in which life and geometric motifs appear.

Because there is considerable use of solids and heavy lines, Apache design has a substantial feeling. It is not overbearing, however, for much of the heaviness is relieved by the use of outlining lines, by balance in mass areas of dark and light, and by the spotting of independent and small elements in the background. Perfect symmetry is often maintained in the basic design. Both repetitive and alternating symmetry contribute to a rhythmic style; a feeling of dynamism is frequent. Design is unified, often bold, and generally simple in terms of the use of a limited number of elements in a single basket. There is no emphasis on any particular number of divisions in a pattern, although four to seven divisions are perhaps most common.

Pima and Papago

Pima and pre-twentieth century Papago coiled baskets were both made of willow. However, the typical Papago basket of this century is woven of yucca. Therefore in the popular eye — and too often in museum and traders' collections — the Papago willow basket is not recognized as Papago. Differences in the two willow types are not always obvious; furthermore, the geographic proximity of the two tribes, as well as intermarriages, have resulted in blendings which further complicate the problem of proper identification.

When Kissell studied Papago and Pima baskets in 1910-11, she noted that Papago women were then making some pieces woven of yucca for sale. But, according to her, these native women would not use such baskets themselves unless they had no other.[41] Contact with white men since the turn of the century has gradually eliminated the need for native pieces, and very few have survived. During the same years, however, more and more baskets of yucca have been made to be sold.

The first serious curb on Papago basket production occurred with the development of cotton cultivation in the Gila and Salt River valleys during and after World War II. Indians received relatively good pay for working in the fields, so entire families

would migrate to the cotton camps. As a result, basketmaking became an increasingly less important factor in the lives of many Papago women. Before this situation arose, these women produced baskets to sell so that they could purchase household items or to earn pin money to satisfy personal desires which ranged from going to the circus to getting a permanent. Some Papagos still work at cotton picking or other wage-earning tasks, but there has been a revival of basketmaking among the women of this tribe. Recently there has been a brisk and healthy production on the main Sells Reservation, except for the western edge, and also on the San Xavier Reservation.[42]

Among Pimas and Papagos, coarse and open-stitch coiling was common in the past, being used primarily for the production of large storage baskets (Fig. 2.25), and secondarily for a few small pieces such as trinket baskets. Both tribes used a multiple-splint foundation; it was wheat straw in the Pima granary basket, while Papagos used wheat straw, beargrass, or ocotillo. A bark binding element derived from the mesquite, willow, or acacia was employed by the Pimas, while Papagos resorted to the leaves of the sotol or mesquite bark. Sewing was wide-spaced, with stitches a half inch or more apart and coils the same in width.

Granaries were undecorated. Rims were finished in braiding or in the same stitch as the rest of the basket except that the stitching was closer and tighter. Smaller Papago storage jars were barrel-shaped; the Pima style was bell-shaped. Larger jars were more globular. All tended to lose their shapes

FIGURE 2.25 Large Pima storage basket. Woven in wide-spaced coiling with a foundation of wheat straw and sewing elements made of mesquite bark, this one is 30″ high, and 31″ at its greatest diameter.

with use. Smaller jars were 1½ to 4 feet high, while the large ones were sometimes 6 feet high and the same in diameter. In weaving the large granary the woman had to get inside to finish the job. Due to its large size, the piece was often woven on the spot where it was to remain.

The open-stitch coil style may or may not be related to a decorative open and split-stitch Papago style which seems to have become popular for commercial baskets produced in the 1930's and still made in fairly limited quantities today. This basket varies in shape and size, but small ones are most common. Straight-sided round and oval forms, some with a bit of shaping in the walls, and with or without lids, were and are produced. Stitching has a vertical or diagonal alignment. When well-executed, this technique has a charm all its own. Sometimes the stitches are split on the exposed surface and splayed open at the top (Fig. 2.26); this adds a decorative touch to many of the open coil baskets. Very recently one woman has done this stitch in such a way as to give it a distinctive curved effect; she calls it the "wheat pattern" (Fig. 2.26).

It is in the close coil that both the Pimas and Papagos have done the greatest quantity of basketry and the most artistic weaving (Fig. 2.27). From a small tied, coiled, or plaited center, the coil then begins fairly tight and small and continues evenly to the rim. Rim coils are finished in the regular stitching of the basket, in oblique sewing, or in braiding. Braiding is not uncommon on many of the older baskets, but it is seldom seen on contemporary Papago yucca pieces.

"Coiled ware of twenty-five years ago was more carefully made than that today," said Kissell.[43] From this statement it seems that even at the early date of her study, 1910-11, some degeneracy had set in. For basketry as a whole, of both these tribes, this trend continued through the years, with occasional betterment of the craft, sometimes at the hands of single individuals. Some excellent work was produced by Pima women in the early 1920's. After the establishment of the Papago Arts and Crafts Guild, considerable improvement in yucca basketry was noticeable, in the late 1930's and into the 1940's. Papagos are doing some good basketry today, yet their best efforts are mostly limited to a few individual craftswomen. Little superior work has been produced by Pima women for some years, and almost no baskets are woven today.

In the old-type close-coil basketry, materials differed more from one locale to another than they did from Pima to Papago weavers as a whole. Shreve indicates this in the careful analysis in her introductory remarks.[44] However, Papagos used either cattail or beargrass for the foundation; when they resorted to beargrass the basket was more durable,

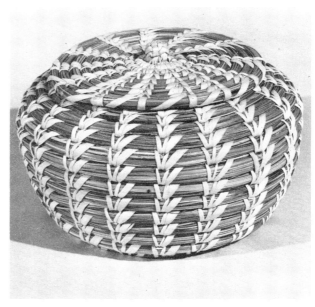

FIGURE 2.26 Split- and open-stitch baskets woven by the Papagos. Popular today are these two styles. The top basket is in a plain split stitch, a style that has been made for many years, while the one below is in what is called the wheat stitch. It is a little more elaborate in the extra stitch to the right of the split stitch.

but also stiffer and more harsh. The Pimas used cattail almost exclusively — their basket was less durable but more flexible. Willow was the common material for sewing the Pima basket, and for all older and later native-use Papago baskets; rarely, cottonwood splints may have been substituted. Papagos traded with their northern neighbors, the Pimas, for the willow, since their dry desert afforded no such material. It was about the turn of the century that the Papagos resorted to local yucca for some coiled baskets, for there are records of the purchase of such pieces in and about Tucson, Arizona, at this early date. The use of yucca and

FIGURE 2.27 Pima and Old Papago baskets. The latter are called "Old Papago" because in this earlier style Papagos used willow as did the Pimas; later Papago baskets are made of yucca. *Top row:* four fine Pima basket trays: two radiate dynamic styles of layout, an allover pattern featuring a squash-blossom motif, and a repeated layout with a "turtle" motif. *Second row:* two Old Papago trays and a wine basket. Note the heaviness of design in contrast to the light and delicate style of the Pima. *Bottom row:* an Old Papago wine basket — exterior and interior — and a Pima water jar or olla. Even in form there is greater sturdiness in the Papago basket, a lighter feeling in the Pima.

the commercialization of the Papago basket go hand in hand. Today the use of willow by this tribe is rare.

Black designs in baskets of both tribes were executed in the native martynia, or devil's claw. The Papagos cultivated this plant in some of their fields, for under these conditions the pods grew longer, thereby supplying better sewing splints. Since willow was precious to the Papagos, they used more devil's claw with the result that there was a dominance of dark over light in the finished basket design.

In general, sewing was tighter in the Papago willow basket than in the Pima basket; this added to the firmness and hardness of the wall of the Papago piece. On the other hand, Papago sewing was more irregular; thus, the better stitching gave the Pima piece a smoother and thinner wall. The Papago basket tended to be more watertight, the Pima less so.

There has been little change in Pima basket shapes through the years except for the addition of the flat plaque; this may well be explained by the fact that the craft was never commercialized to any degree. Jars, bowls, and trays were the three dominant forms. The closest approach to any real commercialization of the craft on the part of the Pimas was the production of miniatures. Baskets are rarely made by Pima women today; when they are, they tend to be reduced in size, of poor quality, and inferior in design.

A few other comparisons between Pima and old Papago baskets point up further details of form.[45] Papago bowls were proportionately wider, more globular, and the base was flatter and broader. The Pima bowl was bell-shaped, more slender in line, and — because the bottom was small — there was a pronounced oblique line from rim to base. In outline the Papago bowl was rounding, the Pima was oval and more subtle. Papago trays were deeper and, again, had a broader and flatter base. The Pima tray outline was almost double-curved, while the Papago was stiffer and straighter.

Changes in Papago basket forms accompanied changes in materials and commercialization of the craft. Although the first yucca baskets copied their contemporary willow counterparts, native forms gradually lost favor. Sizes were reduced. As native-use values were lost, changes in form were aimed directly at the white man's taste and requirements. Flat bottoms, straighter sides, lids, scalloped edges, oval shapes, deeper forms which could be used as wastebaskets, flat plaques and other "curio" shapes replaced the earlier bowls and trays. There were, of course, several additional earlier forms, generally not abundant and rarely found in collections. These include the marriage basket (used to serve food to

the bride and groom) which was a smaller-mouthed, flatter-and-wider-bottomed piece, with blue beads around the rim. It is probable that this was of Pima manufacture because the Papagos did not use these blue beads.[46] This basket was described verbally to Shreve — the original was buried with its owner.

In the old Papago and the Pima baskets, sizes tended to be comparable. Pima trays measured between 12 and 20 inches in diameter and from 3 to 5 inches in depth. Papago trays were of two types, one similar to the Pima, and a second which was not quite so wide and was much more shallow. Papago bowls were as wide as the Pima tray but much deeper.

Coil and stitch counts are interesting in relation to these baskets. Old Papago willow pieces averaged four to five coils and nine to ten stitches per inch, while most of the Pima baskets ranged from five to seven coils and ten to twelve stitches to the inch.

Rims of old Papago baskets vary. Some were in the same stitch as that of the basket and were often black in color; some were overcast in a tight, close, oblique stitching; and about one-third of a sample of twenty-nine baskets had braided rims. Of a sample of 118 Pima baskets, the rims of 88 were braided, 12 were overcast, and 18 were in regular sewing.

In all these respects, the modern Papago yucca baskets are quite different. Forms are more varied, less refined, and less standardized. Rims are finished in the regular sewing stitch and then, quite commonly, overcast in a single slanting stitch, or with one diagonal and one vertical stitch, or in cross stitch. Braiding is rare. Often these rim finishes are in black, sometimes in green or yellow. In coil and stitch count there is some variation: older yucca pieces often have four to five coils and seven to eight stitches to the inch, while a count on a large number of better contemporary pieces revealed that in a majority, coils ran one and one-half to three per inch and stitches six to seven per inch. However, some of the modern Papago basketry is far cruder than this.

Because of the black center which was prominent in many Pima and old Papago baskets, the design layout was often banded (Fig. 2.27). The banded area was treated in different ways by the two tribes, but both used two basic arrangements: first, a simple and continuous theme within the area, and second, repeated motifs. Patterns sometimes emanated from the black center, often forming allover and integrated layouts. When a design moved from the center circle to the rim, the arrangement was either static (went straight from circle to rim) or was dynamic (more action from center to rim).

Deep-bowl layouts were similar to these tray styles in that they were basically confined to wall decoration alone. Jar design layouts are also similar but have in addition an allover, net-like decoration.

As mentioned above, the Papago weaver showed a preference in her designs for masses of dark (Fig. 2.27). Although she was influenced by material available, it is probable that this also expressed an innate feeling for a design style. Papagos attained this end by increasing the size of the center circle, by grouping lines, thus widening bands, or by mass spotting of large elements. Pima lines were narrower, more allover, and other elements were generally smaller and more numerous. Thus Papago design was heavy; Pima was light. Papagos emphasized horizontal and vertical or nearly vertical lines; the Pimas stressed whorls, spirals, obliques, and rosettes, thus utilizing more curvilinear and more diagonal lines. If a Pima weaver used a horizontal line, it was short and secondary, and was definitely overpowered by other lines.

Papago design was dignified, reserved, almost stiff; Pima patterns were dynamic and full of grace. Papago lines were simple, direct, powerful, while Pima lines were delicate and involved. Because of their greater width and size, Papago patterns seem crude and heavy in contrast with the clean-cut and almost perfect lines of the Pima designs. There is beautiful balance in direction of lines in Pima baskets.

Among specific design motifs of the Pima basket were: meanders used in a variety of ways; the squash blossom with three to twelve petals; simple and complex spirals and frets on plain or patterned backgrounds; the swastika (Fig. 2.27); and the maze pattern, usually with the small figure of a man at the entrance. A variety of geometric elements was generally combined with or into the main design motif; these included squares, rectangles, steps, triangles, crosses, lines, coyote tracks (four black squares or rectangles arranged around an open square or rectangular center), and a few others. Some life forms were also used by the Pimas, including men, women, horses, snakes, and the Gila monster. Earlier Papago designs were less varied; among their old willow-basket designs were vertical and encircling frets and horizontal bands. These were made up of wide vertical and horizontal lines, squares, rectangles, and stepped elements. Both tribes used multiple outlines of solids or lines connecting solids.

Designs in the Papago yucca basket are very different from those of the willow piece (Fig. 2.28). The black center is generally missing. Layout is more scattered and spotty and, even at best, lacks the integration of the old style. There is a simpler unity in some patterns. Layouts include spotted, centered, banded (more or less), and radiating styles. Some of the chief design elements and motifs of the modern basket are stars or flowers, diagonals (stepped and spotty, or in bands), short frets, meanders, zigzags, short curved lines, straight and often parallel lines. Individual motifs which may be scattered about include single or multiple coyote tracks, clouds, stars, arrow points, triangles, and life forms. The last includes birds, humans, butterflies, owls, turtles, scorpions, and a few others. All of these themes are simpler, more often separate, and almost always less involved than in older baskets.

Both Pimas and Papagos have made miniature baskets during this century, obviously as a concession to white men, for the Indian had little or no use for small forms. Much of the Pima work was done in earlier years, although there are a few women of this tribe who still make miniatures. Papagos, however, have developed this special craft largely within the past few years.

Sizes of miniatures range from about one-half inch to 5 inches in diameter for bowls or trays with similar dimensions for jar heights. Both coil and stitch counts are also varied, with much of the Pima work finer in quality than that of the Papagos. This is interesting since the Pimas used willow predominantly while Papagos employed both yucca and horsehair in making their miniatures. Some of these Pima baskets had counts of twenty coils and twenty-five to thirty stitches to the inch; the Papago yucca pieces, in the examples observed, seldom exceeded nine coils and fifteen to sixteen stitches to the inch. Quite naturally the count in the horsehair baskets exceeds that of both Pima and Papago pieces woven from other materials, but the workmanship seldom equals that of the best Pima willow examples.

Regular coiling is used to produce most miniature baskets. Occasionally the Papagos do a piece of open coiling, or even use the split-stich technique. Most rims are finished in the regular stitching although several examples of braiding and overcasting have been noted.

Forms of miniatures include flat plaques, shallow and deep bowls, jars, and life forms (Fig. 2.29). Jars vary from simple types without necks to wide- and narrow-necked types. The favored life form of the Papago is a cat — complete with whiskers!

As a whole, designs tend to be simpler in miniatures than they are in other basket forms — this is particularly true of Papago pieces. Comparatively, many of the earlier Pima examples have rather elaborate designs in relation to size; interestingly, each tribe features in its miniatures the general qualities of design in the larger forms. Pima patterns in these small pieces include meanders, sun-

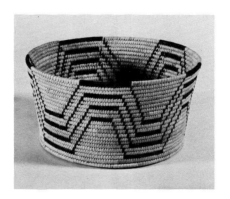

FIGURE 2.28 Recent and contemporary Papago yucca baskets. When the Papagos first used yucca in the early twentieth century, they often copied the old forms (top). Today the baskets are very different, as the three straight-sided pieces (second row) indicate; designs in these are also spotty in contrast to the integrated older designs. Very modern are lids and handles and simple patterns (third row). Life forms, such as the dog and the lady have been quite popular in recent years. All designing in these baskets is in black on the bleached white yucca.

flower or other blossoms, plain and slightly elaborated swastikas, curvilinear lines, and men. Some of these designs are allover. Papago miniature decoration is much simpler, more spotty, and features lines, coyote tracks, short meanders and stepped lines, and, rarely, a maze, a flower or star pattern, or a bird.

FIGURE 2.29 Papago miniatures. All of these baskets except the top right and second from the right in the bottom row are made of horsehair; the other two are made of yucca. Generally, black is used for the design, although the second and third from the left, top row, have "negative" patterns, that is, the design is in the lighter material. All patterns are simple but follow the styles of larger baskets. The two cats at the ends of the bottom row are quite complete with facial features, ears, whiskers, and tails. The larger basket is 3 3/8" in diameter and the smallest is 3/4" high.

Miscellaneous Pueblos

The puebloans are the final group of weavers of coiled baskets. Today only the Hopi are producing baskets in any quantity, although an occasional man in the Rio Grande has produced baskets in the recent past or is producing some today. The consensus is that more examples of this craft were produced in the past, but the record is very incomplete. On the other hand, there has been unbroken continuity in coiled basketry from prehistoric times to the present among the Hopi Indians. And, due to the activities of the Museum of Northern Arizona, Flagstaff, there is a healthy production of fine coiled baskets by this tribe today.

Zuñi baskets collected in the 1880's were of a two-rod-and-bundle bunched foundation, and they were close coiled. Mason illustrates a coiled basket jar from this village which has a short and inward-sloping neck, flat shoulders and bottom, and almost straight side walls.[47] The main decorative theme is a wide zigzag made up of rectangles. Mason suggests that the piece may be of Apache origin, but his illustration of the basket shows side walls which seem too straight and a bottom too flat to fit into Apache types. Also, the shape is not unlike other old Zuñi pieces examined; one such piece in the Southwest Museum is crudely coiled and a little more rounded in body form.

A Zía coiled jar illustrated by Mason[48] is quite like several others which were examined — small-mouthed with little or no neck and a squat and rounded body. Coiled baskets were made at Zía until about 1955. The tray form made there is illustrated by Ellis; of the three examples, one has repeated and two have continuous layout styles.[49] One of the latter designs calls to mind old-style Navajo baskets — a wide red zigzag outlined in black and with a ceremonial break. Ellis reports that Zía baskets are made of sumac- or willow-rod-and-yucca-bundle foundation sewed with one of the first two materials. Sewing is fine and even, with eight to eleven stitches and four or five coils to the inch. Diameters of the trays are from 11½ to 15½ inches while depths range from 2 to 5 inches.[50]

A large tray basket woven by Alcario Gachupin of Jémez was displayed at the 1962 Gallup Ceremonials. It was decorated in green, red-orange, and black, with a geometric motif repeated eight times. This motif was composed of an "eye-beam" element to which was attached a diamond. Gachupin is the only basket weaver at Jémez, although several other men of this village know the craft.

Hopi

Hopi coiled baskets are produced in the three Second Mesa villages of Mishongnovi, Shipaulovi, and Shungopovi. All use the same materials. Most commonly, finely shredded yucca forms the large round bundle over which tight and close sewing is done in narrow and evenly cut yucca splints; sometimes shredded grasses serve as the foundation. The remarkably even coils average about two to the inch. Stitching, which is exceptionally regular and even, counts about fourteen to the inch. It is amazing how very consistently this latter stitch count appears. This figure is not only applicable to the present time, but also to baskets forty or more years old. A simple coil starts the basket, and the rim is finished in the same sewing stitch as the rest of the piece. Commonly the design is carried into the last coil; thus there may be some alternation of color in the rim.

Colors used in the Hopi coiled work include a soft red-brown, black, and yellow (Fig. 2.30). The red and black are dyed as are the splints for wicker basketry, but the yellow is usually of yucca which has been partially bleached. Ground color is the natural off-white of the yucca leaf. Green is sometimes used; it is the natural-colored leaf from the outer part of the plant. Some years ago aniline dyes were used for the sewing elements in Hopi coiled basketry as they were in wicker; the two popular colors for the former were sickly reds and greens. Natural colors or native dyes used today are far more pleasing.

FIGURE 2.30 Hopi coiled plaques, bowls, and jar. Both life and geometric decoration are represented in these examples. Hopi kachina masks are portrayed in the top center and bottom left baskets, and possibly in the bottom right. A Hopi woman is depicted in the center basket, bottom row, while the remaining baskets have geometric designs. The common colors in the Hopi coiled basket — black, dark red, and yellow on a natural ground — appear in all pieces. (*Photo by J. H. McGibbeny*)

Hopi basket shapes and sizes in the coiled weave are much more varied today than they were formerly. Natively, a plaque, a shallow tray, bowls, and jars were produced. All of these forms are made now in quite a variety of sizes. Smaller versions of the older shapes are especially popular. Deeper forms which serve as wastebaskets, oval bowls, square-topped and round-bottomed forms, and a few other shapes have been added through the years.

Design layouts in Hopi coiled baskets are of several types (Fig. 2.30). One favored style, particularly on plaques, is a centered one with a kachina mask, a kachina, bird, butterfly, or other theme centrally placed. There is almost always left and right balance in this layout, but balance above and below only when geometric motifs are used. Banded layouts are common, particularly on the deeper bowl and jar forms. Bands may be vertical or horizontal; the latter may be single or multiple. On jars and bowls there are also repeated layouts, such as a cloud design duplicated four times on walls of bowls. Radiate arrangements are not uncommon.

Designs vary greatly in Hopi baskets, with some related to form (Fig. 2.31). In flat shapes, both symmetrical and asymmetrical patterns are used; life forms, clouds, and geometric motifs appear in these plaques. Trays, bowls, and jars are more commonly decorated with symmetrical and repetitive geometric patterns. Early and late there was and is much alternation of color in designs; this may be simple, as in the use of two colors only, or it may become very complex in the introduction of one more color. When repeated and alternating motifs are added to the latter, the end result is rather complicated design.

Design elements and motifs in Hopi coiled basketry are extremely numerous. In addition to the above, there are, in the first place — as in all other Southwestern Indian baskets — designs built up of squares or rectangles, rarely of lines. Clouds with or without dripping rain and lightning are very popular, as are stars, rainbows, and whirlwinds. So too are kachinas and masks. Women, deer, butterflies, birds, and a few other life themes are common. Various geometrics, such as diamonds, zigzags, meanders, and odd forms are also used. The beautiful tray which a bride weaves for her groom — and which he must have in order to get into the next world — is a large piece with a star or circle design or an "arrow" repeated four times.

Some comment relative to older (1850–1900) and more recent (1930–1965) Hopi basketry is of interest. In some older pieces, coils are thicker but stitching is about the same as in more recent work (Fig. 2.32). Designs in earlier pieces tend to be simpler, more generalized, and allover; in later ones they are more definitive, more detailed, and better planned and executed. Most of the basket is covered with pattern in early pieces; later the design may be allover but there is more undecorated area. Color is handled in a simpler way in earlier work; later it becomes very complex, not so much in number of colors as in elaborate alternations and repetitions.

Today the Hopis are producing better coiled basketry than ever before.[51] They continue to use baskets to decorate their homes, give them as wedding presents, and use them for ceremonial purposes. These native-use pieces are well-made; also a great many baskets made for commercial purposes are perfectly woven and beautifully designed.

Summary

It is the abundant and refined product of the Hopi weaver today, and to a lesser degree that of the Papago basket maker, which indicates that this craft is not dead. To be sure, one could not predict

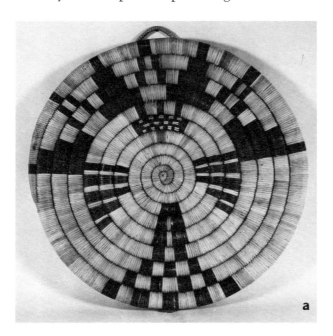

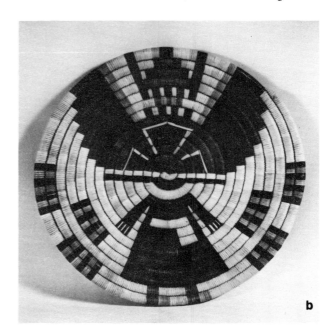

FIGURE 2.31 Contemporary Hopi coiled baskets. Although all of these baskets are woven with fat coils, the sewing elements are regular, and the stitching is close and even. Flat plaques (a and b) and shallow or deeper bowls (c and d) are the common forms. Designs may be life themes, such as the Crow Mother (b) and deer (d), or geometric (c). Colors are varied, too, from black and red on white (c) to the elaborate combination of (b): light and dark yellow, red, brown, and natural. Design is usually carried into the rim (a and b).

a future for basketry in the face of changing economies, revived interest in native crafts (as in the case of the Jicarilla Apache), efforts on the part of whites to change the direction of Indian arts, and a multitude of other influences.

Viewing the picture as a whole, it can be seen that baskets were used by all Southwestern Indians. A decline in their popularity, particularly among the puebloans, occurred in pre-Columbian times when pottery was introduced. A spurt in production resulted from Spanish needs after 1540. But as later Spaniards, then Mexicans, and finally Anglo-Americans brought substitute utensils to the Indian, basketry declined or disappeared (relative to significance of contact). Since 1900, the potentials of commercialization have greatly influenced the quantity of production; museums, native craft guilds, traders, and other individuals have affected quality of Indian baskets. Where baskets are used natively, there is more continuity in shape, size, and design. And, to repeat, basketry is the oldest of the craft arts.

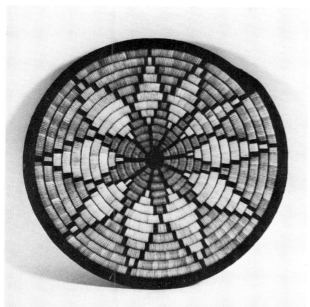

FIGURE 2.32   The old and the new in Hopi baskets. The old style (above) used very large coils; they measure almost one inch in diameter in this piece. They are much smaller in the one below. Designs tend to be diffuse in the older pieces; they are much more ordered and concise in later work. Earlier patterns were generalized, now they are definitive. Colors were aniline red and green, now they are natural dyes and often vary in range.

Textiles  *Chapter III*

PERHAPS one of man's most significant discoveries was textile weaving. Although the basket industry laid firm foundations upon which this later craft was to build, its limitations prevented development beyond a certain point. Textile weavers were to discover new and delicate materials which in turn were to offer potentials in refinement of techniques and artistry. In the Southwest, the textile weaver explored new avenues in the field of clothing which were totally impossible in basketry and its associated technologies and materials.

True weaving is defined as "a technic distinct from basketry [which] may be said to begin where the fineness or the flexibility of the material employed compels (or at least renders advisable) a resort to some device which facilitates manipulation of the component fibers."[1]

Prehistoric Background

Spinning of fibers is perhaps the first step in the direction of true weaving. Back of this, of course, would be the ability to weave larger elements, such as reeds and splints, into mats and baskets; the manual dexterity expressed here is of no small consequence in the development of textiles. Probably spinning was done by hand at first; later it was done on a long slender stick with a whorl — a circular disc — placed below center to keep the stick in motion as the thread was spun (Fig. 3.1).

The terms "warp" and "weft" are basic to any discussion of true weaving. Warp is the stationary element, the foundation — warps are the threads strung on the loom before weaving begins. Wefts are the moving elements, the filler, the elements woven over and under the warps to form the fabric (Fig. 3.2).

Woven bands from Basket Maker times have been found with round sticks serving for the attachment of the warp threads. Perhaps these sticks were secured in some manner so that the warps were held in a taut position. Simple as this device was, it may well have anticipated the loom. Another mechanical aid of sorts is suggested by Kidder and others for the making of crescent-toed sandals; a loop of cordage may have been suspended from a stationary limb or similar device, and from the loop were hung warp threads upon which the fine weaving of this sandal type was executed.[2]

Briefly, small weaving includes a variety of sandals, bands, bags, tump straps, and a few miscellaneous items. Some sandals were produced in basketry techniques, such as the plaited type, but the above-mentioned crescent-toed Basket Maker III sandal was a finely woven piece. Sometimes in the best work there are as many as thirty or thirty-six warp elements in the sandal width. So fine are the weft elements that they resemble cotton. These sandals were made of apocynum or yucca cordage; both plants were native to the Anasazi area. Designs were woven in, produced either in the plain natural color in a variety of weaves, or in colored cords, or additional elements were inserted or knots tied in such ways as to produce raised designs. Tapestry weave, in which warp threads are concealed by the wefts, was typical of this well-made sandal and many other small pieces. This weave is described in greater detail below.

Bags were both coarse and fine in weave. Some were made of wide strips of juniper bark coarsely woven. Others were in fine cordage and decorated; these were textile-like in quality. Netting was commonly produced. Needles have been found with occasional nets, thus indicating the use of such a device in making some of these pieces. Nets were made both large and small; some of the largest measure over two hundred feet in length.

As indicated, designing was not unusual in much of the small weaving. Horizontal bands and stripes were, perhaps, the most common elements, with considerable variety in alternation in widths of each. The prevalent colors were reddish-brown and black. In sandals and a few bands, additional designs included steps, zigzags, meanders, diagonals, triangles, and short lines.

A crude, but interesting, piece of weaving in the Basket Maker period was a robe or blanket made

FIGURE 3.1   Wooden spindle sticks and whorls and wooden comb used by modern Indian weavers. The upper stick and whorl are Navajo style, about 20″ long; the lower one Hopi, about 22 1/2″ long. Both were inherited from prehistoric times. The comb is 8 7/8″ long and 1 1/2″ wide.

of fur (Fig. 3.3) or feather cord. Turkey feathers were split down the middle, or rabbit skins were cut into narrow strips; either of these was then wrapped about a yucca cord, or the feathers were twisted into the two-ply cordage as it was produced. Lengths of the resultant soft cord were stretched close together in a frame, then twined at intervals with plain yucca string. Fur cloth goes back in time to the Desert Culture,[3] while fur robes are still made by the Hopi Indians.[4] Feather cord, on the other hand, seems to have been introduced later; it was short-lived, with relatively few small pieces made of this material in the prehistoric Pueblo periods.

Whether the true vertical loom developed in the Southwest or whether it was introduced from Mexico is still a question. At any rate, it had appeared by Pueblo III times and made possible the outstanding fabrics produced by pre-Columbian weavers.

The true loom was simple (Fig. 3.2): two upright poles supported two horizontal poles. In some pueblo situations the top pole may have been suspended from ceiling beams or from some other device. Floor anchor loops have been found in prehistoric kivas and rooms, indicating that the lower bar was secured to these and not to upright poles. To the upper and lower bars of the loom were tied the warp selvages. The latter were formed as the continuous, figure-eight warps were secured with

cordage at each end. Generally a heddle (a long slender stick) was attached to the warps to facilitate the insertion of large numbers of weft elements at one time. In a simple weave the heddle was tied loosely to alternate warps; a second slender stick served as a shed rod as it was inserted between threads in such a way as to bring forward the warps not tied to the heddle. Shed rods and heddles, too, often unspecialized in nature, would be difficult to identify archaeologically. A comparable but horizontal loom was known in southern Arizona.

The waist or belt loom had the far pole of the strung warps attached to a tree limb or some other more or less stationary point while the closer end was fastened about the waist of the weaver. Warps were wound about each end bar in a continuous, figure-eight fashion, as in the true loom set-up. Narrow textiles, like belts and bands, were also made on a continuous warp; this warp could be moved like a roller towel. Modern Hopi men have learned to secure the near end of these warps to the floor and not about the waist. In the true loom, the warp or stationary element is vertical, in the waist loom it is vertical or oblique; the weft or moving element is horizontal.

Cotton was cultivated in prehistoric times, a fact known from the seeds, bolls, and raw cotton which are found widely in ancient sites. Martin reports cotton thread from before the opening of the Christian era.[5] Spinning of fibers is attested to

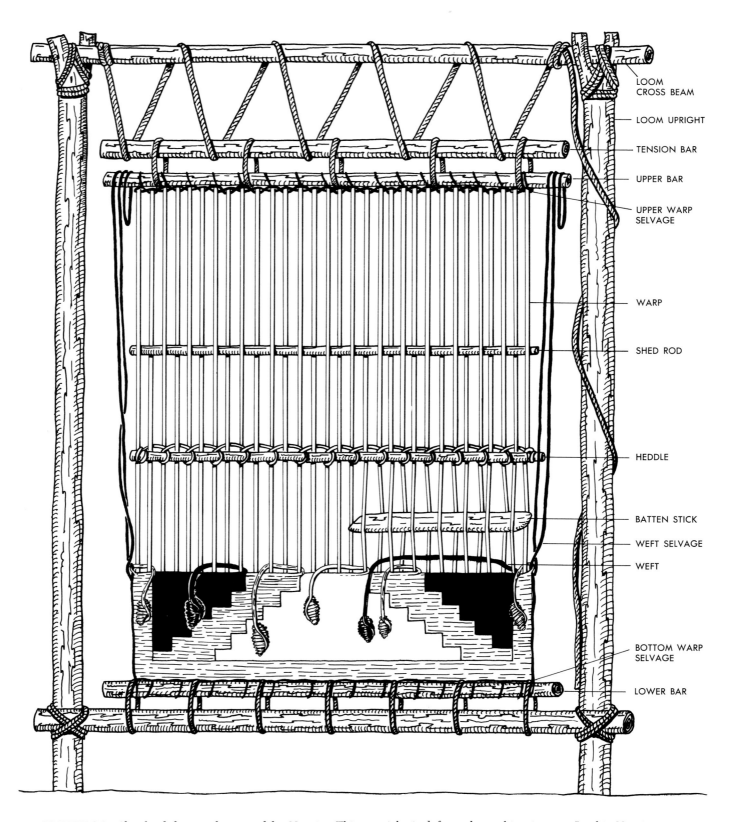

LOOM
CROSS BEAM

LOOM UPRIGHT

TENSION BAR

UPPER BAR

UPPER WARP
SELVAGE

WARP

SHED ROD

HEDDLE

BATTEN STICK

WEFT SELVAGE

WEFT

BOTTOM WARP
SELVAGE

LOWER BAR

FIGURE 3.2 Sketch of the true loom used by Navajos. This was inherited from the prehistoric past. In this Navajo type, beams are set up in the hogan or in the open, with cross beams securely tied to them. From the top horizontal beam is suspended a secondary and smaller beam (tension bar); to the latter is attached, in turn, the bar to which the warps have been secured. The opposite warp bar is attached to the bottom beam. Weaving begins at the bottom, with weft threads inserted largely by hand; sometimes the thread is wound on a long stick and passed through a number of warps. To aid in opening warps (or shed) for this purpose are the heddles and shed rods. For example, the heddle is pulled forward (the batten stick inserted to hold it open), and all threads attached thereto will be in front of the wefts now inserted. The batten stick may also be used to pound down the weft threads, or, if the space is small, the wooden comb may be used for this purpose. The rope at the top of the loom can be used to lower the loom so that the weaver can always sit at her work.

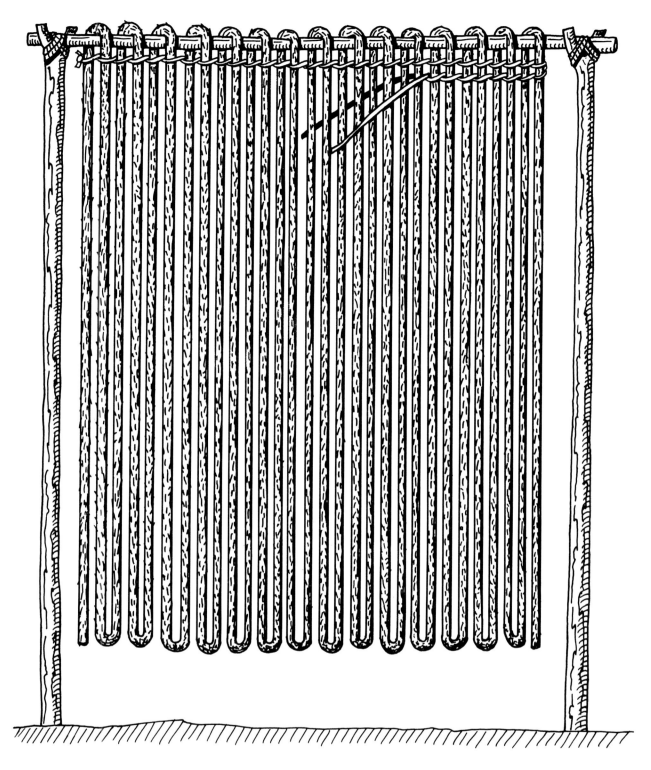

FIGURE 3.3 Sketch showing how a fur robe is woven. This piece is still made by the Hopis. A simple loom set-up is used for the production of this robe. From a single top cross-bar, held by two upright poles embedded in the ground, are suspended the strips of fur twisted about a core of heavy woolen thread. The strips may also be fastened at the bottom, usually to a slight pole. The strips are simply twined together at about four-inch intervals, starting at the top.

later in spindle sticks and whorls, some with cotton attached. In prehistoric sites circular and usually thin whorls of stone, clay, or wood are found. No wool was used in pre-Columbian weaving, although some animal hair was combined with other materials, such as mountain-sheep wool.

In weaving, design and technique are closely related. Among the most important techniques were plain, tapestry, and twilled weaves (Fig. 3.4); to a more limited extent the ancients also used additional weaves but these did not survive into historic times.

Plain weave in natural-colored threads has no particular artistic merit except for the regularity of the alternation of weft over warp throughout the fabric. However, colored threads may be added in either warps or wefts or in both; if in warps alone, vertical stripes or bands result, or if in wefts alone, the same themes appear in horizontal arrangement. If the colored threads are used in both warps and wefts, checks or plaids result.

One of the most important weaves in connection with design is tapestry; it was most commonly executed in an over-one-under-one alternation of both warps and wefts. Twilled tapestry was also developed, with different rhythms such as over-two-under-two, or over-three-under-three, and other variations. Inasmuch as the wefts were battened down so as to completely conceal the warps, they carried the burden of design. Because of the nature of tapestry weave, new threads may be added anywhere in the fabric, thus greatly increasing design potentials. Despite the limitations placed on the

weaver through tradition and technology, tapestry designs offer variations from simple stripes and bands to a wide variety of geometric figures, many in complex arrangements.

The form of the fabric was predetermined by the loom, narrow in the belt type, and square or rectangular in the true loom. Within these limitations prehistoric people produced a variety of belts and bands, kilts, skirts, breechcloths, shoulder blankets, robes, and a few other items (Fig. 3.5).

Uniformity and symmetry are the natural results of good textile weaving. Conventionality of design is typical, due to the nature of the crossing of elements, with some variation relative to thread refinement. The Southwestern aborigine never reached the point of curvilinear design in woven pattern. Even in embroidery and painting on finished fabrics he was more influenced by traditions of the decorative arts than by the potential of creating new (and curving) designs in freer techniques of decoration. The only approach to curvilinear design was in tie-dye, and this was more the result of technique than of creativity. (In tie-dye, predeter-

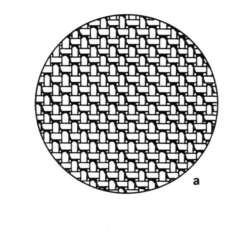

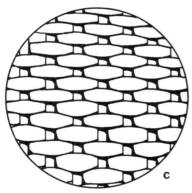
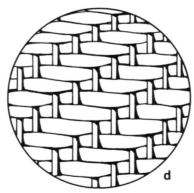
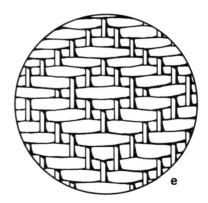

FIGURE 3.4 Sketches of the major textile weaves used by the historic Southwest Indians. (a) Plain weave is used in many cotton fabrics, with a simple over-one-under-one alternation of elements in the weaving process; warps and wefts are both visible. (b) Plain weave, twilled, simply means that the alternation of threads varies from (a). Often there is an over-two-under-two variation; diagonals, zigzags, and other simple geometrics can be created in varied twills. (c) is a simple tapestry weave, the most common used by the Navajos today. As the wefts are pushed or "battened" down, the warps are concealed, thus all design is created in the weft. Again by alternating threads, as over-two-under-two, or over-three-under-one, and others, the so-called twilled tapestries are produced — (d) diagonal twill and (e) diamond twill.

FIGURE 3.5 Characteristic pueblo fabrics. A wedding dress (a) is in plain weave, and of white cotton; later it is embroidered when the owner uses it for ceremonial purposes. The woman's shoulder blanket (b) has longer dimensions from side to side and shorter ones from end to end; diagonal twill weave is used in this piece, with woven dark blue and red borders. The wide white cotton sash (c) is in plain weave and is decorated with embroidery (or brocading). Plain-weave cotton and bright-colored wool embroidery at the sides are combined in the usual kilt (d) worn by the men for ceremonies. Red belts (e and f, the latter 87" x 4") and small bands ornamented with white and dark green are still woven by Hopi men. The small bands are used for head ties or garters. The woman's everyday dress (g) is of wool; it is wide from edge to edge — this piece is folded; the indigo blue border, the detail of which is shown in (h), is in diamond twill while the black center is woven in a diagonal twill; red and green twisted wool cords are usually placed at the junction of these two areas.

mined parts of a fabric are tied, then the entire piece is dipped in a dye bath; the cloth absorbs color where not tied and remains white in the tied positions.)

The basic design elements of textiles were simple. From them were created units or motifs which became typically Southwestern. In turn, simpler or very complex designs grew out of combinations of elements, units, or motifs. Among the more commonly used themes were rows or other arrangements of triangles (plain or hooked), steps, squares, rectangles, rhomboids, frets, and lineal themes. The ancient weaver was clever, for he created variety in design by varying the size and spacing of warps and wefts, by utilizing varied techniques and colors, and by employing endless combinations of the basic design elements. Predominant colors included the natural cotton plus black, brown, red or red-brown, blue, green, and yellow.

As in basketry, there was considerable choice in arrangement of pattern in relation to the total fabric. The field of decoration was decided in the mind of the weaver, then the design adjusted to the area.

Blankets, robes, breechcloths, and sashes presented a great variety of decoration, with styles varying from simple to complex, and with woven, painted, or embroidered designs. On blankets and robes were stripes and bands at the ends or all over the piece; narrow or broad borders of simple or complex geometric motifs; centered themes of single or multiple design units; allover designs of simple repeated single motifs or complex single- or multiple-unit designs. Some of the ornate arrangements appeared also on other garments, such as breechcloths, shirts, and on what appear to be dresses. Most elaborate were some of the bordered or allover patterns on kilts which are well illustrated in the Awatovi murals,[6] and in pieces found in excavations of prehistoric sites.

The inheritance from the prehistoric past in textiles was rich. In techniques and equipment, materials, forms, design units and designs, the pueblo folk followed in the footsteps of their ancestors. It is in refinement of technology and design, in the use of a wider variety of colors, and in more creative and imaginative design that the historic puebloan and Navajo weavers have excelled. Despite high attainment in weaving among the Hohokams, the Pimas and Papagos seemingly produced little along these lines.

Historic Background

Perhaps the two most important changes through historic years have been the virtual disappearance of textile production from all puebloan groups except the Hopis, and the gradual development of the craft by the Navajos in the years since 1700. Other changes occurred, of course, such as the substitution of wool for cotton, and the shift from weaving blankets to the production of rugs. The latter trend has won worldwide fame for the Navajo Indians. Numerous other lesser changes are mentioned in the following discussion.

Throughout historic times puebloans have continued to use cotton for ceremonial items and for a few other objects. All puebloans cultivated or traded for native cotton for years. The Rio Grande villagers abandoned this trait quite generally in the last decades of the nineteenth century, although a few individuals continued cotton cultivation into the 1930's. Hopi Indians raised cotton on a large scale for a long time; some of the men at Moenkopi continued the practice into the decade of 1930-1940. Commercial cotton batting was substituted by some Indians for their native product. Also, commercial cotton string was available from about 1890;[7] it was first used for warps, but in time it came to be employed for the entire cotton object. Rio Grande belts and Hopi products of today are woven of the commercial string.

After Spanish contact and the introduction of sheep, wool became important; puebloans were using it in the 1600's. Since the Navajos did not even learn weaving until around 1700, they have used wool from the beginning of their weaving career.

During the entire historic period, the ancient forms of loom products continued to be made with minor alterations in the pueblo area (Fig. 3.5). Wide and narrow belts were woven; shorter and quite narrow ones served as head ties and garters. Kilts, dresses, shoulder blankets, larger blankets, and footless stockings were produced, largely by the pueblo Indians. Navajos were limited primarily to blankets and blanket dresses, although they did make a few belts and, eventually, some cinches for their saddles. It was the Navajo blanket which became a rug toward the end of the nineteenth century in response to the demands of white men. This was accomplished basically by thickening the blanket, or making it coarser and heavier. Other than this, in all the years of white contact, no significant additions or changes have been made to native weaving in terms of the form of the products of the loom.

A few changes were made in technical equipment in the weaving craft by the Spanish when they introduced sheep to the Southwest Indians. Two important additions were the metal-toothed carder (curry comb-like, for straightening wool fibers) and metal shears (Fig. 3.6). Otherwise the Indians continued to use the same loom and equipment they had known for centuries. Wool was spun as cotton had been aboriginally, that is, on the na-

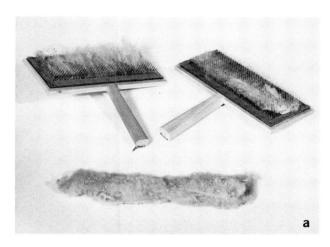

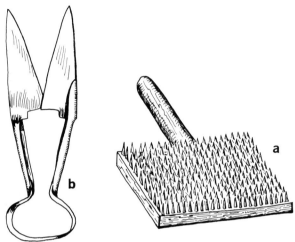

FIGURE 3.6 Metal carders (a) were necessary to prepare wool for weaving. When sheep were introduced to the Indians by the Spanish, these were also brought along. The wool is pulled back and forth, straightening and cleaning fibers in the process. Then it is pulled off in rolls ready for spinning. Metal shears (b) for shearing sheep were also introduced by the Spanish.

tive wooden spindle stick and generally with a wooden whorl.

In technology, some aboriginal styles have disappeared completely while others have not only survived but also have been developed to a higher degree. Plain weave, tapestry, embroidery, and brocading have been more highly developed during the historic years. It is quite generally thought that limited and simpler types of weaves continued to be used down through historic times to the last several decades of the nineteenth century. Since that time, and more recently, some experimentation has occurred with loom weaves, particularly among the Navajos.

As far as the Rio Grande puebloans are concerned, most of them continued with simpler weaves until this craft died out among them. They did, however, develop embroidery to a high degree in the several decades preceding the 1880's. Mera calls these last efforts the "classic" work of the Rio Grande folk. After 1880 almost no weaving was done with the exception of an attempted revival about 1920; again the emphasis was on embroidery. Nothing came of this, and today practically the only work done in New Mexican pueblos is the weaving of belts in a simple floating-warp technique.

Quite a different story is true among the Hopi Indians. Probably all the techniques in use by this tribe at the opening of the historic period have been continued down to the present or at least into recent years. Also, rugs have been made in recent years in a simple tapestry weave. Diagonal and diamond twills and plain weave are used in a variety of blankets, robes, dresses, kilts, and sashes. On the other hand, the Navajos have featured plain tapestry for all rugs, but employ several varieties of fancy tapestry and twill weaves for saddle blankets.

Rio Grande Pueblos

The major outside influences brought to bear on all puebloans of New Mexico can be summarized again in relation to Spanish-Mexicans and Anglo-Americans. Both Spanish and Anglos brought sheep to these people. Some of the puebloans were far less interested in raising this animal than others; thus there were differences in the emphases on native wool weaving. Anglo-Americans also brought a quantity and variety of commercial wools which were particularly important in the development of embroidery. Some of the New Mexican Indians became justly famous for their work of this type.

Students of Southwest Indian weaving believe that the native upright loom prevailed throughout the history of the Rio Grande. However, in 1948, the writer observed a Spanish-type foot loom in use at Jémez Pueblo for the production of cotton cloth about the width of a kilt and in a continuous piece — this is in contrast to the finished single kilt produced on the native loom. Although it is quite generally thought that men did the weaving in the Rio Grande pueblos, this foot loom was used by a woman. Surely it is the exception which proves the rule!

It should be emphasized here that the textiles produced at Isleta, Albuquerque, Santa Fe, and in the Spanish-American (Chimayo) villages of the Rio Grande have nothing to do with Indian crafts, although Indians are sometimes employed in these places. All of these ventures are different from the typical native efforts, particularly in the use of a foot loom.

A general analysis of the clothing of the puebloans will set the stage for the types of garments worn by them. Form was dictated not only by the hand looms but also by the fact that cutting and sewing were almost unknown to these people. This remains true in native products to the present.

Women's dress centered about the blanket. The typical pueblo form was a wide rectangle wrapped about the body, secured over the right shoulder and under the opposite arm, and caught at the waist with a fairly narrow and long belt (Fig. 3.7). For colder weather or for ceremonial occasions, a second and smaller blanket was thrown about the shoulders; this tended to be less wide in proportion to its length than the dress. After the white man came, the Indian woman added a sleeved cotton dress under the blanket; commonly she let the embroidered or lace bottom of a new undergarment, a petticoat, show below the native dress. In time the inevitable happened — in place of the native woven blanket, a piece of commercial cloth was cut in the same form and worn in its place. Today, of course, current styles of white woman's dress are seen more and more, but middle-aged and older women still favor the traditional forms.

In historic years, neither footgear nor headgear for Indian women has been produced by weaving techniques. To be sure, the shoulder blanket may well have been used to protect the head when necessary. Cotton or silk head coverings were Spanish-inspired and became popular upon the introduction of commercial fabrics.

Actually, men's clothing (Fig. 3.5) presents much more variety than that worn by women, a circumstance not unusual in primitive societies. This is due in part to the fact that the man is the ritualist, predominantly, and special types of garments are requisite for this important aspect of native life.

The most common garment worn by Indian men was the breechcloth — it is still worn by many ritualists. In addition to this, and also worn in ceremonies, is the kilt, a garment which reaches from the waist to about the knees; it is a simple rectangle of cloth. One belt or, very commonly, two belts or sashes may be worn with the kilt. Robes used to be common, and might be made of anything from dressed animal skins to rabbit fur, or cotton or wool blankets. In time, Navajo and Hopi products replaced the native Rio Grande puebloan styles. Almost all native styles of men's dress, too, are disappearing or have disappeared today for other than ceremonial wear. One interesting survival, in substitute materials, occurs at Taos where sheets or commercial cotton blankets are worn at all times by the men.

Shirts with sleeves formerly were woven by some of the New Mexican puebloans, and later on by the

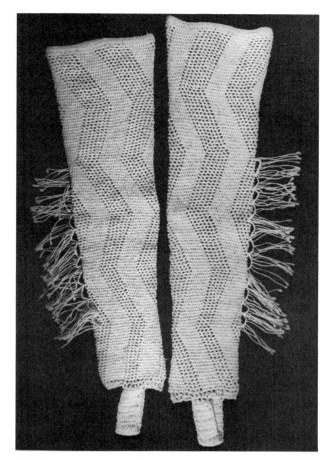

FIGURE 3.8 A pair of contemporary crocheted cotton leggings made at San Juan. These are typical in their design and fringe. They are still commonly worn at certain pueblo ceremonial dances today.

Hopis alone. The latter traded them to the more easterly puebloans. These shirts have all but disappeared although they are to be seen rarely, as when worn by ritualists, for example. The shirt was made of three pieces: a long, narrow body cover with a hole cut for the head, and two smaller rectangles forming the sleeves. The latter were sewed, or rather, tied to the body piece.

A few lesser articles of dress were worn by the men, either for everyday or ritual use. Headbands were commonly woven; today however, pieces of colored cloth have replaced them. Garters were similar to the headbands but smaller in size. Footless stockings were woven of wool, while more elaborate ones were knitted or crocheted of cotton or wool (Fig. 3.8). Needless to say, the garters and stockings have been replaced by commercial items except for ceremonial use.

Although rugs were and are woven in limited

FIGURE 3.7 Zuñi women in native dress. Black wool hand-woven dresses are worn over garments made of commercial fabrics. Note that the wide native garment is wrapped about the body, under the left arm and fastened over the right shoulder. Several manta pins show down the right side of the dress. The very large pieces of silver and turquoise are favored by Zuñi women, particularly the cluster rings and bracelets and the heavy necklaces. White buckskin boots and heavy leggings are native-made. The great jar on the head of the woman to the left is a typical Zuñi piece, but the other two are excellent examples of Acoma vessels. (*Photo by Ray Manley*)

numbers by the Hopi Indians, it should be noted that they have been woven but rarely in this century in the Rio Grande. This, of course, is in keeping with the fact that most weaving of any significance ceased in the Rio Grande by the 1880's, and the transition to the rug occurred after this date among the Navajos.

Tewa Villages

When Douglas made a survey of weaving among the Tewa villages in New Mexico in the 1930's, he found nothing but a memory of this craft activity.[8] In one of his publications, he summarized the Tewa situation as follows. Weaving was never particularly important among these villagers, possibly because of their relative proximity to the Plains folk, which may have influenced them to wear skin clothing. Seemingly there were never more than three or four weavers in any of these villages at one time. The coming of the railroad in the early 1880's put an end to what little weaving there had been, except, of course, for a few belts and occasional other items. Men did both weaving and embroidery, with women doing some of the latter. In earlier years the upright loom was set up in the home or kiva, and on it were produced plain, diagonal, and diamond weaves.

A few words about each individual Tewa pueblo will reflect the differences in weaving from village to village.

SAN JUAN

At San Juan, traditional weaving seems to have ended about the year 1885. A few of the conventional woolen dresses, which were black, or black with wide blue borders, were made here, as well as a limited number of striped blankets. Black wool shawls were embroidered in red and green. Although cotton reputedly was not grown at San Juan, it was imported from the south and used in the weaving of kilts, shawls, leggings, shirts, and for braiding of belts. Kilts and shawls were embroidered, and leggings were crocheted in openwork patterns (Fig. 3.8).

For years a narrow red belt has been woven at San Juan, the last piece to be made in this village. Other striped belts were formerly produced here, with a combination of narrow and broad bands running from end to end. Some had simple geometric themes repeated at the edges and in a central band, all running from end to end.

SANTA CLARA

Santa Clara weavers followed traditions comparable to those of San Juan, although the craft may have lingered in the former village to about 1890. The list of Santa Clara products differs somewhat, and includes woolen blankets decorated with

simple stripes, women's black dresses, men's plain dark shirts, and sashes brocaded in conventional designs in red, green, and black. Reputedly, cotton was imported from Chihuahua, and from this material were made braided rain sashes (Fig. 3.9), embroidered shawls and kilts, and maiden's shawls. The latter, a small, blanket-like piece, had composite edges, each consisting of an outer blue and an inner red band, with the center of the blanket in

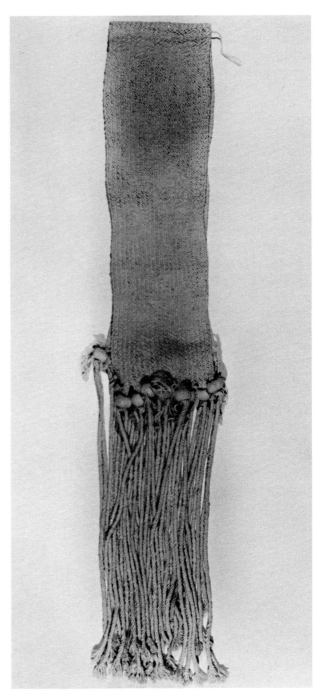

FIGURE 3.9 A Hopi rain sash of braided cotton. Two pieces are sewed together and ornamented at the ends with balls and long fringe. These are made for brides but are also worn by men on special ceremonial occasions. Each piece is 27″ long with a decorative ball-fringe area of 24″.

white. The entire piece was woven. Openwork cotton leggings, with allover designs, were also made. Footless stockings of wool were knitted by both men and women.

The textile craft ceased at San Ildefonso in 1887 with the death of its last weaver, an old man.[9] In general, the same traits as described above prevailed here, with a few additional points of interest. Wool shawls were embroidered in red and yellow; the last weaver made very fine white shawls of wool and embroidered them. Openwork leggings were made in cotton but apparently none were knitted in wool.

NAMBE AND TESUQUE

Weaving, except for belts, ended close to 1870 in the Tewa village of Nambé and about 1880 in Tesuque. Both groups made the woman's black dress and the man's shirt from wool. The black wool shawl embroidered in red and green or red and blue was also produced in Tesuque. Nambé knitted leggings were of wool. Embroidered cotton shirts were made in Tesuque. In these two pueblos, as in all other Tewa villages, the cotton rain sash was braided. In recent years in Nambé there have been produced small and narrow cotton belts, usually in two colors, such as red and white or black and white.

Rather typical pueblo motifs appear in the embroidered and brocaded patterns on this Tewa weaving. Among them are stepped terraces with pendant short lines, often interpreted as clouds and falling rain; diamonds, some with checkerboard interiors; pointed-stepped terraces, frequently on shawls; and narrow and wide stripes and bands on blankets and belts.

Keres Villages

In the Keres villages weaving presents a picture comparable to that of the Tewas in many respects. However, all too little is known about the subject in the former pueblos. There are a few Spanish references to Keres weaving in the seventeenth and eighteenth centuries, but there is little in the way of actual fabrics to support this brief documentation. The craft seems not to have been highly developed among the Keres, although the number of workers was, perhaps, greater than in the Tewa villages. The same loom and techniques were used by the Keresan folk as described for the Tewa.

When Douglas reported on the Keres in 1939, he said that there was one man in the village of Zía and one in San Felipe still weaving cloth. Belt weaving was being done in a number of pueblos. Furthermore, he noted that, "The teaching of weaving in Indian Service schools has resulted in the de-velopment of a new generation of women textile workers in the last 10 or 15 years."[10]

SANTO DOMINGO

In conservative Santo Domingo, striped blankets and women's black dresses were woven in wool. A fairly wide wool belt was also woven; it had a narrow stripe at the sides which ran the full length of the piece, and central spotted and repeated geometric patterns. Apparently some cotton weaving was also done.

ZIA, SANTA ANA, SAN FELIPE

Zía produced the typical pueblo blanket of wool, coarse in texture and with white, black, and blue stripes. The woman's black dress and a wide brocaded sash also were woven in wool. According to Douglas, in 1939 cotton was still being cultivated to a limited extent; its use had been more extensive in earlier years. Belts were braided and kilts and shawls were woven of cotton. Kilts were embroidered and shawls were either embroidered or had woven red and blue borders. Wool leggings were knitted. Many women continued to weave narrow belts with end-to-end stripes composed of short repeated elements; these general styles and designs remained popular for sales items throughout the 1940's and later. They were produced by various Rio Grande pueblos.

Apparently all of the wool and cotton items produced at Zía were also made in the nearby Keres villages of Santa Ana and San Felipe. A few additional points should be made regarding the latter. For one, a little cotton was cultivated at San Felipe in the late 1930's. Also one weaver in particular was making a breechcloth with an unusual embroidered design at the same time. Furthermore, Douglas reported that crocheted "openwork cotton stockings . . . are made by one woman"; this is a trait much more typical of the Tewas.[11]

COCHITI

It is thought that the cultivation of cotton continued in the village of Cochití until about 1900; therefore, it is quite probable that weaving survived until this date. However, it dwindled rapidly, and nothing but belts were woven in later years.

LAGUNA

Quite a different story prevails in Laguna. The villagers claim no knowledge of cotton weaving in later historic years, but they did use wool until 1915 for the production of women's black dresses, men's blue shirts and breechcloths, and the usual puebloan striped coarse blanket. Knitted footless stockings also were made in wool. Lovely embroidered shawls and women's dresses, the latter with wide bands of red, blue, and green decoration down the sides, were made until 1875 in Laguna. Another object, and one not found elsewhere, was a white shawl woven in wool instead of cotton and with the usual outer blue and inner red borders. However, the red was very different: it was in three striped blocks in place of the usual plain red band[12] (Fig. 3.10).

ACOMA

The last of the Keres group, Acoma, is perhaps the most important in the story of weaving in the Rio Grande, for some of the most beautiful decorated fabrics were produced in this village. Men seem to have been the chief weavers. However, it is reported that women sometimes wove large pieces, and certainly here as in many other Rio Grande pueblos, they made all of the garters, belts, and headbands. It was the women of Acoma who did the rich embroidery on their textiles, while in other pueblos men usually applied this decoration. Many of these villagers, both young and old, still do belt weaving; some have learned at school, some carry on the traditional styles passed down through the years.

Since the cultivation of cotton ceased around 1850-55 at Acoma, it seems that some articles normally made in cotton were produced in a very finely spun wool. As in other pueblos, shawls were embroidered in wool. Most of these wools were commercial. In the better and older pieces, red ravelings were derived from bayeta (a European-manufactured material), American wool blankets, American bolt flannel, or Saxony; occasionally some was handspun. Blues and greens which were popular in embroidery were handspun, although some of the yarns may have been derived from ravelings of

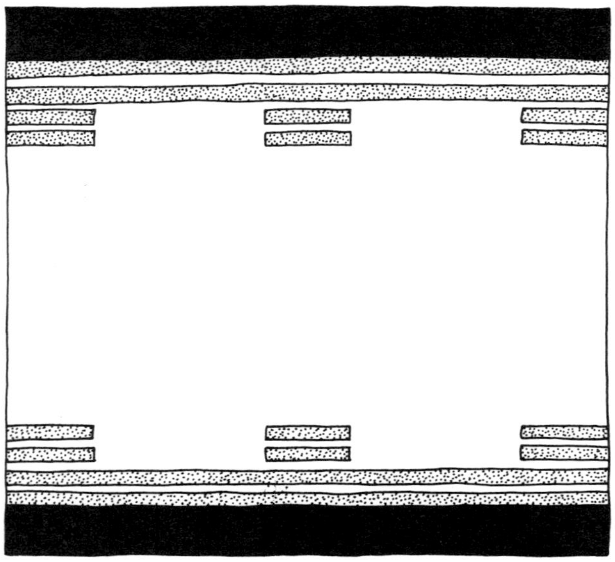

commercial cloth. At Acoma, yellow was derived from rabbit brush and dark blue from indigo.

Embroidered cotton mantas (large shawls) in Acoma are similar to those from other pueblos except that the colors and designs are often more elaborate. Colors include black alone on some pieces and rose and green on others. Design arrangement (Fig. 3.11) involves a wide band at the bottom, solid except for narrow lines of the base fabric which show through as simple white geometric themes or as wider vertical bands. From the band extend several arrangements of pairs of equilateral triangles, their points dipping down-

FIGURE 3.11 Sketch of the top pattern of the Acoma woman's shawl. It is different in that it has these unusual arrangements of old motifs plus two white spaces down the center of each pattern.

wards; this is, perhaps, the most characteristic of all manta decoration. A simpler but similar band ornaments the top of the piece. So far, this decoration resembles that of a number of other pueblo mantas, but here the similarity ends. Acoma decorators add another theme pendant from, or near, the top band. Characteristic are two central birds, highly conventionalized, and tied to the top decoration by means of two white bands which extend from the edges of the blanket through the bird themes.

Breechcloths are wide, 6 to 8 feet in length, and of white cotton except for a band of embroidery at the ends. This decoration may be in red, brown, and blue wool and features solid work except for fine lines of white showing through as described above.

Quite a different style of decoration appears on some of the Acoma cotton shirts, although the shirt form is typical of all pueblos as previously described (Fig. 3.12). At the bottom of the body piece, over the shoulders, and at the ends of the sleeves appear continuous bands of embroidery. Often each band is made up of alternate dark and light blocks rather than the continuous dark bands so common on mantas. Another feature of this garment is the spotting of repeated geometric motifs over the body and sleeves.[13]

Acoman blankets and women's dresses of wool were similar to those of other pueblos, but the em-

FIGURE 3.10 Sketch of a Laguna woman's shawl design. It differs from the usual pueblo style in that the inner band is broken into clusters of stripes.

FIGURE 3.12 Sketch of man's embroidered shirt from Jémez. These shirts of wool or cotton, formerly woven in many of the pueblos, were made in three pieces: the main body part with a hole cut for the head in the center, and two sleeves. Red and black are the two favored colors for embroidery on these shirts.

broidered shawls were outstanding. In the dress, as at other pueblos, a dark central portion in diagonal weave was combined with wide end bands in diamond weave and in a bright blue Diamond-dye color. It was customary to re-dye these dresses from time to time, as well as the plain shawl, with the notion of freshening the black color. Oddly enough, the re-dying process turned the wide borders a dull brownish tone. This feature was distinctive of old Acoman dresses.

One of the most beautiful pieces of all pueblo weaving and embroidery was the Acoman shawl of wool. The central portion was in diagonal weave and the ends were most commonly in plain blue, sometimes in red and green. Designs were spaced slightly apart and were geometric in style, although some were suggestive of floral patterns. The general effect was rich.

Tiwa Villages

Of the four Tiwa villages — Taos, Picuris, Sandía, and Isleta — the first three seemingly did no weaving, or at least they have not done any within the past hundred or so years. This is understandable in the first two villages, for their clothing tradition was in skin garments. Proximity to the Plains would explain this. On the other hand, Sandía, which is so much farther south, simply had no tradition of weaving. Parsons speaks of "home-grown cotton" in Isleta for the weaving of kilts, leggings, and belts. She also refers to both men and women as weavers of wool blankets.[14]

Jémez

One other pueblo in the Rio Grande should be mentioned in connection with weaving — the Towa-speaking village of Jémez. Cotton-growing survived here into the twentieth century, and a few items such as shawls, kilts, and braided sashes were produced in this native material or in commercial string. Within the last thirty years they have made a cotton belt for commercial purposes. A well-woven piece, it is decorated with small geometric elements — lines, squares, or bands — which run the length of the belt. Colors are black, red, green, and white.

Sometimes additional colors appear in belts made by school girls from this village. During the 1940's a number of these belts were made by girls from Jémez, Nambé, and other villages, in colors such as lavender and pale blue and with occasional new designs.

Western Pueblos

Zuñi

Textiles produced by the Zuñi Indians in the past were very much like those of the Hopis, with some individual traits marking each tribe. Although Douglas reported "a number of weavers at Zuñi" in 1935 and 1936,[15] Rummage saw little or no weaving during the late thirties.[16] Seemingly, all weaving has disappeared from the Zuñi villages today, with no trace of even belt weaving to be found.

One of the first differences to be noted in Zuñi weaving is that it was done primarily by the women, although some men could and did weave. On occasion, the same situation applied to embroidery. However, only men did knitting. The native upright loom was used, but a device peculiar to the Zuñis and Hopis was a measuring rod attached to the warp threads. This rod served the purpose of maintaining the same width throughout the fabric; it was moved upward along the warps as the weaving progressed.

Basic techniques at Zuñi included plain, diagonal, and diamond weaves. Belt weaves were of two kinds. In one, there was a continuous warp which could be moved so that the work was always directly in front of the weaver; warps were left unwoven for about a foot, then cut in the middle of the unwoven space. This left fringes at both ends of the belt. The second type was a loom in which a band encircled the waist of the worker and the warp was fastened to a fixed point opposite the weaver. Both looms produced belts in which the warp alone showed and was the carrier of design.[17]

The Zuñis cultivated little if any cotton; seemingly, the Hopis supplied them with at least some fiber. It was cleaned and the fibers partly straightened by hand, then the preparation was completed by using a carder. Spinning was done in the traditional manner, with a spindle stick, 16 to 18 inches long, and a wooden whorl. Commercial cotton cord was used in later years, but wool came from the

Zuñis' own sheep. About the turn of the century, Zuñis were using indigo and some native plants for their dye colors.

Several types of cotton shawls were made in Zuñi. One was the familiar large white one with a heavily embroidered lower band and a lighter top band, all done in colored wool (Fig. 3.5). In the lower band, which was predominantly black, or black and green with fine white lines showing through as design, large diamonds — usually four — were embroidered in brighter colors. Rising from each diamond and above the total band were two triangles. A second and smaller shawl had colored bands of wool woven along the top and bottom. In an older style the band was blue alone and done in a diamond weave. A later version had the more familiar dark blue outer band and an adjoining red one at each end (Fig. 3.5). The white center of this shawl was done in plain or diagonal weave, the red in diagonal weave, and the blue in diamond weave.

The usual pueblo cotton kilt was made in the village of Zuñi, with embroidery on the sides and a very narrow band at the bottom. The kilt and the braided ceremonial cotton sash were both being made in Zuñi in 1935-36[18] (Fig. 3.5).

There are several interesting points in connection with wool weaving in Zuñi. For one thing, the Zuñis made a large all-black blanket which no other pueblo produced. This was in coarse weave and had no decoration. It is not to be confused with the dark blanket dresses also made in Zuñi, and often at other pueblos. With the coming of commercial blankets in 1885–90, weaving of the black blanket ceased, despite the fact that it was customary to bury the dead in this native piece. To this day, Zuñi men assisting in ceremonies wrap themselves in large black blankets, but most of these are commercial pieces. Another Zuñi blanket had a white ground against which were woven dark blue and black stripes; often these appeared in clustered bands. The Zuñi blanket was more nearly square and fuzzier than those from other pueblos.[19]

Women's dresses also point up some differences in details. Two types were made; both were black or dark brown. The latter looked as if it were woven of natural black wool, which, when undyed, had a brownish cast. Both were woven in a diagonal weave except for plain-weave borders. Dark blue embroidery appeared on plain-weave borders of the older style, while the later dress had about 6 inches of decorative diamond weave in the same place. Both presented a very subtle type of decoration. Although basically dresses, these pieces could be worn as shawls. The main embroidery themes, which appeared in bands about 3 inches wide, were simple geometric designs and highly conventionalized butterflies and flowers. Embroidery was usual-ly in dark blue; rarely red was used. Another difference appeared in the diamond-weave bordered type: in the Zuñi dress it was usually black, while in other pueblos it was dark blue.

Shirts of the usual pueblo style were made in Zuñi. They were of black or dark blue wool, in diagonal weave, and undecorated. Kilts were of diagonal weave, blue or black in color. One type was plain, while a second style had dark blue embroidered ends. Breechcloths were similar to kilts in weave and decoration. Wide white sashes with brocaded ends (Fig. 3.5) were made of either wool or cotton, and their designs were like those produced at other pueblos. Black or dark blue footless stockings were knitted in wool. Peculiar to Zuñi alone were regular knitted socks with bands of blocks or zigzag designs.

Embroidery materials at Zuñi were quite generally like those at other pueblos. In addition to native dyes, Germantown yarns were available to them from about 1879 on, while bayeta appeared earlier and continued to be used to about 1881.

Hopi

Hopi weaving is extremely important in the story of Southwest Indian crafts, for it presents one of the most continuously practiced and abundantly represented of the native arts. There is no reason to believe that it has ever not been practiced since its inception among the Hopis' Anasazi ancestors shortly after the opening of the Christian era. To be sure, there have been periods of advancement and retrogression, both of these represented in the historic as well as the prehistoric periods. The Hopis must be credited with the preservation of this important aboriginal craft of weaving.

When the Spanish arrived in the Hopi country in 1542 under the leadership of Tovar (Tobar), who was sent by Coronado to visit "Tusayan," they were given bits of cotton cloth by the Hopis. Forty-three years later Espejo, upon visiting the Hopi, was presented with what may well have been kilts or even small blankets. It was not until 1629, however, under the first Spanish to establish missions in Hopiland, that sheep were brought to this tribe. No further influences of particular note from the Spanish occurred as far as the Hopis were concerned. Europeans were eliminated from the scene with the burning of the mission at Awatovi in 1700, except for casual and uneventful contacts with occasional priests and several New Mexican governors.

The coming of the Anglo-Americans was also unimportant in relation to weaving. Ives, who visited the Hopis in 1858, noted that it was evident that contacts between Hopis and Americans had been very slight. Two items that Ives mentioned in connection with his visit are of interest: he said that the Hopis had many flocks of black sheep, and that all the people wore blankets of dark and light stripes. In 1871 the Mormons took a Hopi named Tuba, and his wife, to Utah. There the two saw spinning machines, but these made no impression on the Indians. Later, the Mormons established a woolen factory in the Indian country, but it failed. No further Anglo-American influences, other than the introduction of Diamond dyes and commercial yarns, occurred among the Hopis until well after the turn of the twentieth century.

Men are, and apparently always have been, the weavers among the Hopis except for the production of the fur cord blanket, which is a woman's task. In 1931, Jeançon and Douglas reported that there were close to two hundred weavers among the Hopis, and that weaving was done in all villages, with Hotevilla the center of this activity.[20] Although there are not as many weavers today, there are a few in each village, with Hotevilla remaining the center of this activity.[21]

The loom, a simple frame stretched upright between ceiling beams and floor, is set up in the home or kiva. Among the Hopis, the kiva is as much a "club" for the men as it is a ceremonial chamber. It is here that the men gather to gossip as well as to practice and present rituals. It is here also that the young men spend much time, and it is here that they generally learn the craft of weaving. The rabbit-fur robe, according to tradition, had to be made in secrecy; therefore a woman sought a less-frequented portion of the home to pursue this craft.

Cotton has been the material used by the Hopis and their ancestors since it was first known to the latter about the eighth century. It is used today for the weaving of ceremonial garments, even though they may then be ornamented in wool. The chief variety of cotton used by this tribe was *Gossypium hopi,* the same type cultivated by all Southwest Indians who grew any. Kent says, "The Hopi were the last to relinquish large-scale cultivation of the plant."[22]

In 1938, Colton reported that all handspun cotton fabrics were becoming rare, due to several influences. For one, the Hopis stopped growing their own cotton. Commercial cotton batting was then made available to them by traders; it was too difficult to handle and took too long to spin, so the Hopis turned to commercial string. To counteract the loss of another native factor, the Museum of Northern Arizona tried to induce the Hopis to use Pima long staple cotton grown in the Salt River Valley of Arizona by trading it to them.[23] But this still involved the tedious task of spinning which may explain why string continued to grow in popularity. Cotton string was long used for the warp

with a handspun weft for filler. Today commercial cotton is used exclusively for both warp and weft.

Andalusian sheep were introduced to the Hopis by the Spanish. Some other blood has been added to that of the original animals, but the Hopis have fought several efforts to "better" their flocks in certain directions. They have not been interested in improvements which would bring about better sales of the animals, because they keep sheep so that they may use the wool for weaving — and not to sell the animals. Hopis have used some commercial wool yarns, particularly for embroidering and brocading their own hand-woven pieces.

In the preparation of native materials, the Hopi used the methods peculiar to his ancestors. Cotton bolls were laid out on clean dry sand and beaten. Further cleaning and the straightening of fibers were done by hand. Both cotton and wool were spun on the native spindle stick with the circular whorl attached. Men did this between the hand and thigh, rolling the stick away from the spinner. It is said that, in general, the Hopis did a better job than the Navajos of wool spinning, producing greater uniformity in thickness and evenness of the yarn. Hopis often used a corn cob for rubbing the yarn to assure a smooth surface. As a rule — and always in wool — there are differences in the thickness and tightness of yarns according to whether they are to be used for warp, or weft, or for binding, or according to the nature of the piece to be woven. Warps are usually spun several times which makes them smaller and tighter, therefore stronger than the wefts.

Considering wool weaving as a whole, there is not as much color in Hopi work as there is in the Navajo. However a great deal of color is used for embroidery or in brocading. Wools of natural colors were, and still are, most commonly employed, including white, gray, much black, and dark brown, although imported indigo was popular with this tribe from early years. It was the cotton which was generally embroidered or brocaded in bright red, green, black, and other colors. For years the sources of these colors were native vegetable and mineral dyes. Aniline colors came to the Hopis about the same time as they did to the Navajos, after 1870, and although not abundantly used, they contributed to the degeneracy of the craft.

By the late 1920's, Hopi textiles were at low ebb. The Museum of Northern Arizona then took a hand in improving the native colors as well as improving the materials and workmanship in this craft as a whole. Both indigo and cochineal had been traded from Mexico to the Hopis in historic years, but poor substitute colors from commercial dyes replaced them. The Museum obtained natural indigo and

sold it to the Hopis; this was a boon to them for they greatly favored this color.

The Hopi man weaves in several techniques and produces a variety of pieces. Number and arrangement of heddles account for the former; use dictates the form of the piece. The woman's white wedding dress (a large robe, almost square), other ceremonial dresses, and kilts are made in plain basket weave and in cotton (Fig 3.5). All these pieces are embroidered, usually in bright-colored wool yarns. Woven in the same plain weave, but in wool, are baby blankets, usually striped; a black and white shoulder blanket for boys; a wide white sash with brocaded ends; and a few other pieces. Maiden's shawls of cotton or wool are done in diagonal twill, plain or basket weave. The woman's everyday wool dresses (Fig. 3.13), baby blankets, and men's plaid blankets are woven in some combination of basket, diagonal, and diamond weaves.

The woman's dark dress, which is a wide and short wrap-around affair, has a black or dark brown center in diagonal twill weave with broad borders of dark blue in diamond or diagonal twill weave (Fig. 3.5). Where the two weaves and/or colors meet, heavy red and green yarns are sewed onto the dress. This dress survived the longest at Hotevilla; today it is worn almost exclusively for ceremonials.

A checked or plaid blanket (Fig. 3.14) for men and boys is one of the most interesting pieces that the Hopis make. It is in a black and white combination, or brown and white, or sometimes in all three colors. The color design is dominant, but beneath it can be seen, upon closer scrutiny, a subtle patterning in the weave, usually in a combination of diamond and diagonal types. This unusual piece is woven only by the Hopis.

Blankets for beds and everyday wear continue to this day to preserve the native style of simple edge-to-edge stripes, often in dark blue and black. Subtle touches of other colors may be used. The Hopis, more than other puebloans and certainly more than the Navajos, tend to favor in blankets a predominance of dark colors, particularly dark blue from indigo (or its substitutes), and black. In addition to this heavy blanket, a few rugs comparable to simpler Navajo styles have been made by the Hopis.

Men's shirts were woven of wool, sometimes in a black-and-white checked pattern; more commonly, they were plain and in dark blue wool. The em-

FIGURE 3.14 Hopi man's plaid blanket. This is a very subtle piece of weaving for not only is there the obvious black and white plaid patterning, but also there are several weaves — plain, diagonal, and diamond twills — incorporated in this one piece.

broidered shirt which found so much favor in the Rio Grande pueblos was woven occasionally by the Hopis, but generally it was less elaborately decorated.

The Hopi maiden's shawl, with the wide red and blue woven borders (Figs. 3.5 and 3.13) is like that of the Rio Grande. So, too, are the kilts and wide sashes, with embroidered or brocaded designs resembling those of other pueblo pieces. The wedding dress (Fig. 3.5) is of interest in that it is all white for this first ceremony, but is usually embroidered later on with a wide band at the bottom, double triangles coming out of the band, and with a narrow border at the top. All of this is in the typical black and green mass-type embroidery, with other colors favored for diamond inserts in the lower border. The Hopi woman *must* have a wedding dress, for when she dies it insures her passage to the world beyond.

Hopi men do all of the embroidery on all fabrics. They also make the complicated braided wedding or "rain" sash, which is white. Large balls are formed below the braiding and from these rounded elements fall long tassels, the latter simulating rain.

FIGURE 3.13 Hopi Indians in ceremonial dress. Each of the women (maidens as indicated by the "whorl" hairdos) wears the typical old-style wool blanket dress and shoulder blanket of white cotton with dark blue (or black) and red borders. Their white buckskin moccasins with the heavy uppers are typical. The men wear the native handwoven red sash with black and green decoration. All of these are worn only on ceremonial occasions. Note the abundance of turquoise, shell, and coral beads. The large but squat drum is one of the forms favored by the Hopis. (*Photo by Ray Manley*)

FIGURE 3.15 Hopi men's knitted footless stockings. Made by the men of this tribe, these stockings are white, dark blue, or black wool.

Women who weave the rabbit-skin blankets (Fig. 3.3) use a rough loom which is secured to a ceiling beam and to the floor. Strips of rabbit fur are wrapped about a wool cord to form the continuous warp; this is finger-twined with a stout, doubled wool yarn.

Sashes were woven on a small waist loom. Douglas summarizes the use of this loom as follows: "Smaller looms based on the same general plan [of the true loom] are used for weaving brocaded sashes . . . ."[24] Diamonds, nested chevrons, outlined crosses, and bands are among the patterns favored for sashes (Fig. 3.5).

Many belts or small belt-like pieces are made and worn by the Hopis (Fig. 3.5). Most of these are in red with simple end-to-end patterns in black and white. Occasionally a bit of green may be added, particularly to the wider belt, which also has small geometric patterns, such as triangles, squares, lines, and narrow bands. These are repeated from end to end, in clusters or in a continuous fashion. Garters and head ties are similar but simpler.

Hopis learned to knit at some unknown time. In particular, they have knitted dark blue or white stockings which are footless (Fig. 3.15) and reach only to the knee. Wooden needles were used in earlier years but commercial types of other material

replaced them as the latter became available at the traders.

Non-Pueblo Tribes

The Navajos are the only non-pueblo tribe doing any textile weaving today. Apache Indians never did any, despite the fact that they are the language brothers of the Navajos, and otherwise show certain similarities in their culture. But all recorded evidence points to the Apache wearing skin clothing until he encountered white men. As a result of the Pueblo Rebellion of 1680, some Rio Grande puebloans lived with the Navajos for some time, and the latter apparently learned weaving from this contact. Since the Apaches were definitely enemies of other tribes, the chances of learning weaving from them would have been slim. Moreover, the southern groups with whom more Apaches came in contact did only limited weaving.

Ute and Paiute

Although their culture as a whole was very simple, the Ute and Paiute Indians did produce rabbit-skin robes (Fig. 3.3) within historic times, although they no longer practice this craft. These robes are not textiles in the proper sense of the word, yet they have a distinct place in the background of weaving in the Southwest, as mentioned in the prehistoric summary above. Actually, they were products of finger weaving rather than of true loom weaving, even though a loom frame with top and bottom poles was used. Historically, strips of rabbit skin were wrapped about wool cordage, then this was strung between the two poles. The rabbit cord was twined together at intervals with two strands of plain cord — a heavy brown wool yarn in several pieces examined. The end result was a warm, soft blanket or robe.

Pima and Papago

Pimas and Papagos formerly wove belts and blankets of cotton. Women did the spinning, men the weaving. These two tribes used quite a different loom, a horizontal one which was raised but a few inches above the ground. Not too much is known about this craft among these two tribes, for neither has done any weaving since the latter part of the nineteenth century. Little has been preserved from earlier years.

Probably the Pimas and Papagos cultivated cotton into the historic period, perhaps to the close of the nineteenth century. A simple, solid white or red cotton blanket was produced in plain weave, leaving both warps and wefts exposed (Fig. 3.16). No designs were woven in nor were they otherwise applied. However, a reddish or dull brown border or selvage gave a little contrast to the white blanket.

These tribes also produced belts. Quite a variety

FIGURE 3.16 Pima cotton blanket. This plain weave all-natural blanket, except for a light red thread just within the edge on all four sides, probably served as body blanket and dress alike. This piece is 80″ long and 62″ wide and is dated 1877. (*Courtesy United States National Museum, Washington, D.C.*)

of colors was used, including some bayeta. One example had black, white, green, and yellow zigzags which ran from end to end. Two Pima belts in the Peabody Museum, Cambridge, Massachusetts, collected in 1851, combine blue, white, and red (Fig. 3.17). One belt is striped, the second has a complicated geometric pattern — resembling the basketry designs of this tribe — with triangles, frets, and lines extending the length of the piece.

Yuman Tribes

Among the various Yuman tribes little or no weaving was ever done. The Yuma proper did some crude and uncomplicated work, utilizing a simple upright loom. A variety of materials was used, including cotton, bark, and rabbit-skin strips; in one or several of these materials they produced crude blankets, robes, or skirts.

The general nature of aboriginal dress, and therefore of weaving, of several of the Yumans is indicated in the following statements by Spier: "Mohave dress was much like that of other Lower Colorado tribes but differed in some particulars. In general Mohave men and women wore only loin coverings, were barefoot and bareheaded, and covered the upper body only as inclement weather dictated."[25] More specifically, Spier described women's dress as consisting of a front and back apron

of willow-bark strips which hung from a cord, with the simplest twining in two or three rows just below the cord holding these strips in position. Beneath this apron was a shorter one made of fine willow bark. Men wore a breechcloth of wide willow-bark strips woven in checkerboard style.[26]

Spier further reported that neither men nor women wore shirts, but he indicated that those who were wealthier did trade for Navajo "ponchos." These he described as only 18 inches wide and with a slit so that they could be slipped over the head.

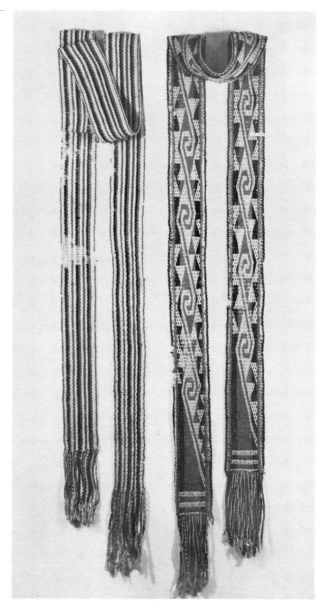

FIGURE 3.17 Two belts of wool made by the Pima Indians. The simpler striped pattern on the left is more typical. The belt on the right is designed with elements borrowed from basketry and pottery decoration, as the triangle, meanders, and interlocked motifs. Favored colors were red, blue, and white, although others were used. This specimen was collected in 1878. (*Courtesy Peabody Museum of Archaeology and Ethnology, Harvard University*)

Like the Yumas proper, the Mohaves wore rabbit-skin robes which they wove themselves or obtained from the Walapais in trade. The Mohaves made them of twisted strips of skin of jackrabbits or cottontails; as among other tribes, the strips were twined together. Thus it may be concluded that, except for the belt, true textiles were not produced by the Yumans of the lower Colorado River.

An example of a Cocopa cradleboard tie (Fig. 3.18) in the Arizona State Museum is of interest. It has a pattern of small black and white checks which zigzag from end to end against a black background.

Perhaps one of the last bits of weaving to be done by the Yuman tribes were the belts made by the Maricopa Indians. Spier reported, "The weaving art is now moribund, only cradle bands being made and but few of these."[27] To all appearances, the Maricopas learned true weaving from the Pimas. In the 1850's, Bartlett reported that the Maricopas made cotton blankets like those of the Pimas, women's skirts, and head- or waistbands, and belts. Old men did the weaving; either men or women did the spinning. The introduction of white man's clothing put an end to any weaving efforts on the part of this tribe.

Maricopa cradle belts were decorated, most of them having designs in color. Spier reported that only commercial yarns were used in 1932, but that there were dyed yarns, including a bright red made from a native plant, and that clays were used to produce dull reds or blacks or a faded orange.[28]

Interestingly, it was on the regular horizontal loom that most Maricopa fabrics were woven. This loom was made by driving four stakes into the ground, a pair supporting a warp bar at each end. For all Maricopa pieces, the warps were strung in figure-eight fashion on these two bars. Size was the main difference, with smaller looms for belts and larger ones for blankets. Occasionally a true belt loom was substituted. For the most part white cotton was used, but sometimes colored threads were added at the edges so as to produce decorative selvages in the blankets, or they were variously placed for belt designs.

Reportedly, the Havasupais produced no woven garments except, possibly, the rabbit-skin robe. They wore clothing made from skins, some in the tradition of the Plains Indians. White man's garments were adopted rather late. Also, a belt woven by the Hopi Indians was commonly worn by Havasupai women.

Navajo Weaving

Navajo weaving is a complex example of the textile craft and an oft-confused one. In the hope that some of this confusion can be eliminated, a back-

FIGURE 3.18 Cocopa cradleboard tie. Simply woven, these narrow ties were used to secure the infant on the cradleboard. Patterning, as the zigzag here, was in simple color combinations, such as this black and white example.

ground of materials, technology, history, and the developments of regional styles is given here (Fig. 3.19). In earlier years there were few or no regional styles but there were distinct forms and periods of development. Today regional styles are common and a few early forms have persisted.

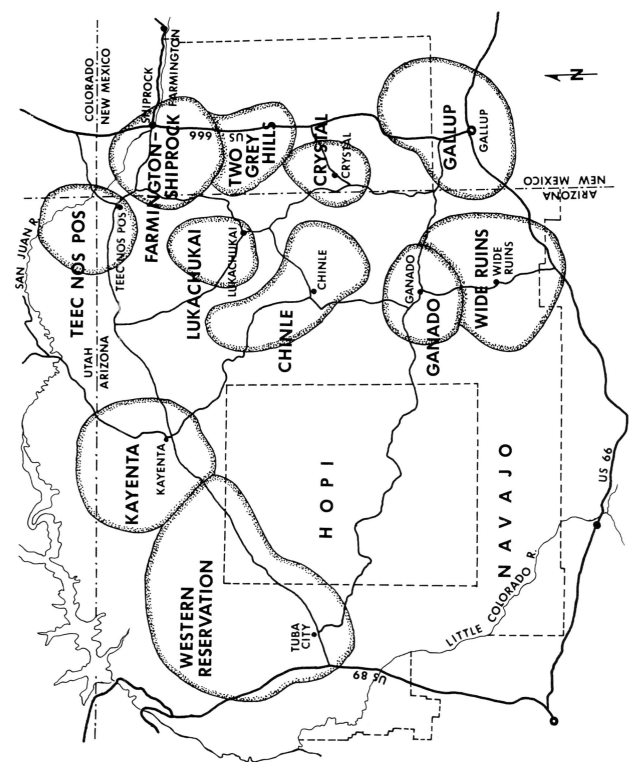

FIGURE 3.19 Map showing the general distribution of the major types of contemporary regional styles of Navajo weaving.

Materials

A knowledge of materials is important for these have been influential in both design and quality of loom products.

By the end of the seventeenth century, the Navajos reputedly had large flocks of sheep. Descendants of the Spanish-introduced animals received additions of new blood through the years (especially as varied breeds were given to the Navajos by the United States government), from the early Merino to the Rambouillet sheep. Today the Navajos herd an animal of mixed heritage, but one which has been bred to some of the peculiar needs of the tribe. Their reservation nurtures many small sticker-bearing plants, thus animals with long wool are not desirable, for the pelts become too matted to be hand carded. Since sheep were for many years the main source of what little meat the Navajos consumed, meat was another consideration. These and other requirements resulted in the breeding of an animal which has relatively short wool, is sturdy, and yet has some meat on its bones. This is a "Navajo sheep;" there is still no uniformity in characteristics or appearance of this animal.

The first diversion from the use of native wool resulted from the introduction of small amounts of bayeta shortly after the opening of the nineteenth century. Bayeta was a baize-like material manufactured in England, traded to Spain, thence sent to Mexico. It reached the Southwest in bolt or yardage form, or in uniforms of Spanish soldiers. Navajo women unraveled the cloth, respun the threads, and used them in combination with native wool. Bayeta was sparingly used at first, but by the mid-eighteen hundreds greater quantities were available and the Navajo weaver used more of it. Its use again dwindled after 1870 with the growing popularity of other commercial yarns and dyes. C. A. Amsden, in his classic book, *Navaho Weaving*, seems dubious about the reported use of bayeta from 1890 to 1920.[29]

Imported into the Southwest around 1850 were two other colorful materials favored by the Navajos — Saxony and Zephyr yarns which were manufactured in Europe. Saxony, a three-ply yarn, generally, which came in reds and other bright colors, was especially popular. This material has quite a distinctive sheen. Germantown yarns, from the eastern United States, were most popular from 1875 to 1890, but small amounts were still used after 1890.

From about 1865 to 1890, still other commercial wools found their way into the hands of Navajo weavers. Bed blankets, red flannel underwear, and flannel cloth were all unraveled to be rewoven on the Navajo loom. Red was favored, but this and

other colors were distinguishable from the fine bayeta because they were aniline-dyed and of garish tones. The red of the bayeta was obtained from cochineal; other bayeta shades were green, blue, and possibly yellow. The red bayeta was used almost exclusively by the Navajos. Indigo, probably from Mexico, provided the source of a dark blue color popular among the Navajos as it was among other Indians.

The first Navajo weaving was in the natural colors of the sheep's wool — white, brown, and black. Whether the earliest black was dyed or not is a question; in later years it was, for the natural wool is never a real black. It is questionable also when the first gray was employed; certainly there is no indication of its use in the earliest known examples of weaving. Gray is produced by carding black and white together.

Although several native dyes were known to the Navajo possibly as early as 1800, there was no appreciable exploration of the idea of using them until the twentieth century. Especially after the introduction of bayeta, native dyes held small charm for these Indians. About the time Germantown yarns became popular, aniline dyes were also available. Thus it is easy to understand why native dyes were rarely used for so long after their first introduction.

During the 1920's, Cozy MacSparron of the Chinle Trading Post, in cooperation with Miss Mary C. Wheelwright, urged the Navajo Indians of northeastern Arizona to revert to the use of vegetable dyes. Some weavers did, and a limited number of soft and varied shades of tan, green, yellow, and pink resulted. Further experimental work at the Wingate Vocational High School resulted in additional natural colors.[30] Then in the 1930's the William Lippencotts of Wide Ruins Trading Post began a similar venture. Their work among the Navajo weavers resulted in even more varied colors than had the MacSparron experiment. In time there developed at this second center a tremendous variety of the less dull colors, and more varied and sophisticated designing.

Several other experiments in color for Navajo rugs occurred during the 1930's. A wide range of interesting tones was produced by the DuPont Company especially for Navajo use. Among these were a rich medium blue and a bright rosy red, the two sometimes used in a single rug. But these dyes were a little too complicated for the Navajo woman to use in her hogan; thus they were short-lived. The Diamond Dye Company also produced some more muted aniline colors which they labeled "Old Navajo," but they, too, were not used for any length of time.

Today the Navajos use wool from their own

flocks as the chief material for rugs. Unfortunately, some few weavers use cotton for the warp. Occasional bits of Germantown yarn will be employed for decoration in some pieces. In one rug observed several years ago nylon replaced wool. Some rugs at the 1963 Gallup Ceremonials utilized another commercial yarn. It is to be hoped that such new materials will be used with caution — or not at all.

Women are the weavers among the Navajo. However, on several occasions Navajo men have done special types of weaving.

Techniques

The majority of Navajo rugs have been woven in plain tapestry weave (Fig. 3.4). Twill weaves have been known from early years, but have never been used to any great extent. Today, some twilled tapestry weaves such as the diagonal or diamond types (Fig. 3.4) are used in the saddle blanket; occasional large rugs (such as one 56 by 88 inches) have been woven in this style. In fact, the fancy tapestry weaves are so typical of saddle blankets that many traders refer to them as "saddle blanket weaves." The term "reverse weave" is also applied to these techniques, for in the fancy twill tapestries, designs are the same but colors different on the two sides of the rug.

Although completely different, the "two-faced" blanket is often confused with the "reverse weave" blanket, the former term being loosely applied to either technique or finished product. In actuality, the two-faced blanket is a piece with completely different designs and colors on each face (Fig. 3.20). Again, a basic tapestry weave is employed, but the difference lies in the heddle-shed-rod number and arrangement. Three heddles and one shed rod are used, the same number employed in some twill weaving.

Twill weaves for the most part are made with a loom set-up of two, three, or more heddles and one shed rod; alternations of wefts over warps may be as follows: over-two-under-one (two heddles), over-two-under-two and over-three-under-one (both, three heddles), and over-three-under-three (five heddles). These alternations, or combinations of them, produce zigzags, diamonds, hexagons, and other geometric forms.

The heddle set-up for the two-faced weave throws wefts over three warps on one face and under one, then over three and under one on the reverse face. Obviously, the three exposed or floated wefts on each face will be the carrier of color and design, while the single weft will be lost to sight by the battening down process of the tapestry weave. Color can be changed at any point on either face — thus the designs can differ. Apparently the Navajo women who use this technique spin the weft yarn for the double-faced rugs quite loosely, thus aiding in the "hiding" of the single weft.

If the weaver so desires, in making a two-faced piece she can have a design on one face and a perfectly plain reverse face, or the same design in different colors, or entirely different designs on each face. The weaving of this elaborate rug has never developed widely. Today there are still a few Navajo women who can and do produce the two-faced blanket. Two such rugs were displayed by the Navajo Arts and Crafts Guild at the Heard Museum, Phoenix, Arizona, in 1965. Both had a design in conventional colors on one face and a different pattern in vegetable-dye colors on the reverse side.

Rare examples of still another weave, double cloth, have been reported. Amsden describes one such piece,[31] and the writer saw quite a different example in 1940. Apparently two separate warps are used in weaving double cloth, and the resulting two pieces are caught together at intervals by catching a warp of one face into the opposite fabric. Small squares, which are arranged in bands in the blanket described by Amsden, are one color on one face and a different color on the opposite face, with allover squares on both faces. Bonding is done at the corners of the squares, and the cloth can be pulled apart between points of joining. The second double weave was grey with indistinct red bands and no difference in the two faces. The two fabrics were bonded at irregular intervals.

Formerly the Navajos used another unusual trick in weaving called "tufting;" but this is rarely seen today. Long tufts of Merino or Angora goats' wool were attached over warps in one of several possible ways and at regular intervals, leaving long ends projecting. The end result was more like a goat's pelt than a rug, but it was, of course, a woven piece. Tufting appeared on either plain or twill weave.

One last feature should be mentioned in connection with the technology of Navajo weaving, one peculiar to their saddle blankets. This is the addition of a tassel at the corners. Sometimes they are small and in the same subdued tones of the blanket. In other instances they are long and full and bright in color. Not uncommonly, commercial yarns will be used for this purpose. Quite generally bright green or red tassels decorate a single or double saddle blanket at two or four corners.

Origins and History

There is as yet no precise date for the beginning of the textile craft among the Navajos. The consensus is, however, that it was somewhere around the opening years of the eighteenth century. After

Tuba City-Storm Pattern

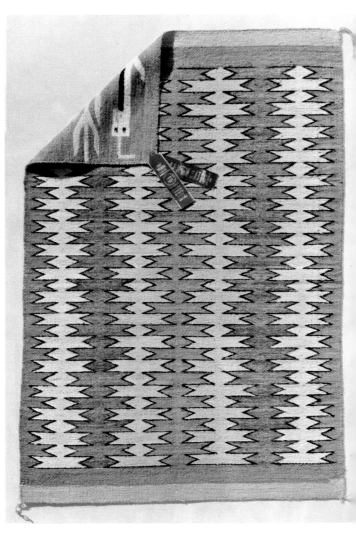

Two-Faced Rug

Pictorial Rug

Ganado Rug

the Pueblo Revolt of 1680, a number of villagers from the Rio Grande went to live with the Navajos in the Governador country of northern New Mexico. This is attested to in the direct association of Navajo hogan rings and pueblo ruins in the area in question. It was probably after this date that the Navajo actually learned to weave, but how soon thereafter is still unknown.

The first mention by the Spanish of Navajos actually possessing hand-woven blankets is in the year 1706. The question is, however, who made these blankets — Navajos, or the puebloan folk who lived with them? The fact that Navajos learned the craft from the puebloans and that they acquired the pueblo weaving traditions in so doing does not help to answer the question, for the first Navajo products were probably more like the puebloan than those of any other time. Kent states that, "Some time before 1700 the Pueblo people taught the art of weaving to the Navajo."[32]

There are several points of technique, artistry, and other aspects to support the puebloan source of Navajo weaving. In all of the following traits there are acknowledged pueblo origins or associations. Wool has been and still is spun on a spindle stick-whorl device which is typically native. There seems to be no question regarding the non-European vertical loom with its heddle and shed-rod attachment, a type which goes back into pre-Columbian times. Batten stick and comb are also puebloan. Navajo belt looms are constructed, set up, and used in the pueblo manner. Pueblo techniques were and are employed by the Navajos, with plain tapestry dominant; variations on this weave, such as diamond and twill styles, were well developed among the puebloans.

The form of the Navajo loom product is cited as another evidence of puebloid origins. Striped shoulder blankets worn by Navajo men and women in early years repeated the wider edge-to-edge, or weft, dimensions of the pueblo manta which served as the woman's dress or as a blanket worn by both sexes.

Kent says that the Navajo woman's dress, which has a narrower weft dimension, is also "based on pueblo models."[33] Since the dominant form of the pueblo woman's dress was a rectangle with the wefts forming the greater dimension, this would not

seem to be the inspiration for the Navajo style. Perhaps the latter tribe adapted the puebloid blanket which has the greater dimension along the warp length. This is a feature always found in the Navajo woman's dress as well as in all other pieces except the chief blanket and the early shoulder blankets for men and women.

Another historic incident is of interest in relation to Navajo blanket weaving. The Spanish in New Mexico had long depended on slave labor (reputedly native women in the colonists' households) for the production of their fabrics. These pieces were woven in the native tradition, by hand and on the upright loom. Then about 1750, a horizontal foot loom of European origin was introduced into New Mexico; however, it was not until early in the nineteenth century that it became widely known and used.

The products of this foot loom, which were the work of the Spanish-Americans and not the Indians, were characterized by several features important to this story. The dimensions were greater along the warps and smaller from edge to edge. There were points of significance in relation to design, also. In addition to stripes, which resembled those in pueblo pieces, there were other designs in the New Mexican blankets, such as geometric elements between stripes, horizontal zigzags across the piece, or bands of vertical zigzags. Some pieces dated around 1870 have both end and side borders, and some dated 1860-70 and thereafter have a dominating central diamond motif.[34] This Spanish-American development, then, seems to have been an important influence on Navajo weavers, not only in design, as has been noted by many authors, but also possibly in the dimensions of the loomed piece.

Perhaps one of the reasons why so little is known about the earlier work of the Navajos is because much of it was used by the Spanish for export to Mexico. The Spanish-Americans in New Mexico did not use their imported horizontal loom to any extent until after the arrival of instructors from Mexico in 1806. Thus, Navajo weavers remained important to the Spanish to the end of the eighteenth century. Their blankets were highly prized in Sonora and Chihuahua, Mexico.

The earliest known pieces of Navajo weaving

FIGURE 3.20 Contemporary Navajo rugs. The Storm pattern rug, made largely on the western part of the reservation, favors the colors illustrated here, red, black, gray, and white. The central box is the center of the world, zigzags emanating from this are lightning, and the rectangles in the four corners are the "Houses of the winds;" in the center ends are highly conventionalized "water bugs." The two-faced rug is unusual in that it is of vegetable dyes; one face has this sophisticated geometric pattern while the opposite face is decorated with ritual subject matter. The pictorial blanket is well illustrated here: color and form which balance throughout the greater part of the rug are less typical than the lack of balance in the top and bottom rows. Typical designing of the Ganado rug is represented in this piece: a large central motif surrounded by lesser geometrics on either side; the double border is also quite usual. (*Courtesy Read Mullan Gallery of Western Art, photo by Herb McLaughlin*)

are the famous Massacre Cave fragments from Canyon del Muerto, northeastern Arizona, dated 1805. Illustrations of these in Amsden show plain and twill tapestry weaves and edge-to-edge striped patterns, with a tendency to group the stripes into bands.[35] Natural wool colors of white, brown, and black, plus indigo, and stripes of bayeta were used, the last "so thin, indeed, that they convey the mute suggestion of a material rare and highly prized."[36]

Despite the fact that there are as yet no earlier examples of Navajo textiles, the Massacre Cave pieces indicate a tradition of long standing in materials and decoration. Mera believed that there was no change in either of these until about 1840 or perhaps 1850.[37] The consensus is that plain tapestry weave, natural wool colors, a little native dye, indigo, and bayeta, and simple striped patterns predominated until the middle of the nineteenth century.

The year 1850 inaugurated the Classic Period of Navajo weaving which continued to 1875. Tremendous strides were made in both technology and artistry during these years. Mera thought that Spanish influences, particularly from Oaxaca, San Miguel, and Saltillo, Mexico, affected, or least inspired, some of these changes.[38] All the new materials, such as Saxony and Zephyr, were introduced, and bayeta became more abundant. By the end of this period bayeta was not common; some say that it was gone by 1875.[39] Suffice it to say at this point that design was "classic" during this period — sophisticated combinations of edge-to-edge stripes and geometrics.

During the 1850-1875 period, Navajos not only were producing their own clothing on their looms, but also were supplying other Indians with the same. Some of their blankets were still traded or sold into Mexico or to American soldiers. Contact with Mexico was of long standing, to be sure, but in the opening years of the second half of the nineteenth century it was furthered by the beginning of trade of Navajo horses.

From the early 1870's on, influences affecting the Navajo craftsman were so numerous that only the more important can be discussed. First and foremost was the establishment of more and more trading posts on the Navajo Reservation, many during the 1880's. These brought new materials, particularly aniline dyes and Germantown yarns, as well as many new ideas of designs and styles in weaving. Commercialization of the Navajo loom product eventuated from the trading post as well as from other white contacts.

The coming of the railroad in the 1880's also greatly influenced the Indian for it brought new materials such as yardage goods and clothing. Many of the Navajos substituted the fabrics for their native dress. By 1890, as a matter of fact, this trend had become so well established that the Navajo blanket was becoming a rug, an occurrence which may well have saved the craft from an early death. Needless to say, weaving degenerated during this period.

It must be stressed that many of the dates given herein are relative and not absolute. Actually, the traditions of the Classic Period lingered beyond 1875, and undoubtedly for a longer time in some areas than in others. Moreover, it took some years for the blanket to become a rug. Substitution of materials, changes in design, and changes in use were very slow in this vast Navajo country.

The great elaborations which had occurred in designing and in the use of commercial dyes and yarns were curtailed with the beginning of the rug. Once again the Navajo turned to natural colors of wool — black, white, brown, and grey — with a few touches of red. Designs were static and borders on all four sides became standard. The quality of weaving degenerated. Certainly some of these trends were not only encouraged by, but also continued because of, the traders' custom of selling rugs by the pound. Nor did this custom encourage artistry, or develop technology. Results were quite the opposite, with degenerative qualities to be seen in dirty and poorly spun yarn, uninspiring designs, and poor weaving. This trend continued to some degree until the 1920's. There were, of course, some exceptions such as the J. B. Moore activities at Crystal as described below.

During the third decade of this century, further personal interest on the part of white men was expressed in Navajo weaving. This took significant form in the work of Cozy MacSparron at Chinle. Not only did he encourage the Navajo women of this area to return to the use of vegetable dyes, but also he directed their interest towards the revival of the old style edge-to-edge patterning and borderless rugs. The result was a pleasing product which grew in popularity through the years.

By the time of the 1938 Lippencott revival of vegetable dyes at Wide Ruins, experimentation had improved the dyes. As a result, many of the colors from this area had a fresher, cleaner appearance. Today some of the Chinle rugs retain the softer and duller shades, but in many another example one cannot tell the origin of the rug. Also, during recent years, largely as a result of encouragement from the Navajo Arts and Crafts Guild, the area where these vegetable-dye rugs are produced has been expanding. It centers in the Wide Ruins and Chinle regions but extends around and beyond them.

Among the many important incidents which contributed further to the improvement of the Navajo textile craft were the creation of the Navajo Arts and Crafts Guild in 1941 (the Wingate guild, established in 1939-40, was the nucleus for this); the research and experimentation of the Home Economics Department (begun in 1934 at the Wingate Vocational High School) to determine the sources of native dyes;[40] the establishment of the sheep laboratory at Ft. Wingate; and the organization of the United Indian Traders Association in 1931. It should also be mentioned that several off-reservation traders became interested in and featured vegetable-dye rugs, thereby encouraging their sale. Thus, between these efforts, and those of the Navajo Arts and Crafts Guild whose aims also included finding markets for Indian arts, a greater public interest was created in the vegetable-dye rug in particular and in improved Navajo weaving in general.

Several other interesting efforts to better the quality of the Indian crafts, usually on the part of the white man, began in the 1920's and have never stopped. Drawings or pictures of the best old pieces of weaving were shown to Navajo women to encourage them to improve their designs. State fairs, the Gallup Indian Ceremonials, and special art and museum exhibits have been greatly influential along these lines, particularly in offering prizes for superior craftsmanship. New ideas have been suggested by traders, ethnologists, artists, and others to help the weaver improve her product, especially in the direction of creativity in design.

Again it may be said that today the Indian is living in a rapidly changing world, meeting many and varied challenges. His craft arts, including weaving no less than the others, are vital reflections of these cultural contacts.

By the 1920's a few people had begun to use such regional terms as "Chinle rug." The latter referred, of course, to the revival vegetable-dye style. Through the years traders have used such terms as "Ganado Red" rug, or "Teec Nos Pos" style. To these have been added quite a few others, most of them originating among traders and gradually disseminating to off-reservation clientele. Today the phrase "regional styles" has become an accepted term in rug identification. Formal publications referring to a synthesis of such styles are very recent. Foremost among them are the map of the Gallup Indian Trading Company and three booklets, Kent's *The Story of Navaho Weaving*, Dutton's *Navajo Weaving Today*, both published in 1961, and Maxwell's *Navajo Rugs — Past, Present and Future*, which appeared in 1963.

It should be added that today, even though there is not as *much* weaving done as in former years, there is more *good* weaving than ever before. Not only is there a great variety of styles, but also excellent preparation of materials, high standards

of weaving, and a continued superiority in designing. At the Gallup Indian Ceremonials of 1965, more than one expert remarked about the "finest quality ever seen in Navajo vegetable-dye rugs."

Styles of Weaving

"Old Style" (Non-Regional)

Many pieces of weaving executed by the Navajos before the turn of the century were characteristic of the entire reservation. These are designated here as "old styles" or non-regional types. A few of these are still woven. However, since shortly after the turn of the century, there has been a continued increase in weaving styles peculiar to more limited parts of the reservation; these are called "regional styles." Over the entire reservation, too, there is woven today a variety of rugs which may be called "commercial" for want of a better term. Most of them are black, white, and red; some may have gray or brown added. They are decorated with conventional geometric patterns and are bordered.

The first non-regional style is the simple robe or body blanket. The exact nature of this piece in its earliest manifestations begs description, for accounts are too brief to allow one to say more than that the Navajo wove and wore garments of wool. Knowing the historical contact with the pueblos, the chances are very good, as mentioned before, that this robe or blanket was either plain or simply striped.

The earliest known Navajo body blanket had alternate brown and white stripes; later came black and white stripes, then other color additions. It was not long before the Navajo had elaborated upon the simpler, pueblo-inspired styles. Even before 1850 there was considerable variety in the use of limited colors and edge-to-edge motifs on body blankets. There were thin stripes and vari-widthed bands; either these were of solid color, or one color might be outlined on both sides with a second color. Stripes and/or bands were arranged in groups or units; they were balanced but rarely were they evenly distributed over the entire surface, for the monotony of exact duplication throughout a craft piece does not appeal to the Navajos.

In addition to the blanket, it seems that Navajos may have woven plain shirts at an early date; Amsden describes one which could be dated as early as 1800. Belonging to the same time, also, is a woman's garment of the puebloid type, with a plain black center and the two borders of indigo blue in diamond twill weave.

Into the second half of the nineteenth century the Navajo woman's shoulder blanket and dress were more ornate than the coexisting and preceding pueblo styles. Before the end of this half century the former was very decorative (Fig. 3.21). It had a wide band at each end and a central one, with narrow stripes grouped between them. Within each of the wide bands were geometric themes, such as meanders, diamonds, zigzags, or crosses. Gray was used as background for the stripes in place of the white in the man's comparable piece, but more colors might be used in the other three areas, such as a red background with yellow and blue designs.

From as far back as is known, the man's shoulder or body blanket was larger and bolder than the woman's piece (Fig. 3.22). In time it came to be known as the "chief blanket" (Fig. 3.23), but certainly it was not worn exclusively by men of rank. By 1850 the chief blanket seems to have been well established. Typical broad central and end bands appeared, some with touches of red within them. These bands were elaborated through the years with more color and emphasis on designs. Red

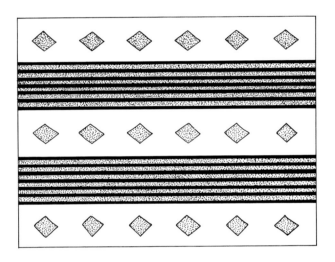

FIGURE 3.21 Sketch of the Navajo woman's shoulder-blanket style. Probably inspired by the puebloan form, this style had its greater dimensions from edge to edge. It featured three decorative areas, a central one and one at each end, with simple repeated geometrics in each. Between these areas were bands filled with narrow stripes.

became dominant, with some indigo added, and a diamond was the main motif within the three areas. Both above and below the central band were two broad black bands on a white ground.

Although these decorative motifs in the chief

FIGURE 3.22 A sketch of the Navajo man's simplest shoulder blanket. It was broad-striped, with black and/or dark blue, bands on a white ground, often with narrow red stripes within or between the dark color.

blanket became more and more elaborate through the years, they retained certain qualities. In each blanket or rug a single motif was used, with the broad black bands always there. Some variation occurred in the geometric theme, as, for example, in the diamond, which was most popular. A full diamond ornamented the center of the middle band, half diamonds appeared in mid-edges and mid-top and bottom, and quarter diamonds filled the corners. If one folded the piece from edge to edge or top to bottom, the diamond was completed, and the same was true if all four corners of the blanket were folded into the center.

Other decorative themes in the chief blanket included squares, rectangles, or hexagons, with possible elaborations of any of these geometric designs. Through the years the geometric themes became larger; by the late 1800's many of these motifs had overpowered the stripes (Fig. 3.24). And, although bands remained broader than in the woman's blanket, they served merely as background against which appeared the blown-up geometric patterns. Classic and simpler types have been produced from the inception of the chief blanket to the present time.

One other point should be stressed, namely, that the chief blanket, and to a lesser degree the woman's manta, reflected the changes which occurred in the greater periods of development of Navajo weaving as a whole. Thus the chief blankets were better woven, generally, in the 1850-75 period; they became rugs in the 1890-1900 years;

FIGURE 3.23 Modern styles of Navajo weaving. The chief blanket, upper left, represents the peak of the development of this type, with the geometric themes so large as to almost touch. A blue lighter than usual was used in this piece. Upper right is a Kayenta rug; like the Ganado style it has a large central motif featuring red (usually not as dark as the Ganado red). The central rug is a fine example of Teec Nos Pos weaving; colors are largely natural except for limited touches of red, green, and a purplish shade; and design carries out the usual patterned border and outlines of all major themes in the main part of the rug. In the lower left is a good example of a Chinle rug. On a colored ground, bands run from edge to edge and consist of multicolored stripes and geometric elements; the latter are typically made up of triangles. The last rug, in the lower right, is a double saddle blanket; allover concentric diamonds are created in the twill weave. (*Courtesy Read Mullan Gallery of Western Art, photo by Herb McLaughlin*)

Chief Blanket

Kayenta

Teec Nos Pos

Twill Weave
Saddle Blanket

Chinle

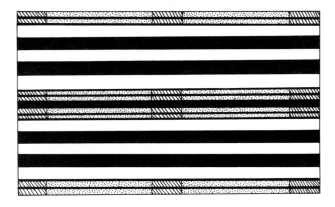

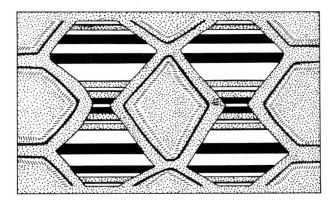

FIGURE 3.24 Sketches of the three major types of designed Chief Blankets. The earliest style (a) featured a design within bands, sometimes just barely extending beyond the band. Later (b) the design definitely broke from the confines of the bands. The latest development (c) shows the geometric design completely overpowering the bands. The last two styles have remained the more popular ones through the years.

they were made of commercial yarns and were more colorful with aniline dyes after 1875, and so on. Red became and remained a prominent addition to the black, dark blue, and white background bands; it was used either in the central and end bands, or in the geometric designs within them, or in both.

The woman's shoulder blanket followed the same general period changes, usually in a reserved fashion. The central, top, and bottom bands reflected artistic change, while between them there remained the grouping of narrow stripes. Sometimes these stripes became incorporated in the central and end geometric patterns, as in the case of the use of large crosses against the extension of such a striped ground. More often there were small diamonds, triangles, zigzags, or other geometric elements, plain or in combination, confined to and running the width of the central and end portions, while the massed stripes were restricted to the areas between them. In the true manta and the chief blanket the larger dimension followed the wefts. The woman's manta averaged 45 by 60 inches, while the chief blanket averaged 50 by 70 inches.[41]

The Navajo woman's dress (Fig. 3.25) presents a style quite different from that of the puebloans. In the first place, the single and weft-wide pueblo dress is replaced by two weft-narrow blankets, one to be worn in front, one on the back. It is possible that this difference existed from the beginning, inspired by the Spanish-American weaving mentioned above, or perhaps by the Navajo custom of wearing two skins in a comparable manner.[42] It may be that the first Navajo dress simulated the pueblo style in an allover dark blanket. According to tradition, the first deviation from plain styles was the addition of indigo stripes at each end of a blanket, but no example of this type exists. Mera illustrates a very early dress which has such stripes but they are outlined with red.[43]

The typical Navajo blanket dress that is known today is characterized by a black (or brownish-black) center with a wide red border at each end. The center is handspun while borders have been of bayeta, flannel, or machine-spun yarns. Designs in borders could be in dark blue, which is homespun, or in other colors which are usually commercial. Border patterns include stripes with or without small geometrics attached to them, rows of repeated diamonds, crosses, zigzags, and occasional other forms. The blanket dress persisted until the end of the nineteenth century. It was woven only rarely after this date.

Another product of the Navajo loom which probably goes back to early years and which sur-

FIGURE 3.25 Two regional types of Navajo weaving and a Navajo woman's dress. The top rug comes from the Ganado area; it is a little unusual in the more quiet central design, but it does have the fine rich red so typical of this area. It is both beautifully woven and designed. The Farmington-Shiprock yei rug here illustrated is woven in vegetable-dyed wools. The lack of borders and the surrounding Rainbow goddess are typical features, as is the fine weaving. The lower illustration is a Navajo woman's dress; it is made in two parts and fastened at the sides (top and bottom in the picture). Center of each part is black, and in wide red borders are simple geometric patterns in dark blue. (*Courtesy Read Mullan Gallery of Western Art, photo by Herb McLaughlin*)

Ganado

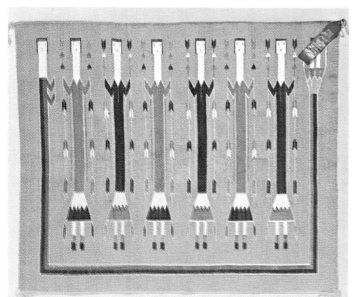

Farmington-Shiprock Yei

Navajo Woman's Dress

vived into late times, is the so-called "dougie" (Fig. 3.26). Just before the turn of the century traders were using this term for a coarsely woven shoulder blanket which the Navajos made for themselves and for other Indians. The word is a corruption of the Navajo "di-yu-gi," meaning a thick, soft, fluffy blanket.[44] This type of blanket was made of a coarsely spun native wool and was loosely woven. (Reminiscent of this weave is the saddle blanket still made on the western part of the Navajo Reservation, largely for commercial trade.) The dougie was simply decorated in natural-wool combinations of black, white, and brown. Kent refers to them as being common in the 1850's and 1860's,[45] while Amsden tells of a trader advertising them in the late 1800's as one of three main types of Navajo loom products.[46]

The shape of the majority of the remaining types of blankets made by the Navajo from 1850-1875 was rectangular, but with the greater dimension along the warps and not along the wefts. Several distinctive artistic styles were produced, and, as previously noted, technically some of the best weaving was accomplished in these pieces, as well

FIGURE 3.26 An early piece of Navajo weaving. It could be a shoulder blanket — called a Dougie — or, possibly, a saddle blanket. The piece measures 34″ in width and 46″ in length. The darker and lighter tans which serve as background are very coarse threads while the red and blue are finer. Most of the narrow stripes are in dark blue, red, and light blue.

as in the manta and chief blanket, during these years. Poor work was done, of course — as in the dougie — just as some equally fine or finer weaving has been done in the past twenty to thirty years.

Superior wearing blankets of Classic years (Fig. 3.27) were made of various combinations of finely spun native wool, bayeta, and Saxony. Other commercial yarns appeared in the later years of this period. Thread counts in some weaving range from 40 to 55 wefts and 8 to 12 warps per inch. To be sure, some were finer and some were not so fine. Among the design styles were: a subtly striped background against which were placed edge-to-edge and allover or zoned geometric patterns; or the same patterns and arrangement minus the striped ground; or a dark ground which had more severe banded patterns and sometimes a centered diamond. Terraced or stepped elements and rectangular figures, all built upon right-angles, dominated Classic motifs.

The style with the striped ground presented a diversity of geometric themes in its decoration, although large and small zigzags and diamonds were featured. Navajo ingenuity asserted itself, however, so there was great variety in their use. One common style was edge-to-edge zigzags with end treatment like the chief blanket; the zigzags might be confined to bands, or might be so used as to meet at their points and form diamonds. Diamonds varied, too, for they might be clustered across a wide central area or appear in wide sections toward both ends. Duplication was unknown. Endless additional elements were used, but never too many in a single blanket; the essence of good Navajo design prohibited cluttering with more than two or three basic elements or motifs in a single piece. Diamonds might be of three different sizes or vary in shape, but along with them would be lines and triangles in one blanket, or chevrons and crosses in another. Even zigzags were used in various ways — in horizontal position and across the fabric, or in short verticals which formed bands. Stripes were subordinated to other design elements in all cases.

The second type of blanket in this period lacked the striped background. Rather there was a perfectly plain ground, often red in color, against which were featured terraced patterns. Zigzags and diamonds were popular in this style also, with the latter often formed by the meeting of the points of the zigzags. A feeling of greater simplicity characterizes these blankets, due in some instances to the absence of the striped ground.

A type of weaving which is important in the history of the craft among the Navajos is the so-called "slave blanket" (Fig. 3.28). This product was the result of Navajo weavers combining the use of their own upright looms and certain of their weaving

FIGURE 3.27 A fine example of a Classic Period Navajo blanket. The complex arrangement of edge-to-edge stripes and bands and stepped diamonds, zigzags, and triangles is in indigo, red, and white with small touches of green. This piece represents not only a peak in designing but also some of the finest of Navajo weaving. This blanket is 49″ wide by 64″ long. (1850–1875).

traits with aspects of the Spanish craft which they learned as slaves. Because of the use of Spanish dyes, many of the striped blankets had a non-Navajo feeling. Mera also notes that the two-ply warp, when found in combination with unquestionably Navajo weaving features, would indicate "the work of some captive weaver."[47] Too, the large central diamond is typically Mexican. There is some question as to the time of this development. It would seem likely that the slave-blanket trend spanned the end of the first half and the beginning of the second half of the nineteenth century. Slavery continued after this date, of course, for Amsden quotes its documentation as late as 1866, when an Indian agent said that "no less than 400 Indians are thus held in Santa Fe alone."[48]

Decoration of the slave blanket runs the gamut from a very simple edge-to-edge design featuring bands (which perhaps reflects the pre-1850 style) to more elaborate styles reminiscent of the Classic blanket (1850-1875), and on to large central diamonds made up of small elements and with a distinctly Mexican flavor. Some also have large areas made up of allover small elements, another Mexican trend. In describing one of these blankets, Amsden mentioned that the colors, a red central figure and

stripes of purple, grey-pink, red, and orange, are suggestive of the Chimayo blanket made by Spanish-Americans in New Mexico.[49] He also stressed the dimensions, 53 by 82 inches, as being less Navajo and more Spanish-American.

Another blanket favored by Navajos during the Classic and post-Classic Periods was the so-called "Moqui" (Hopi) style (Fig. 3.29). It included many variations, but featured a dark ground, usually of indigo, with a few or many stripes and occasional other decorative elements. This type of blanket was favored by the Hopis, hence its name, but was woven also by the puebloans of the Rio Grande and by the Spanish-American weavers of New Mexico. In many instances technical features alone distinguish the Indian piece from the Spanish-Colonial loom product; the latter has a center seam and lacks the extra yarns twisted along all selvages of Navajo loom products (Fig. 3.2).

From the standpoint of design, the so-called Moqui-style blanket produced by the Navajos paralleled other traditions in some respects, but featured finer stripes and, often, finer weaving. Earlier ones had simple and narrow stripes of

FIGURE 3.28 Another example of Classic Period Navajo weaving which demonstrates the use of many colors. In the usual manner are bands of plain colors or with repeated geometrics. Colors include dark blue — probably indigo — red, gold, pale green, very pale yellow, and brown. Weaving is fine but the edges are irregular. Dimensions are about 38″ wide and 52″ long. (1850–1875).

FIGURE 3.29 Beautiful example of Navajo-woven "Moqui" type blanket. This piece is so named because it simulates an old-style Hopi (called Moqui) blanket decoration which features narrow background stripes in indigo. It assumes, however, the usual Navajo vigor in the addition of the two great crosses and the laced squares, both in red and white, against the indigo and lighter blue stripes. This piece measures 60″ by 80″. It is a "Hubbell" type, dated around 1900.

brown or black and indigo blue between wider white bands and, most distinctive of all, some "beading" in the stripes. Beading is an alternation of tiny blocks, usually of darker and lighter colors, rather close together and in one stripe. In time, red was added, then other colors, and, in sequence, wider bands, terraced figures, and finally serrate styles appeared. Withal, the very dark indigo ground was favored until the end of the nineteenth century when a revival of the Moqui style at Hubbell's Trading Post, Ganado, Arizona, introduced in rugs a substitute aniline purplish color for the indigo.[50]

There was a lingering of design styles and of good weaving too, after the end of the Classic Period. As a whole, however, new trends developed from the early 1870's which resulted in very different blankets as compared with the Classic and earlier types. Kent refers to the years from 1875 to 1890 as the "Transition Period;" it is transitional in the sense of the carryover of many design styles, and it is also a period full of new vigor in color, new styles of design, and at the end, the shift from blanket to rug weaving.

Although some foreign and commercial materials,

such as bayeta, Saxony, indigo, and cochineal, had penetrated the Navajo country before the establishment of trading posts in the early 1870's, it was not until after this time that an appreciable amount of dye stuffs, such as anilines, and yarns — Germantowns in particular — appeared in Navajo weaving, as a greater influence on design. It is quite possible, too, that Fort Sumner days introduced the Navajos to commercial blankets in larger quantities in the form of government-issue blankets which the weaver could unravel, respin, and put to use at her loom. These influences were responsible in some measure for the changes which occurred in post-Classic times.

It is tempting to postulate that the easy accessibility of dyes and materials in this period sent the Navajos off on a color and design spree. Certainly designs and colors changed greatly. Every color in dye packets appeared in blankets, many in one piece, and usually in larger designs. In many instances designs themselves ran riot, no longer confined to bands but spreading out over the fabric. Some of the more exuberant included large end-to-end themes, such as diamonds and zigzags (Fig. 3.30); pictorial subjects including cows, men, horses, trains, birds; and very broad bold complex bands of designs.

Adding to the vigor of patterning was a common substitution of acute angles in place of the right-angle style of previous years. This developed about 1880. The smooth line made possible by the acute angle of this serrate patterning opened up new design potentials still favored today by the Navajo weaver, particularly for true diamonds and triangles. Previously, diamond patterns, large or small, were always built up in stairstep fashion.

It would be impossible to describe even a representative group of these Transition Period blankets, so varied are they. Several examples of each of the above trends will have to suffice.

Banded decoration was still popular early in this period (1875-1890), and often it utilized the new serrate style of designing. Simple zigzags of earlier styles assumed vigor as they were made of a number of acute-angled units. In one blanket, vermillion, pink, brown-black, white, and grey added variety of color in its series of grouped zigzags. Kent illustrates an example of banding which shows the lingering old style combined with the new. "The blanket shows a pattern of simple stripes, some beaded, on which is superimposed a diamond motif worked in serrate style."[51] Banded styles of decoration are extremely popular today, particularly in the vegetable dyes and in Crystal rugs.

End-to-end patterning may well have been the result of sheer desire to create a new style, or it may have been encouraged by the increase in size and elaboration of serrate diamonds. One example in Mera's book would seem to support the latter idea. A large central diamond reaches from edge to edge. Half diamonds extend from the inner points of the full one, with their "cut" edges touching the end borders.[52] Again, color added vigor. A late example of this style combined orange, black, and white on a red ground.[53] When made today, end-to-end patterns are often enclosed by borders on all four sides.

Pictorial blankets rarely appeared before 1880. In the early pieces figures were highly conventionalized, and the relative coarseness of Navajo weaving made all of them angular. Although most of the animals, humans, and other figures were arranged in rows, some few were scattered. One example shows men on horseback, other quadrupeds, birds, and a scorpion-like figure, all in bands.[54] Another example is more allover in arrangement and has a conglomerate of scattered geometric and life forms. The latter include a man on the back of a tapir-like animal (?), front part black and back part white; quadrupeds (cows?); various sized multi-colored birds; men, one obviously in cowboy dress; women in long full skirts; two trains, complete with smoke coming out of the stacks; and a scattering of small geometric elements. This blanket, too, is woven in a variety of colors — red, lavender, yellow, green, black, white, and blue.[55] Pictorial rugs have been made occasionally through the years and are still being made in the 1960's (Fig. 3.20).

Shortly before and during the last decade of the nineteenth century, several significant changes occurred in Navajo weaving. The most important was the shift from the blanket to the rug; another change was stylistic — the addition of a border to Navajo loom products. Less significant were the shift back to colors of the natural wool plus a little red, and a return to more reserved patterns. The bordered, plain-colored, simply designed rug persisted until about 1920; a few are still woven.

The shift from blanket to rug was undoubtedly encouraged, if not inspired, by traders on the Navajo Reservation. Trade with the Mormons in Utah and with others preceded and perhaps anticipated this potential. In the early 1880's, agents noted a brisk trade in Navajo blankets, some to traders, and a growing reputation for this tribe's weaving ability. It was the dougie, or shoulder-type blanket, which was most widely traded; this is important since it was the dougie style which became heavier, thicker, and larger to serve as the first rug. And it was the transition to the rug which made possible the further development of Navajo weaving as a significant trade item. The larger, better-woven,

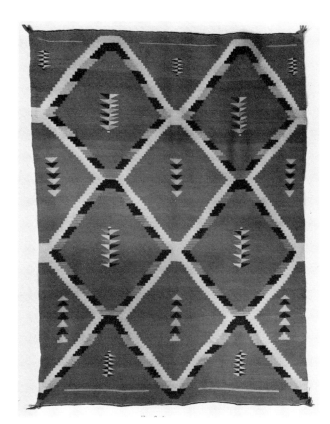

FIGURE 3.30 Transitional Period Navajo blanket. This piece is not as well woven as the Classic examples. The arrangement of the great outlines of allover diamonds breaks from the tradition of edge-to-edge patterning which prevailed to 1875. The large figures have double outlines, one in white, the other in alternating indigo and pale green. The same colors are used in the stacked diamonds and triangles.

and artistically more elaborate blanket was, even in the 1880's and 1890's, a collector's piece, with far less potential for general use and sales. It was the trader who realized the potential of the dougie-turned-rug; he has been and still is a very important individual in the story of Navajo weaving.

During the 1920 revival of vegetable dyes by MacSparron, Navajo weaving again took on new life. The predominantly somber products of the preceding two decades were far below the standards of Classic weaving; so, too, were some of the revival styles. Thus it was primarily through improvement of, or change in, the craft that interest could be revived. Further improvement followed in the 1930's and has continued to the present; during these years there have been developments in the craft along many lines.

Regional Styles

The term "regional" as applied to Navajo weaving began to assume significance during the 1920-1930 period of change, despite earlier trends in the direction of local styles. Among early and familiar types were the Chinle and Wide Ruins-Pine Springs vegetable dyes, Ganado Red and Teec Nos

Pos, Crystal, Two Gray Hills, and others. Sometimes a geographic location gave the name to the rug, or a trading post, or sometimes a characteristic trait, such as color or design. Most of these regional names have come into use rather carelessly or unconsciously. With a few exceptions, regional rugs are rectangular, with the longer dimension along the warps.

In his 1934 publication, Amsden mentions an earlier Crystal rug and says, as of that date, "One no longer hears mention of the Crystal rug. . . ."[56] James illustrates in color a number of early Crystal rugs, and these make very plain the connection between this and the Two Gray Hills types.[57]

It is important, then, to turn back briefly to pre-1920 years. An early trader at Crystal, J. B. Moore, became interested in the improvement of Navajo weaving in his area, and actively worked at this from about 1897[58] to 1911-12.[59] He sent wool to the east to be scoured and carded and, after it was returned, supervised its dyeing. He supplied the ideas for the designs and had the best weavers produce the rugs. Many of Moore's suggested designs were in keeping with Navajo traditions, while others were new to the Indian.

These early Crystal types are worthy of a few comments as far as design is concerned. Ground colors featured gray or brown, but may have been red in some instances. Single or double borders were used, with one or both carrying a design; the border background was often red. Design enclosed by the border or borders was allover and quite generally heavy, with many wide-line motifs in black or some in white or brown, large outlined geometric forms, and a tendency toward a prominent central motif which was roughly diamond-shaped.

The connection between this early Crystal rug and the Two Gray Hills, the latter well established by 1925, is obvious. Amsden says of the Two Gray Hills rug in 1934, "Here the Moore tradition flourishes today, . . . and this small corner of the reservation has a widespread reputation as the home of the best of modern Navaho weaving."[60] Although for a time native wools in black, white, and gray prevailed in the Two Gray Hills rug, there have been years when the wool was imported. Today the majority of the wool is native and handspun, and it is the finest in the Southwest.

Quite naturally the early Two Gray Hills rugs were more in the Crystal tradition than are the styles of the period beginning about 1950. Many had single borders with quite heavy designs; heaviness and simplicity also characterized the central motifs. Some had gray center grounds; others may have had complete red grounds for both border and center. However, there were some Two Gray Hills rugs in the 1930's more like the contemporary product, with delicately patterned double borders and more intricate and finer designing in the center.

A classic Two Gray Hills rug of today (Fig. 3.31) could be characterized by the following traits. It is woven of the finest carded and spun materials, with a thread count as high as 110 wefts to the inch in some of the best examples. The pieces are very light weight, more like blankets than rugs. One rug woven in 1962 is so thin that, if hung in a window, it looks like a geometric picture. Colors may be natural wools or dyed; much of the brown and more, if not all, of the black is dyed, while the gray is usually black and white carded together. Soft tan or beige tones are brown and white carded together. The number of shades of beige, brown, and gray, even in a single rug, is astounding: six shades of beige were counted in one example. A few other colors may appear in Two Gray Hills rugs today, usually in very small quantities; these may be vegetable or commercial dyes.

Modern designs in Two Gray Hills blankets are typically complex, far more so than in the early pieces. Borders may combine a plain black one with a second which is white or light with a black design in it. The entire center is commonly gray with intricate and involved allover designing which features a large centered theme with lesser motifs between it and the borders. Solid black, brown, and white motifs of large or small size may be combined with outlined or line themes.

There is still a feeling of architectural design in the Two Gray Hills, as there was in the early Crystal rug. Design elements in these rugs include steps, diamonds, plain and complex crosses, swastikas, meanders of various forms, plain and recurved frets, stars of various sorts, plain and complex lines, rhomboids, hooks, triangles, squares, and rectangles. Balanced symmetry prevails, both above and below center and to right and left.

The Two Gray Hills rug is without question the finest product of the Navajo loom today. Within the past ten to fifteen years the quality has greatly improved. As early as 1947 Mera noted that, "From

FIGURE 3.31 Navajo rugs in regional styles and all in vegetable dyes and natural colors. The beautiful colors in the Wide Ruins rug (top left), deep pink and yellow, are favorites in this region, weaving in the piece is excellent. There are at least six shades of tan or beige in the Two Gray Hills rug (top right); typical patterning is represented here: a large central motif with several outlining elements, small repeated themes in the four corners, and a triple border. In the lower left is a Raised Outline rug from the western part of the reservation. An additional thread outlines the edges of all design elements. In the Crystal area, the rugs are characterized by edge-to-edge wavy lines (lower right); there are no borders; and bands are plain or have simple, repeated geometrics within them. (*Courtesy Read Mullan Gallery of Western Art, photo by Herb McLaughlin*)

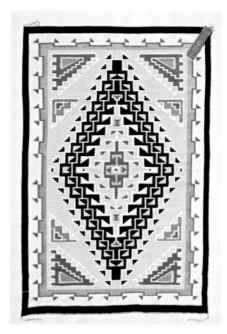

Two Gray Hills

Wide Ruins

Western Reservation-Raised Outline

Crystal

a purely technical standpoint these rugs generally average somewhat higher than the directly ancestral type."[61] Today they have gone far beyond the early Crystal rug both technically and artistically.

After the early Crystal tradition moved east into the Two Gray Hills area, the weavers in the former region did not produce any outstanding products for some time. However, by the late thirties, Crystal-area Navajos were weaving entirely different and very distinctive rugs. The main feature of the newer Crystal rug is a wavy line which is produced by changing each successive weft color and battening each down so that one color alternates with the other in the same row (Fig. 3.31 and Fig. 3.32). The wefts are loosely inserted. Another feature common in these rugs is a use of vegetable dyes of dark shades of yellow, almost-mustard green, tans, red-browns, and black. Also, designs are edge-to-edge, with geometric elements occurring between the bands of wavy lines.

This Crystal wavy-line technique is spreading a bit into other areas. It has crossed over from extreme western New Mexico into the Chinle, Nazlini, and Wide Ruins areas of northeastern Arizona. This illustrates the contemporary trend among Navajo weavers to be influenced by each other.

The revival of vegetable dyes and old-style edge-to-edge patterning, first in the 1920's, then on into the 1930's and 1940's, has proved to be one of the most important developments of this century in Navajo rug weaving. Any pre-1900 use of vegetable dyes presented a very limited number of colors; later developments extended color variation and quality far beyond all knowledge of earlier years. Dutton reports a recording of over 250 recipes for making vegetable dyes today.[62] Varying shades can be obtained by dipping the yarns once or several times in the same dye bath as well as in different colors. Natural wool colors and aniline dyes may be used in combination with vegetable dyes in rugs.

Chinle vegetable-dye rugs today (Fig. 3.23), which are made at Nazlini also, are characterized by subdued shades of green, yellow, rose, brown, and greenish gray. Some of these colors have a somber cast — especially in earlier work. Black and white are also used. Some pastels and brighter colors are used at Chinle, but not as many as in the Wide Ruins area.

Typical designing in Chinle rugs can be characterized by several major features. Lines, bands, or a combination of the two, usually arranged in clusters, are placed between rows of geometric patterns or used as a background for these elements. A feeling of openness prevails, perhaps due to plain white or light bands between those with geometric designs. Among the geometric elements used are serrate-edged diamonds, a line with stubby diagonals above and/or below, and a slightly modified H-figure. Quite often the geometric elements are large in size.

The vegetable-dye development in the Wide Ruins-Pine Springs area (also known as Kintiel), fostered by the Lippencotts, resulted in some of the most sophisticated color and design combinations of all Navajo weaving. Coupled with this has been an increasing improvement in preparation of materials and in weaving. Excellent weaving was already established at Pine Springs when the Lippencotts started their work about 1938. The Navajo Arts and Crafts Guild, which has been located at or near Window Rock since 1941, has been another factor in the development of this vegetable-dye rug, particularly after the departure of the Lippencotts in the early 1940's.

Soft and often light but rich tones of a wide variety of colors are quite generally used in these rugs (Fig. 3.31). Combinations of pleasingly blending shades of pink or rose or yellow, with touches of white and gray, are one favored arrangement. Other combinations include: deep rich gray, light brown, light olive green, and white; light and medium gray, white, two shades of tan, and pink; soft yellow, tan, pale brown, and white. In the latter three combinations, the white is limited sometimes to very narrow stripes or is used as a fine outline. The colors named beggar description, for their subtlety is often beyond descriptive words.

It is in the handling of color and design together that the Wide Ruins-Pine Springs weavers are such past masters. Not only is there perfection in the combination of subtle shades, but also expert use of beading, outlining in color, line designs, small design units, and simpler designing as a whole. Less use of sharply contrasting juxtaposed bands results in softer, more blending effects. Further, white and black are used sparingly and often in broken sequences.

As a commercial piece, the Wide Ruins vegetable-dye rug has been one of the most successful of any type of Navajo weaving. This is due in part to its esthetic qualities, but it is also due to certain practical values. There is enough variety in color to please, and the colors do not have the shocking qualities of other types of Navajo rugs. The rugs are beautifully woven. They will fit into

FIGURE 3.32 A portion of a beautiful Crystal rug. The beauty of this wavy-line technique is greatly enhanced by the use of subtle vegetable-dye colors throughout the piece, plus very fine weaving. (*Courtesy Read Mullan Gallery of Western Art, photo by Herb McLaughlin*)

a modern and sophisticated home. And yet, withal, they have the beauty and strength of an outstanding Navajo trait — the Navajos' great feeling for abstract design.

The Teec Nos Pos (also Tees Nos Pas, and other spellings) rug (Fig. 3.23) comes from the extreme northeast corner of Arizona and from a small part of the northwestern-most section of New Mexico. This rug is commonly called an "outline rug," for it is characterized by fine-line color outlines for all of the major and many minor decorative elements or motifs. Red, black, gray, and white are dominant, although touches of other colors may be added, such as greens and blues. Some Germantown wool is combined with the basic handspun. Technically, this is often a well-woven rug — it takes skill to produce the very fine outlines. A fairly wide border is also typical, and generally this carries a heavy design. Among design units and motifs are hooks, rows of serrate elements, arrows, diamonds, triangles, feathers, triangles with stems, and various line themes.

Around Ganado, Arizona, particularly to the southwest and east, an outstanding type of rug has been made for some years (Figs. 3.20 and 3.25). The rug employs a fair amount to a large quantity of deep and rich red; hence the piece has come to be known as the "Ganado Red" or "Ganado" type rug. Designs are often massive, with large areas of red either in the background or in the design itself. Quite large areas of white are typical also. Designs tend to be on the simpler side; they also lack any feeling of being cluttered. Single or double borders may be used, and both are usually plain, perhaps one black and one red.

Another style of Navajo weaving which is made more commonly for a tapestry or wall hanging is the so-called yei or the yeibechai rug. The name yei refers to gods or to the personalities in Navajo religion which are intermediaries between man and his gods. They are impersonated in the yeibechai dance, a part of the winter ritual called the Night Chant. As there is a difference between a "yei" spirit and a "yeibechai" dancer, so too is there a design difference in the rug. The yei rug is ornamented with the elongate figures which are so commonly used as decorative themes in Navajo sandpaintings. They are conventional in style. On the other hand, the yeibechai rug attempts to portray the human dancers; therefore, an effort is made in the direction of realism when weaving the latter figures into the piece.

These pieces are incorrectly called prayer rugs; they are neither used by the Navajo nor does he attach any religious significance to them. The late Fr. Stoner reported that John Wetherill said that he had a Navajo make the first yei rug to send to the 1904 World's Fair in St. Louis. James pictures three yei blankets in his book, which was originally published in 1914.[63]

Yei rugs are made in two areas, the Shiprock-Farmington region of northwestern New Mexico, and the Greasewood-Lukachukai section of northeastern Arizona. Characteristically, the Farmington area yei rug has a white background (Fig. 3.33). Through the years these have varied greatly as to quality, size, and colors used. One piece, produced in the late 1930's, was so finely woven that the heads of the yeis were definitely rounded. The colors in this piece were less garish than they are today. Also, through the years there has been a growing use of commercial yarns (Germantowns) and dyes in the making of these rugs at Shiprock. In some pieces, backgrounds are darker (Fig. 3.25).

Contemporary pieces from the Farmington-Shiprock area are characterized by a wide variety of colors in a single piece, such as red, green, yellow, pink, blue, and orange. Often there are three or more figures in a row, with a red and blue rainbow goddess surrounding the line of figures down the two sides and across the bottom. Many of the Farmington rugs are borderless.

In the second yei area, rugs are made largely in and about the trading post of Lukachukai. They differ from the first type in that often they have a gray or dark brown ground or, in some pieces, a red or black ground (Fig. 3.33). The figures are done in a number of colors; reds are favored, but greens, yellows, aniline-dyed blues, and blacks are also used. Generally there are not so many colors in a single piece. Handspun is the common material. One to twelve yei appear in the Lukachukai-Greasewood rug, in one or two rows. The Farmington rug often carries considerable detail for it is more finely woven than the Lukachukai type.

Another rug, which is not particularly regional but is related in certain ways to the yei style, is the sandpainting type (Fig. 3.34). The first of these, reputedly, was made in 1919 by a Navajo medicine

FIGURE 3.33 A Navajo yeibichai and a yei rug from the Farmington-Shiprock and Lukachukai-Greasewood areas. Although the two styles are not quite as distinct today as they were in the past, many of the weavers local to each area follow these two traditions. The Lukachukai-Greasewood style (top) is characterized by a border, homespun (therefore coarser work), and a darker background. This example is a yeibichai rug, for the figures are dancers and not the spirits or yei. In the lower Farmington-Shiprock piece are representations of the yei, therefore this is a true yei rug. Background is white or light; there is no border, but around the figures is a Rainbow goddess. Through the years Germantown yarns have become ever more popular, thus design detail is finer. (*Courtesy Read Mullan Gallery of Western Art, photo by Herb McLaughlin*)

Lukachukai-Greasewood Yei

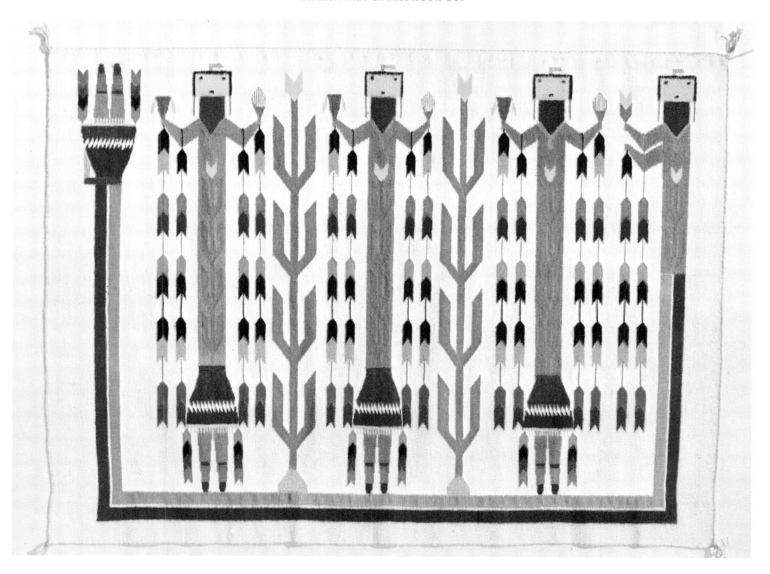

Farmington-Shiprock Yei

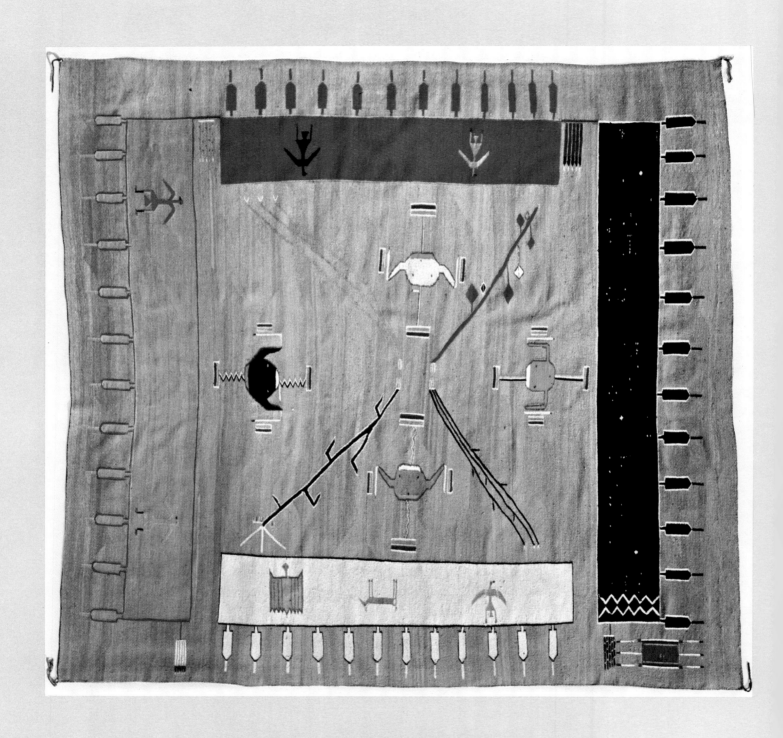

Klah's Sandpainting Rug — "Shooting Chant"

man.[64] The "Whirling Log" has been a favorite subject for several of these rugs; this is one of the paintings made by the Navajo medicine man in the "Night Chant" ceremony. In the rug as in the painting there are four crossed logs, a male and a female deity sit upon each log, and either the four sacred plants or other designs appear between the logs. Other yei figures may appear around the four sides, and a rainbow goddess around the outside, leaving one side open as is done in the original painting. One such rug had a soft tan ground and a simplification of figures which made for an artistic blanket. And "blanket" is used advisedly, for the sandpainting piece is often quite light weight.

In the Gallup area a small "runner" is woven. This piece has become quite important as a commercial item but it lacks the artistry of many another example of Navajo weaving and it is not too well woven. As the name implies, the piece has longer and narrower dimensions. It has a cotton warp, and is often small in size. Colors are apt to be bright, since aniline dyes are used. Often there is a centered geometric pattern with no further decoration. For the most part, the runner is borderless.

Around Kayenta another rug is found which has certain regional characteristics (Fig. 3.23). In some ways it resembles the Ganado rug, although it is not always as bold and simple in design nor does it have the same rich red. The Kayenta rug tends to be more ornate, it may be double bordered, and the red is a lighter shade than the Ganado color.

Two last areas significant in Navajo weaving are the Tuba City and the Western Reservation regions. Coal Mine Mesa, in the former locale, has produced some fine saddle-blanket weaves. Although these weaves are found all over the Reservation, some distinctive pieces have been made at Coal Mine Mesa in recent years. In the same area an interesting raised-outline rug style has been woven (Fig. 3.31). Literally, the main design is outlined with a thread which stands above the rest of the fabric. Sometimes a secondary pattern is created on a neutral ground in self-color in the same manner. These raised outlines appear on the front but not on the reverse face of the rug.

Fine twill-weave saddle blankets also are woven in the Coppermine area of the Western Reservation. Otherwise, rather conventional rugs of black, white, and gray, with occasional touches of red, come from this region.

One of the most interestingly designed rugs of the Navajos is the Storm pattern (Fig. 3.20) which is woven in the Tuba City and Western Reservation areas. Moore pictures one of these in his 1911 catalog.[65] He refers to it as a "special design" and says that it "is one of the really legendary designs embodying a portion of the Navajo mythology."[66] The Storm pattern has certain standard features with individual variation found in greater simplicity or elaboration. Always there is a square or rectangular central motif; from the four corners of this motif zigzags lead out to smaller but comparable themes in the corners of the rug. There are further designs in end and side centers. One explanation for the details of the pattern is that the central motif is the center of the earth, the zigzags are lightning, and the four corner themes are the houses of the winds. The motifs in the center ends of the rug may be geometric or conventional representations of the water bug.

On the Western Reservation many of the rugs are woven in black, white, gray, and red and are not particularly distinctive. Around Inscription House, however, there are some well-designed and equally well-woven rugs in these colors. Also, a highly commercialized saddle blanket comes from this part of the Reservation. A thick and fuzzy type with very simple edge-to-edge stripes, often in garish colors, it is woven in both single and double saddle-blanket sizes.

The saddle blanket is the only piece woven by Navajos primarily for Navajos in recent and present times (Figs. 3.23 and 3.35), and it is the only piece in which the craftswoman has explored beyond the simple tapestry weave used in all other blankets and rugs. Basically, the saddle blanket incorporates variations of the twill weave to produce diamonds, zigzags, end-to-end or edge-to-edge stripes, hexagons, herringbone, and other geometric patternings which are so common in this piece. Sometimes several design elements or units are combined in a single saddle blanket.

The charm of the saddle blanket lies in the subtlety of weave and color. Solid areas of color are almost nonexistent, although they do appear sometimes in bands or lesser geometric themes. Far more common are nests of outlines of the geometrics used. These elements are generally small and allover and are used with simple end borders and/or variations in weave. Side borders are far less common; when they do appear, they may be like the end types. Occasionally a side

FIGURE 3.34 Sandpainting rug — one of the finest — woven by a Navajo medicine man, Hosteen Klah. Directional colors are represented in white for the east, blue for the south, red for the west, and black for the north. Rectangles of red and blue represent clouds, the horned figures are the sun and moon. All other designs are equally symbolic. The piece is beautifully woven — more the quality of the older blankets than of rugs. (*Courtesy Read Mullan Gallery of Western Art, photo by Herb McLaughlin*)

border is more elaborate than those at the ends. Emphasis on the center of the saddle blanket may repeat the end motifs or may elaborate upon them.

In quality, Navajo weaving stands today at one of its high peaks. However, the quantity of weaving started to decline in the early 1950's, then levelled off after the mid-1950's. Since then there has been neither a rise nor further decline, although in the spring of 1963 there were few rugs available. It seems that the craft will never be a significant factor economically among the Navajos, for they are developing and changing so rapidly that the small income brought in from weaving is of less and less importance. More and more women are going into other lines of endeavor, although there are a few young women who are following in the footsteps of their mothers in this craft. At the 1961 Navajo Fair, the first prize in juvenile weaving went to the daughter of the woman who took top honors in the adult category.

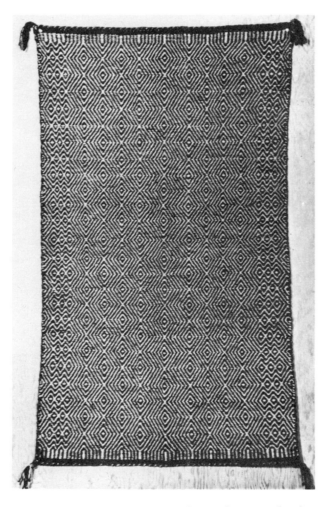

FIGURE 3.35 Navajo saddle blanket. A fine example of a double saddle blanket, in a diamond-twill weave. Colors used in this piece were red, black, and white. Dimensions were 30″ wide and 60″ long.

Furthermore, the percentage of income from rugs to the Navajos has been made minuscule by the vast sums accruing to the tribal coffers by way of uranium, oil leases, and other natural resources. As husbands bring home fatter paychecks, the Navajo woman finds less and less attraction in the small sum she receives for the hard task of preparing materials for and weaving a rug.

Perhaps the weavers at Hopi villages will be discouraged also. A commercial canvas-like material is sometimes substituted for the hand-woven kilt. Probably it is only a matter of time before all the factors of acculturation will combine to eliminate the traditional styles of weaving of both Navajos and puebloans.

Summary

In the broad view, weaving in the Indian Southwest today presents an interesting picture. Descendants of those responsible for the high development of this craft, the puebloans, have ceased to weave except for the Hopis. Rio Grande puebloans passed their peak in textile production before the beginning of this century. Latecomers, the Navajos, borrowed the craft from the puebloans and are now the great weavers of the Southwest.

With few exceptions, the development of weaving represents a continuum, at least from early Christian Era days to the present. The loom, techniques, and forms developed in those prehistoric years prevail to this day. Spanish introduction of wool supplemented the native cotton; Anglo-Americans later substituted commercial cotton, wool, and aniline dyes. Other than this, there has been little change in materials. Navajos use wool almost exclusively, while the Hopis produce the majority of their woven fabrics in cotton.

Design has undergone considerable change, although here again tribal tradition has prevailed. For centuries the Hopis have been preoccupied with designs in fabrics of great simplicity; their historic development in this expression has been in the elaboration of cloud, rain, lightning, and related patterns, this due, perhaps, to higher attainment in embroidery and brocading. Adhering rigidly to tapestry weave, Navajo design has run the gamut from the early pueblo-influenced simple banded patterns to elaborate executions of ceremonial dance and life figures. In the late 1960's, some of the finest weaving is being produced by the Navajos, in preparation of material, refinement of technique, and in sophistication of colors and design.

Pottery   *Chapter IV*

POTTERY is one of the most important of the native Southwestern Indian craft arts. It presents a faithful record of the changes in styles and fluctuations of feeling for form; it gives clues to the activities of its makers by indicating functional aspects, and it presents an unbroken record of artistry from its inception before the opening of the Christian Era to the present. A basket weaver and a textile worker have certain technical limitations placed on their art expressions, but not so the potter. This is particularly true of potters who decorate by painting. The decorator is limited only by form, for his brush is free to make a straight or curved line at will. It is here, too, that the art tradition of the group is reflected.

Prehistoric Background

The problem of the origin of pottery in the Southwest is still an unsolved one. Ceramics first appeared in the Hohokam and Mogollon cultures; the consensus is that this trait probably entered these areas from Mexico. Hohokam peoples were producing a fine grade of pottery by approximately 200 B.C., as illustrated in pieces from the lowest levels at the site of Snaketown.[1] Although undecorated, both form and construction show a refinement which would not be encountered in a potter's first wares. These earliest pieces show thin walls and good texture, and their surfaces reveal some polishing.

Early wares in the Mogollon, although not as refined, also show developed rather than beginning characteristics. These early pieces are dated as of about the opening of the Christian Era.[2] The vessels were neither as thin walled nor as well finished as the Hohokam, but they were superior in both features to the first clay products of the Anasazi. In the latter area, ceramics appeared several hundred years later, probably not before A.D. 400.[3] Here the earliest pottery was crude in form, walls were heavy, and some pieces carried a basket impression, as though they had been molded inside a woven container. It is quite possible that the idea of producing vessels out of clay crept into the Anasazi area from the south, very likely from the Mogollon people. Perhaps one of the first "traveling salesmen" of the Southwest carried this important idea to the more northerly tribes, and some astute women followed it up with the production of the first crude wares of the Anasazis — Mogollon wares are also found in Anasazi sites at an early date.

In the Southwest there are abundant deposits of clay, some of better quality than others. It did not take the native potter long to discover that superior materials produced superior vessels. Local variation in clays aids the archaeologist in distinguishing locally made wares and in determining the sources of trade pieces. To the clay, however, a second substance — commonly a coarser material — must usually be added, to keep the vessel from cracking as it dries and is fired. This "temper" also tells many tales of origins of wares; for example, the Hohokam potters were particularly fond of using a temper which had quite a bit of mica in it.

Technically, the simplest procedures were followed by the Southwest potters. Never did they use a wheel, nor did they know the true kiln. Two methods of firing the wares were known, reduction and oxidation. When the quantity of oxygen is limited in the firing process, this is called a reducing method; the resultant vessels have a gray or white color. On the other hand, if air is allowed to circulate freely during the burning, the atmosphere is called an oxidizing one, and the pottery has a brown, red, or yellow color. The oxidizing atmosphere was commonly used by the Hohokams and the Mogollons, while the reducing atmosphere was the more usual technique among the Anasazis.

In most native pottery the base of the vessel was probably hand molded, but the majority of the walls were formed by building up coils of clay. Two methods were used to smooth and thin the walls. In the first, the hand was placed inside the vessel and a piece of gourd rind was used for scraping and smoothing. A smooth-surfaced and sometimes shaped rock was employed in the second method, the rock serving as an anvil on the vessel interior, while a wooden paddle on the exterior served for the smoothing and thinning process.

Within a basic minimum of forms, great variety was expressed by the prehistoric potters. Fundamentally, bowls and jars served these ancient folk for most of their requirements. However, there is so much artistic variation in these two forms that the expert can identify a pot in time and space on the basis of these differences. Other forms were developed, of course, including pitchers, ladles, and scoops. Several additional types, such as mugs and colanders, were limited in areal distribution.

There are distinct features of form (Fig. 4.1) in each of the three major culture areas. Great simplicity and limited variation are more typical of the Mogollon; more variety in form, with emphasis on the absence of any protuberances, characterizes Hohokam; and in the Anasazi there is great local variation. Hohokam jars usually had no neck or only the barest suggestion of a neck above the orifice; they featured also, for a long time, a beautiful outsweeping and curving line from the vessel's mouth to a low point at which there was an abrupt inward turn forming a shoulder. Many of these "Gila-shouldered" jars were the largest vessels ever produced in the Southwest, past or present. Hohokam bowls also featured specialization such as the lovely bell-shaped forms or the large-shouldered types, both of late years. High-necked jars or those with a flat upper surface leading to a mouth minus a neck, straight-sided or more globular bowls — these would be some of the Anasazi variations in form. A hemispherical bowl and a simple round-bodied, short-necked jar characterize the dominant Mogollon forms.

Only a small percentage of the total pottery of all three groups of pre-Columbian times was decorated; there was, nonetheless, a high degree of adaptation of design to vessel forms. For example, the Hohokam shouldered jars and bowls created banded areas which were effectively decorated. Other styles of adaptation of design to form were equally dynamic in their treatment by the Hohokams, such as sectioned or allover layouts in open bowls or plates. Subdivision of the decorative area was rare, perhaps because it interfered with the natural feeling for flow of line and dynamism so characteristic of this Hohokam group.

On the other hand, divided areas of decoration were featured in many of the Anasazi layouts. Here a more studied, careful, precise style of painting invited such treatment as the popular banded and quartered layouts. Amsden has contrasted these two areas in these words: "She [the Hohokam decorator] is a master of the extemporaneous stroke, using her brush in truly creative delineation, whereas the pueblo decorator used hers as a methodical generator of prim lines in formal geometric figures. The latter is a well-schooled draughtsman, the former an unschooled artist."[4]

FIGURE 4.1 Prehistoric Hohokam and Anasazi pottery. These vessels show variety of form and decoration. The distinctive Gila Shoulder (b) and the long neck of the Chaco pitcher (d) demonstrate the former. Development of a local style is illustrated in the Chaco pitcher too, for here the use of fine hatching lines enclosed by heavier outlines is decidedly peculiar to this area. Decoratively outstanding also are the combination of curvilinear and rectilinear themes and opposed hatched and solid elements in the Anasazi vessel (c), the sweeping scrolls and vitalizing fringes of Hohokam painting (a).

A brief summary of prehistoric developments in colors, design elements, and designs further emphasizes the importance of the heritage of the modern potters (Fig. 4.1). In the Hohokam area, red decoration on a buff ground was the prevailing style both early and late. The first designs featured small elements, in simple straight- and curved-line styles. These evolved into more complex geometric forms; later, life forms appeared and quickly became popular. Delightful and often simply drawn small figures of quail and other birds, dogs, humans, lizards, and horned toads were popular subjects.

The earliest Anasazi pottery designs were inspired by basketry and consisted of endless varieties and combinations of rather poorly executed geometric elements. A brief period followed during which the potters simplified and improved their drawing. Then the puebloans hit their stride in endless and splendid combinations of lines, dots, triangles, steps, scrolls, frets, and a few life motifs. Often the latter were geometric. Refinement of drawing, complexity of motifs and designs, and creativity marked the products of the artist's brush before the end of the prehistoric period. Greater color range was expressed, too, with fine and varied black-on-white or black-on-red combinations. Also there were polychromes of various color relationships such as black, white, and red; buff, red, black, and white; and occasional other colors.

During these prehistoric years, pottery decoration developed motifs distinctive of the Southwest which were carried over into historic decorative arts. Art styles of the Southwest can thus be set apart from others of the New World. The greatest credit for this development can be given to ceramic decoration of the prehistoric period.

One trend in the Mogollon area should be mentioned. From an early, heavy, and simple style, the potters progressed to an intricate geometric style. Later, and perhaps due to Anasazi and/or Hohokam influences, a new expression appeared. This is called the "Mimbres" style, and it is basically a conventional or semi-realistic treatment of life forms. Banded edges and centered life figures or a group of them make up the usual layout. Some of the latter tell a story, an unusual aspect of Southwest pottery painting. This entire development exhibits the potential for creativity which existed and still exists among the native populations of the Southwest.

All in all, a very rich heritage in ceramics was passed down from their prehistoric ancestors to the Indians of today. Vessel forms, layout styles, colors, design elements, and designs were richly explored by the ancients. In design elements alone, the list is endless; little has been added along this line in historic years until very recently.

Historic Development

Development in the historic period, as in the past, has been through creativity more along the lines of slow and often subtle changes in form within the basic styles, new combinations of age-old elements and motifs in decoration, and some experimentation in surface finish.

Thus, there has been an unbroken continuum in ceramics of the Southwest Indians since the inception of the craft about 300 B.C. Today the potter still works as her ancestors did for centuries before her. She is well aware of the better sources of clay, goes out and gathers the chunks, perhaps easing the task by traveling in a pickup truck instead of on foot; she may use a pickaxe to dig the clay; and to pound the material she often uses a modern device such as a hammer instead of a metate and mano. Formerly she winnowed the clay, removing undesirable particles by tossing the stuff in the air on a windy day, and collecting the finer particles on a nearby cloth. Today she may use a sifter purchased at a dime store. Temper is added in the form of sand, ground-up potsherds, or some other foreign matter; all are still native. Clay and temper are mixed with water and the mass is kneaded into a small ball. To start the vessel, the ball is thinned out and formed over or inside the base or part of an old pot, a saucer, or basket — anything that can be turned as the potter works. Only a few Indians have used the potter's wheel in historic times.

The building up of side walls varies according to different sizes of vessels. Small pieces are usually molded from a lump of clay. All of the pueblo tribes make large, fat rolls of clay and build up the walls of larger pieces by winding these lengths around and around to form the vessel. Successive junctures of coils are broken. Often walls are straight at this point. The potter then takes the traditional curved-edged gourd rind, or a substitute tool, and shapes the vessel slowly, building out the desired curves. She also smooths and thins the side walls at the same time. Vessels are then dried in the shade.

After the vessels have dried, they are again scraped and smoothed. Often the surface is then slightly moistened. Today the smoothing may be accomplished with a metal object, such as a baking-powder can lid, in place of the polishing stone used for centuries by the Indians. The Navajos scrape their vessels with a corn cob. When the desired smoothness is attained, a slip is usually added, although some potters do not slip their wares. Slip is a thinned clay mixture applied with a swab (usually a rag), sometimes in several layers. This makes for a smooth surface. In fact, some potters polish the wall as they add the slip. In some pieces of pottery the slip serves as the finished surface — otherwise it is painted. The piece is now ready to be fired.

Although it has been estimated that not more than 7 percent of the pottery made prehistorically was decorated, the percentage has greatly increased in recent historic years. This has been true particularly with the loss in native use and the subsequent commercialization of the craft. Painted decoration is done with a yucca brush. Lengths of yucca leaves, about four to six inches long, are chewed at one end for about an inch. The pulp is thus removed, and the remaining fibers form the brush. If heavy lines or mass areas are to be painted, the brush is ready; for work of varying degrees of fineness, a few or many of the fibers are cut away.

Paints used by Southwest Indian potters are largely of mineral origin. One exception is a black made by boiling bee weed or tansy mustard to a thick paste; dried cakes of the stuff are stored and used as desired. Shades of yellow, red, orange, and some black are derived from ochres or iron ores; manganese is also a source of black. All color materials are ground on a stone mortar and mixed with water. One commercial source of color, poster paints, has been adopted by several Rio Grande pueblos, among them Tesuque and Santo Domingo; this and several other local village developments will be treated below. The basic native color combination among puebloans is black decoration on a white, off-white, or buff ground, with smaller or greater touches of red, yellow, or orange.

According to the habits of different groups, the pot is baked in a variety of simple "ovens." In the Rio Grande, generally, a fire is built and allowed to burn down. Over the hot coals are placed stones, tin cans, or other objects which support a grate. The vessels are then stacked upside down on the grate so that their walls do not touch. Sheets of metal or large chunks of broken pottery enclose the pots, then cakes of dung cut out of the corral are stacked around and over the vessels. Fuel — wood in the Rio Grande and coal among the Hopis — is burned under the pots for a half hour to as much as two hours. Temperatures range from 1200° to 1500° Fahrenheit. When the potter decides the vessels are done, she allows them to cool, removes them with a stick, and wipes off the ashes.

Toward the end of the second decade of this century, María and Julián Martínez of San Ildefonso developed the technique of a matte design on a polished ground. Previously, a plain black ware was made by smothering the fire at its peak heat with a mass of pulverized manure. This created an intense black smoke which penetrated the walls of the vessel. When this principle is applied to a polished and painted vessel, the end result is a dull design on a lustrous surface. This surface finish was one of the most sophisticated developments of historic years, and its potentials have been explored to high artistic degrees by San Ildefonso and other puebloans. San Ildefonso and Santa Clara produce a polished-matte red-ware as well as the black, and San Juan also has borrowed this idea, featuring the redware combination.

Carved wares also have been developed in the Rio Grande, primarily in these same three pueblos, San Ildefonso, Santa Clara, and San Juan. In this technique the decorative area, often a band, and the design, generally a simple geometric or snake form, are predetermined. The background is cut away, leaving the design standing out at the same height as the rest of the pot. Since the vessel is polished before the cutting, all areas except the carved portions are glossy; the cut area is dull (generally painted), thus adding a second dimension to the decorative effect.

Polishing of the surface was, of course, nothing new to the puebloans, for back in prehistoric times this finish had enjoyed a high development. Sometimes the polishing was done before, sometimes after the application of the painted decoration. However, never did it have the high gloss which has been attained in the Rio Grande in recent years. Some of this gloss is intensified by the addition of lard. Prehistorically, in the Rio Grande and other limited areas of the Southwest, glazes were used. Although quite poor, they did add a certain quality to the designs. No all-over glazes were developed. In later historic years, glazes have not been produced by native ceramists except for one Hopi man; other Indians, under more white than native influence, may use this finish.

After World War II, two Hopi Indians, Charles Loloma and his wife, Otollie, studied ceramics at Alfred University in New York. There they learned techniques foreign to the Indians. They returned to her Second Mesa village and put to use some of their newly acquired knowledge. Charles sought native sources for glazes; he used a kiln; and he threw many of his pots on a wheel. He taught some of his tribesmen these new ideas, but then he and his wife moved to Scottsdale, Arizona, taking his kiln and wheel. Thus in some ways Loloma and his wife have been affected by the white man, but the influences felt by these two have not spread to their tribesmen in the field of ceramics. Hopi women still make, decorate, and fire pottery in the traditional manner. Individuals from other pueblos, however, have learned to use the wheel.

One other form of decoration which has been

developed is modeling. This, too, goes far back into prehistory. Through recent years animals, birds, humans, and occasional other subjects have been treated realistically or in a very general manner. Sometimes it is possible to tell that a figure is a specific animal, or, in other cases, the piece may reveal no more than a generalized quadruped or bird form. Life forms may be modeled as independent figures or they may ornament a complete bowl or jar; commercialization in the craft has tended to encourage the former.

Incising, indenting, and other ways for making impressions or cutting simple lines into the clay were additional techniques of decoration known to the ancestors of the Southwest Indian potters. A few villages have carried on or developed one or several of these techniques. Generally, a sharp pointed instrument is used, cutting straight or curved lines into the surface of the clay. San Juan

has produced some fine pieces in this manner. Naturally, all are designs of line. Occasional finger or other indentations appear on the necks of Hopi pottery; simulated hands or bear paws are imprinted on Santa Clara jars.

Vessel forms (Fig. 4.2) have remained true to native tradition throughout most of the historic period; it is within the twentieth century only that significant changes have been made. The railroad — as well as the trader — played its part here, too, for it brought endless and varied pots and pans to the Indians. Within this century there has been a complete abandonment of the craft by some tribes, the production of small amounts of pottery for native use by a few, and a healthy native use along with varying degrees of commercial production by others. Forms have varied according to which of these several situations prevailed in a given tribe or village.

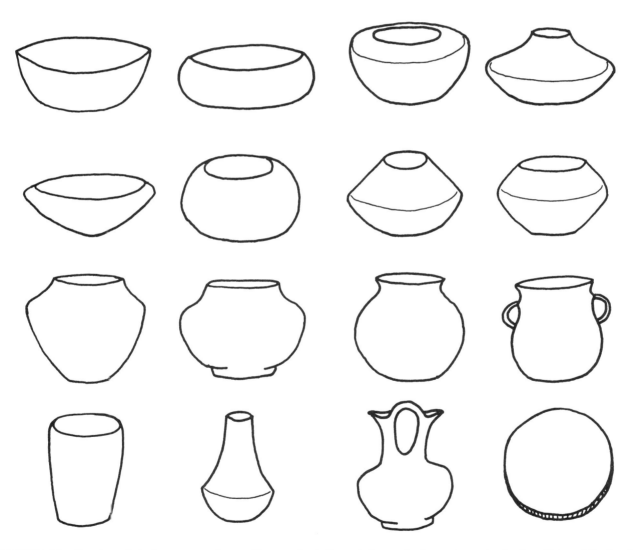

FIGURE 4.2   Sketches of modern pottery forms. The two basic forms today, as in the past, are the jar (or olla) and the bowl. There are more variations of jar forms than bowls; this is indicated in the above wider or narrower rims; taller and shorter necks; bodies with greater diameters high, near the middle, or at a lower point; in the more abrupt line between neck and body, or in a smooth flowing line at the same point.

The two basic forms which have dominated throughout the more than two-thousand-year history of Southwest ceramics are the bowl and jar. The native jar is commonly called an "olla." Large jars were, and still are, used natively for storage of water or foodstuffs. Smaller jars served for cooking and for carrying the daily supply of water. Large bowls might be used for storage on occasion, but, more generally, they held the family food and drink or the same for larger crowds on festive occasions. For example, beautiful old Zuñi bowls were filled with bread at their 1962 Shalako ceremonials. At this same ceremony several Indians jointly ate stew out of a native bowl of smaller size. Seemingly, individual serving dishes were not made by the Indian populations. Any and all of these vessels could also have special uses, particularly of a ceremonial nature. When this was the case, decoration was often of a special type. A serious curtailment of native use of bowls and jars has been noted since World War II.

A few other forms of native pottery should be mentioned. Among the Hopis, dippers are still made and used. A special double-necked jar is produced for use at Santa Clara and a few other pueblos. The Hopis continue to make tiles, while pottery drums are still used by Zuñis and Navajos.

Contact with the white man and subsequent commercialization of the ceramic craft in varying degrees have resulted in several distinct trends. One is diminution in size of vessels; a second is the creation of new forms; and a third is the increase in quantity and variety of decoration. Many of the individual pueblos and other tribes have retained their characteristic forms of bowls and jars but have reduced them greatly in size; some are made in miniature. These are the two outstanding forms made by all native potters today for commercial purposes. Other old forms and the majority of new ones also tend to be small, as those named above, plus ashtrays, boxes, candlesticks, and open forms which resemble plates or saucers.

In spite of changes in such aspects as form or finish, the native potters have adhered predominantly to the continued use of their traditional designs. This does not mean that decoration has become static. Quite the contrary, for in some cases it has continued on a high plane or has developed in more dynamic styles. To be sure, some have degenerated — both Pima and Papago tribes, for example, have carried on nothing of the delightful artistry of their forebears, the Hohokams. Some Rio Grande puebloans, and possibly Zuñi, were influenced to a slight degree through Spanish contact.

Geometric design is the rule in all native Southwestern pottery; although basically rectilinear, with the stepped or terraced theme most common, there is a great deal of curvilinear decoration. Life forms appear, running the gamut from high conventionalization to simple realism. The entire life form or some part of it may appear; the latter is particularly adaptable when designs are highly conventionalized. The full interior of a bowl or other open form may be decorated, but never is the exterior of a jar completely covered with design for always there is a small or large bottom area which is left plain.

Another general point in relation to ceramics among the native Southwesterners is that a great deal of individual village or tribal character has been expressed in their products. Forms, shades of colors, decorative themes and styles, all have been combined to make a pot distinctly Zuñi, Hopi, or Santa Claran, for example. Since white contact, there has been some exchange of ideas. The greatest diffusion has come since the end of World War II: Indians now travel about more readily and exchange thoughts and see the products of others. Commercialization, with the inspiration for one village to copy the popular (and saleable) styles of another, has been a considerable influence in this direction. Undoubtedly the great popularity of the black polished-matte pieces of San Ildefonso encouraged the Santa Clarans to develop a comparable ware. Then the potters of San Juan were influenced in the same direction.

Along with these trends there has been another influence which is tending to re-emphasize the local styles, namely, the rise of personal names in the field of ceramics. This trend began in the 1890's with the Hopi woman, Nampeo. It was accelerated late in the second decade of this century with those first and very important San Ildefonso names, María and Julián Martinez. Other names have been added along the way, with Lucy Lewis of Acoma an outstanding one today.

Formerly, pottery was made by all or most of the women of a village, each one supplying her own household with the necessary utensils. As pottery has been commercialized, Anglo-Americans have been very influential in the promotion of individual names. No native potter "signed" her wares until a white man came along and told her it would help to sell them; today certain signed pieces have greater value than unsigned vessels by the same potter. Of course, in many cases this has also encouraged an improvement of the craft in design, form, or finish, or in all three. The success of one potter in many instances has inspired other potters to execute their pieces with more care. Artists, special exhibits, traders, museums, and other such influences have also played a part in the encouragement of individuals and in the allover betterment of the ceramic craft among Southwest Indians.

Western Pueblos

Pueblo pottery surpassed in all ways all other Southwestern Indian ceramics. Of course there were or are individual pueblos to which this statement would not apply, such as Sandía, where no pottery is made today, nor would it apply to the crude poster-paint decorated wares of the villages of Tesuque and Santo Domingo. But in materials, forms, designs, and quality of painting many other pueblo people have maintained a high degree of artistry during historic years.

There have been differing trends among the puebloans in the ceramic expressions. Some have followed the old traditions, particularly for their own utility wares; if they make pieces for sale, they may or may not follow strict native styles. Some few villages have devised new styles, partly within the traditional, such as the polished and matte wares of the Rio Grande. No puebloan has strayed completely from the native tradition, for even in the garish poster-paint wares, forms may be native, and there is a heavy measure of traditional designs. Some potters combine their own art trends with some outside influence, as, for example, when a Santa Clara potter uses the lovely plain black style in the making of a pair of candlesticks, or when a Zuñi woman uses themes from ceremonial vessels to decorate a small ashtray.

Hopi

Hopi pottery is outstanding today and has been for some years. Mention should be made of a few technical differences expressed by this tribe. To begin with, much of the clay is of such nature that it does not need the addition of a temper. To smooth and thin the vessel, the potter rubs it with a piece of sandstone. Paint may be applied with a rabbit's tail or with a piece of cloth. Black paint is a combination of tansy mustard plus hematite; the red or orange is derived from iron hydroxide; the white is fine white clay. Firing is done with cedar chips and bark, sheep dung, and coal; these materials are used in varying quantities by different Hopi women.

Utility wares are made on all the Hopi mesas and in most of the villages to this day. One of the common pieces is a fairly large cooking vessel, usually quite straight-walled, with a slightly curving bottom, and a mouth as wide as the side walls. The second common utility piece is a storage jar, either rounded or almost straight in its body lines and with a medium to small mouth. Despite its simplicity, the jar has pleasing lines. Both of these pieces are made from a clay coarsened by the addition of

quantities of ground sandstone temper. Both also have rougher walls and are unslipped and undecorated. They are gray, brown, or a mottled orange color. Some jars are waterproofed with a coating of piñon gum. Technically similar to these pieces are canteens (Fig. 4.3) which were formerly made in very large sizes. The latter are characterized by one flat side and a great rounded side. A small-necked mouth is close to the flat base.

It is for their decorated wares that the Hopis are most famous. These are produced on First Mesa today, primarily in the villages of Hano and Sichomovi, although some are made at Walpi and a little at Polacca. There are three main types of decorated wares, a buff-to-almost-orange-base type which is unslipped, a fine white slipped style, and a deep rich redware. The latter may be slipped with a yellow clay which turns red on firing, or it may be made entirely of this clay with the same end result.

Some knowledge of the historic background of modern Hopi pottery is necessary to understand certain styles of design. Toward the middle and end of the second half of the nineteenth century Hopi wares were definitely on the decline. An ethnologist-archaeologist, Jesse Walter Fewkes, was working among the living Hopis and also excavating in prehistoric sites of their traditional homeland. When he was working at Sikyatki, a prehistoric ancestral Hopi home, he employed members of this tribe on his dig. Among them was a young fellow from the Tewa village of Hano whose wife, Nampeo, became interested in the beautiful pottery

FIGURE 4.3 Hopi canteen. There are lugs for carrying this large vessel, and a small neck close to the flat side; the latter facilitates pouring water from the vessel, particularly when the liquid gets low. A rough, unpolished and unslipped surface adds to the feeling of sturdiness in this utility piece which is still made by the Hopis.

which came from the prehistoric site. Inspired by these designs, she decided to attempt a better style of decoration than was currently practiced in her own community and in the nearby Hopi villages. She did not copy the Sikyatki patterns, but very obviously used many of the elements and motifs from this prehistoric ware. The result was some of the finest Hopi pottery made in historic years. Nampeo's designs inspired other Tewa women of Hano and the Hopi women of First Mesa. Her daughters and her granddaughters have carried on her fine style, each in turn expressing certain individual traits. Other women have attained equal ability in ceramic decoration in this area as, for example, Garnet Pavatewa, Sadie Adams, and Violet Huma.

Hopi pottery vessel forms are of two main types, a bowl and a jar. Bowls (Fig. 4.4) are deep or shallow, while their walls are incurving, almost straight, or outcurving. Often the last type is a little deeper than the first two. The distinctive Hopi jar (Fig. 4.5) has an incurving rim, a flattened shoulder, and is shallow; these features are important from the standpoint of decoration. The typical jar has no neck, the small orifice terminating at the same level as the shoulder. Other jar styles may have short or medium necks; a less typical one may be more rounded in body, minus the distinctive shoulder or with a modified one, and may have a neck. Miscellaneous forms include a tall and almost straight-sided vase, ladles, tiles, rattles, and a few "curio" shapes such as boxes, ashtrays, candlesticks, and cookie jars. In the commercialization of their craft, the Hopis have often continued their native ceramic shapes but have decreased their sizes.

Design (Figs. 4.4 and 4.5) on Hopi pottery throughout the twentieth century is very much tied in with the Nampeo story. There is remarkable adaptation of design to the specific vessel form and to the space the decorator wishes to use. Hopi women have been called outstanding masters of line — they are careful and capable painters. Geometric elements include lines and bands, triangles, and scrolls; these elements are commonly found in more formal divided bands. Life forms are very popular, although many of them are so highly conventionalized as to be unrecognizable as such by the casual observer. Among these, birds are prominent, or parts of birds, such as feathers, beaks, and wings. Some kachinas or kachina masks are used, also clouds, lightning, and rain. In the use of most of these elements or units of design there is much duplicating symmetry, a trait rather typical of Hopi pottery decoration.

The main bowl decoration is on the interior, even where the incurved rim is used. Several styles exist (Fig. 4.6). The simplest is a narrow band,

usually just below the rim. Often this appears on the outcurved rim form, and is of a formal type, with or without divisions but with the same element or motif repeated throughout the length of the band. Some bowls have a balanced and mirrored design in the center — usually large in size; sometimes this may be a pair of opposed birds. A third and

FIGURE 4.4 Hopi bowls. The low squat lines of bowls (a) are illustrated here. Even though a slight incurve of the rim is also characteristic, the form invited interior decoration which was often asymmetric (b and c). Vessel (c) is a fine example of modern work by Garnet Pavatewa. (*Bowl* (c) *courtesy Douglas Lindsey*)

very popular arrangement in bowl interiors is a large design pendant from the rim, filling a goodly portion of the upper half of the vessel, but often extending well into the lower half. Curving lines and bird themes are very common designs on interiors of bowls.

The flat-topped Hopi jar presents an interesting design field; an encircling band is formed by the natural divisions in the jar shape itself; that is, the inner lip and the outer turn of the shoulder form the "borders" of the band. Of course there is a great deal of variation here, for there are jar shapes which emphasize the shoulder, there are some which have a more gentle turn, and some which are

FIGURE 4.5 Hopi jars. The high-shouldered jar with more elongate lines (top) is typical of Hopi styles of more than fifty years ago; today jars feature much more curving lines (bottom). The older jar reveals less decorated area; recent and contemporary styles have wide or narrow bands with continuous decoration. In contrast to the full kachina form on the older piece, the newer form features bird-wing motifs coupled effectively with an elaborate line theme.

distinctly rounded. In the earlier sharp-shouldered type the design is more commonly confined to this area, although there may not be a drawn line at the outer edge. Somewhat later the design tended to "dribble" over the edge of the shoulder; today the latter trend is a common feature regardless of shape.

There are several layout styles for the jar. A few larger pieces and many small ones have a continuous band in which there are repeated and usually joined motifs, such as a scroll, or wing patterns. For a second style, this band may be broken into four or six equal sections in which appear repeated and identical designs; the band may be divided in half and contain symmetrical designs; it may be divided into four equal or unequal but balanced sections and be decorated with alternating themes; or it may be divided into eight equal units, these to be decorated with three different but opposed and balanced designs.

One interesting pottery form made by Hopis in earlier years is a drum. A short neck (with an out-flared lip for tying the drum head) turns rather abruptly into a flat and broad shoulder, then the latter turns into an almost straight side. The flat and wide bottom of the drum is unusual for Hopi pottery, but decoration is typically Hopi.

In spite of its dominant formality, Hopi ceramic decoration features rhythm and dynamism. Colors are pleasingly handled, adding to the beauty of the work. The following color combinations are used commonly: black alone on a base of soft buff or buff with indistinct rosy areas; black relieved with lesser touches of red, on buff; black alone or with white on a red base. Whatever the combination used by the Hopi woman, color coordinated with design distinguishes these wares from those of any other pueblo group.

As mentioned above, the Hopis still make and use storage jars, small and large ollas, canteens, and cooking pots. At the time of writing, these are being made largely by Alice James on Third Mesa, although a few are made on each Mesa. One woman at Hano still makes tiles. The First Mesa decorated wares include those listed above plus a little black on white. Plain red or buff wares are also made. Most Hopi women today do not take up ceramics until their children are grown.[5]

In the 1966 Scottsdale show there were some unusual and beautifully made indented wares of red clay. Below the rim of each piece was a wide band of perfectly executed deep indentations.

Zuñi

Zuñi pottery is almost extinct today. In fact, there has been a greatly diminished production since 1879. From time to time there have been limited revivals, such as in recent years with a fairly large production of modeled owls. For many years there have been several Zuñi women producing bowls and ollas, but certainly not in the fine tradition of pre-1900 days. In spite of inferior workmanship, most of the potters have adhered to traditional forms and decoration, with relatively little production of miniature and insignificant curio pieces.

Clay used by the Zuñi potter — even in better days — is heavy and coarse, and the vessel walls have an irregular but smooth feeling as one runs his hand over the surface. A white kaolin slip which darkens with age is decorated with black designs; in some styles touches of red (ranging from orange to blood red) may be added. The base of the vessel is reddish or brownish in color. Shapes are basically water jars, large and small bowls (Fig. 4.7), and owls. Varied decoration is adapted to each specific form. Painting has rarely been as carefully executed as it is on Hopi pieces, and it lacks the duplicating symmetry of the Hopi, al-

FIGURE 4.6 Hopi pottery jar exterior and bowl interior layouts (method of arranging design). In the top row are continuous, repeated, and halved layouts; in the second row jar shoulders may be divided into four parts of equal or unequal sizes and may be decorated with alternating motifs; the third division may be in six — or eight — parts and have varied but opposed balanced motifs. Typical bowl interior design layouts are presented in the bottom row: centered symmetrical, centered balanced right and left, and asymmetrical.

though there is a rhythmical repetition in Zuñi work. There is little in the way of solid painting, for the Zuñis consider this "dirty;" theirs is a design of line rather than surface.

A definite break appears in jar decoration between the neck and the body (Figs. 3.7 and 4.7), or the "stomach" as the Zuñi calls it. Entirely different designs are used in the two areas; in fact, tradition dictates that the elements of one part of the jar are not to be used on the other. The neck, which slopes gently to the fairly abrupt turn into the body, is segregated by one or two broad lines which are broken at one point. This is called the "life line," because many Southwestern Indian groups believe that the line must be left open so that the spirit of the maker and decorator will not be caught inside the vessel. A Zuñi tale relates that the potter will die if the line is not open at one point. Decoration within the neck band is usually made up of simple, alternately repeated elements.

FIGURE 4.7 Zuñi jars and a bowl. Two major layouts were used for jar decoration, divided (a and b) and undivided and integrated (c). Both styles have separate neck and body decoration; the former is banded and generally repeats two motifs twice each in an a-b-a-b manner. In jars (a) and (b) the two vertical panels are filled with one medallion each, and the two remaining areas are divided into two (a) or three (b) horizontal bands. The deer motif is favored; birds are a little less common. Arches appear above and below the deer. The allover decoration is geometric and may be more elaborately or more simply (c) conceived and integrated. The shape of the Zuñi bowl is pleasing with its gentle constriction close to the rim (d). A banded pattern of alternate repeated simple geometric units is typical. Interior design is more elaborate, usually with a banded area near the rim and a more — and often asymmetric — ornate design filling the center.

Zuñi jar body decoration may be one of several styles (Figs 3.7 and 4.7). The simpler one has all-over painting, usually in a single repeated motif which is integrated, or in a band of large, repeated elements. The second and composite style requires a division of the design field generally into two larger and two smaller vertical fields. Each larger area is further divided into two or three sections. In the former, the areas are equal while in the three-divisional plan upper and lower bands are of equal size and a central band is narrower. Heavy lines mark off all these areas except in the case where the decorator substitutes a medallion for the two smaller vertical sections. Arches are common above and below the horizontal areas.

Birds and/or deer appear in the three horizontal bands or in one or two of them, with geometric elements in the remaining band or bands.

Zuñi birds are squat little creatures with long tails; they are often represented with the beak touching a conventionalized flower. The deer is drawn in black, always with a red "heart line" running from its mouth to the animal's interior; here the line commonly ends in an arrow point or just a blob.

The rosette or medallion is the third common motif; it is most usually black with varying amounts of red added. This motif is quite different from native pueblo design and may well be a Spanish-influenced theme. It is not beyond the realm of possibility that these and other non-Indian designs found on several types of pueblo pottery were inspired by embroidered altar cloths.[6] Another common design unit is a large hook which has long triangular points on the outside curve. Additional elements or units often used as fillers include circles, triangles which are plain or end in a simple scroll, steps, spirals, squares, and diamonds. Some of the geometric outlines are filled with hatching, either in parallel or crossed lines.

Modern Zuñi jars are decorated with the same designs. But the painting is much sloppier and the designs are not as well balanced. The vessel form is awkward, too; often it is longer in body lines and disproportionate, thereby losing the beauty of its classic shape. There are, of course, occasional better pieces; several fine examples were noted at the 1963 Gallup Ceremonials.

Zuñis have made both decorated and undecorated clay drums. They are large in size and accommodate quite a wide skin head. One example of a Zuñi clay drum was decorated with a series of animals.[7]

The Zuñi bowl is no longer made. In typical pieces there were elaborate interior designs and simple exterior bands. The latter band almost always consisted of one or two geometric elements forming a unit which was repeated two or three times. The interior design was made up of two parts, a simple geometric band with repetitive design just below the rim, and a much more elaborate band or allover design covering the greater part of or the rest of the bowl interior. The latter combined angular and curvilinear motifs in sweeping designs or life themes. Many of the elements listed above, such as circles, triangles, and hooks, were used in dynamic arrangements. Bowls averaged about 6 inches high and about 14 inches in diameter. They were straight, sloping-sided, or bell-shaped.

A delightful piece made for years by the Zuñi (some were collected about 1879) and a popular item today is the modeled owl (Fig. 4.8). This figure ranges in height from 2 inches to about one foot. The bird is painted all over with curved black lines to simulate feathers. Other painting in black and red and a bit of modeling too, may be used to stress the eye circle and pupil, ears, feet, wing feathers, and other such detail. Quite a bit of variety appears in the modeling of the owl today, such as the addition of one or several small birds on the parent's back (an early treatment too), or one on each wing, or a snake on the back with the head of the startled bird turned all the way around looking at the reptile! Through the years much careless work has appeared in both modeling and painting. Relatively poor painting today contrasts, for example, with that of an old piece in the Southwest Museum, Los Angeles, which shows very fine allover line work delineating feathers; wing and tail feathers are black-tipped while all others are in black outline but carefully formed. This bird dates back to the 1880's.

Rio Grande Pueblos

In the Rio Grande, pottery continues to be produced today for both native consumption and for sale. For the past twenty-five years or so, however, there has been more of the latter and less of the former. Before 1920, many of these pueblos produced little or no commercial ware. In the early years of the twentieth century, pottery had died out completely among some of the Rio Grande natives but was important in many other villages for the production of storage and other utility wares.

Before 1900, the basic color tradition of the Rio Grande was black decoration on a white, cream, or red ground. Some polychromes were produced, mainly by adding red to one of the first two combinations. A plain or dull blackware was made at Santa Clara and probably at San Ildefonso before this date. By the turn of the century, several pueblos were producing polished black or redwares or both.

Then, toward the end of the second decade of

FIGURE 4.8 Zuñi owls. These owls have been made for years in very much the same manner, with some additions, as the small one on its mother's back. On the dull white slip are added black lines for feathers and some small detail about the face, while ears, beak, and eyes are largely red.

this century, came the development of the currently popular style, the matte-polished combination. Chapman says, regarding its first expression at San Ildefonso, that "the bowl was simply mopped all over with the red clay slip, as if it were to be given an allover polish. The avanyu (water serpent) figure was then produced by polishing only that part of the bowl, but in smoothing the outline of the avanyu Julián found it necessary to use a brush, dipped in the dilute red clay, and so soon discovered that it was possible to produce the entire matte surface by painting . . . the relatively large matte surface made the bowl look crude and unfinished, and it was unattractive to the touch."[8] This first procedure resulted in a polished pattern on a matte surface, the opposite of the more popular styles of today.

"So Julián improved the design by confining the avanyu to a band in which relatively little matte was needed. The avanyu and the feather design are the two outstanding examples of Julián's motifs developed on the polished surface. Later, Julián developed numerous motifs in the matte itself, from simple to more complex."[9]

Dutton says of the matte-polished styles at San Ildefonso and Santa Clara that, "The first pieces made at both pueblos had the mass dull and the design burnished." Further, she says that even after this was reversed the serpent motif still is always a polished design on a matte ground.[10]

Marriott tells quite a different story of the origin of the matte-polished ware at San Ildefonso. The

first plain black pieces were produced by María and Julián quite by accident: in a regular burn, two pieces came out black. Then after much thinking on the problem, Julián came up with the current method, namely, smothering the fire toward the end of the burn with pulverized manure. The heavy black smoke thus created penetrated the walls of the vessel, making them black inside and out. The vessels were still plain.[11]

Some time later, around 1918-1919, the decoration of the first of these vessels occurred. Late one afternoon Julián came in from the fields tired and restless. On the floor were many pots María had just polished. He picked up one of these and painted a design on it; María was a bit startled when she saw this. But when the pot came out of the burn several days later both were pleased with the matte black design on the shiny black background.[12] It did not take long for the white man's appreciation to make this a popular style and the technique spread to other women in San Ildefonso and eventually to other villages.

Colors vary in the polished-matte wares, with the usual combinations being black on black, red on red, or various pale tones such as blue or blue gray, tan, pink, or white on red or tan. San Ildefonso continues to feature the black style. In recent years María has achieved a gunmetal and highly polished finish on her vessels.

Compared with the past, there is today only a limited Rio Grande village production of the native black-on-white, or black, white, and red ceramic wares. There are, however, a few cases of new color developments. Most of these are limited to a single group and will be discussed in connection with each pueblo. Poster paints were introduced to the pueblo of Tesuque during the 1920's and became widely used there; later they spread to Santo Domingo, Cochití, Isleta, and Jémez where they are used in limited quantities.

In the Rio Grande the native bowl seems to have disappeared first, but the jar, and particularly the large storage jar, lingered into recent times. It has been reported that there were many of the latter used in native homes throughout World War II years, but that they have been fast disappearing since then.

On the other hand, there has been a continual increase in variety of forms for sale, with smaller sizes growing in popularity. During the earlier years of commercialization the tendency was to produce medium-sized versions of the basic native pieces. But it did not take the puebloan long to learn that she could sell an ashtray faster than a jar and perhaps for the same price. Thus, in many of the Rio Grande villages today there is made, virtually by the thousands, a variety of small bowls, jars, ashtrays, boxes, candlesticks, and various knicknacks. Most of these pieces have little if any individual village character except for remnants of design or colors. In bowls and jars there may be some resemblance to the village forms.

Design in Rio Grande pottery seems to have followed the trends of other aspects of the craft. In other words, as long as the products of the ceramist were for native use, design followed heavily traditional paths. But when commercialization began, design became more simplified, often was executed with less care and artistry, and many times degenerated into a real curio style. Some individuals did and still do maintain high standards and certainly this comment does not apply to them. In fact, it is they who are keeping Southwest Indian ceramics within the realm of a true and highly artistic craft expression.

San Ildefonso

San Ildefonso is certainly one of the best known of the Rio Grande pueblos for its pottery, primarily because of the work of María and her late husband Julián. They were the first to popularize the craft; María has remained outstanding and the best known in the field of pottery. She has continued to develop through the years, and has influenced a great many Indian women in her own and other villages. At the age of 80 in 1965 she was still demonstrating to the public the process of pottery production.

The older wares produced at San Ildefonso were of three styles: black on red, black on cream, and black and red on a white (or cream) ground. In the polychrome wares red was used sparingly. Whereas the clay in the modern black ware is coarse and porous, and walls are thick, the earlier vessels were produced of better clays and were thinner walled. Smooth walls were and are typical of San Ildefonso pottery.

Artistry in the older San Ildefonso vessel was vested in form, arrangement of design, and the design itself (Fig. 4.9). In the recent blackware and its red counterpart, the beauty of the work is in the perfection of the finish and in the careful modeling of the vessel. Design is more complex in the black-on-cream and polychrome wares; in the black and red polished styles there is just enough decoration to offer contrast so as to bring out the beautiful high burnish of the surface. Shapes differ in the two wares, the old and the new; old styles were primarily very large storage jars, smaller jars, and quite large bowls. In the black and related wares there are some smaller versions of the jar and bowl, and there are new forms also — platters, vases, boxes, a long-necked

vase, trays, and the usual ashtrays and candlesticks.

Traditional designs in San Ildefonso polychrome may be strictly geometric and are often curvilinear (Fig. 4.9). Jars are divided into decorated neck and body sections; in these areas, designs are integrated or they are made up of separate repeated themes. Often a simple scallop pattern appears just below the lip. Although the neck line slopes rather gently into the body area, there is a design break between the two. Again, a scallop or other simple geometric motif may decorate the divider line on

FIGURE 4.9 Old-style San Ildefonso jar and bowl. Neck and body of the jar have separate decoration but both utilize relatively simple and alternating geometric motifs of black and red on a white slipped ground. Base and inner rim are also red. The jar is 8 3/4" high and 12" at its greatest diameter. The interior bowl decoration is a rather unusual combination of typical elements in yellow-brown and black on a white ground.

one or both sides. Body decoration is more ornate; it may consist of horn-like arrangements made up of sweeping and curve-sided triangles, simpler triangles, and other geometric units, each motif repeated several times; or composite leaf-like motifs, also repeated several times; or great striding birds and animals almost chasing each other around the pot. Cloud themes and other small elements are sometimes added here and there. Some of this subject matter, such as the life forms, may well have been inspired through contact with Europeans.

In these polychromes there is much variety. Red is used sparingly in some vessels, more abundantly in others. Black and red may be balanced or not, and red elements are sometimes outlined in black. Black-on-red ware, is old at San Ildefonso. It features more solids in designs, and patterns are simpler and more scattered. Geometric themes predominate, with angles dominant over curves.

The simple decoration of matte-polished (Fig. 4.10) and related wares at San Ildefonso features one or two geometric elements combined to form a repeated motif, or the vessel is commonly decorated with the horned-serpent design. Among the most popular of the elements are frets, scallops, terraced figures, triangles, feathers, and leaves. There is a formalism in this style of decoration, yet it is not stereotyped. The quality of work is usually good in both black and red styles, with accurate spacing, true lines, and an evenness in the surface paint and in the polishing.

Despite the popularity of this style, the San Ildefonso potters have maintained a high degree of skill in their craftsmanship and simplicity in their designs. In addition to María, other women who have attained superior ability in making these wares include Juanita Gonzales, Rose Cata, Santayana, Blue Corn, Desideria Sanchez, and Lupita Martínez.

One of the latest developments of the matte-polished combination at San Ildefonso is exemplified in a piece made in 1966 and signed by Popovi Da, the son of María and Julián. This jar is black in its lower portions while the upper section is finished in a pleasing burnt sienna tone. In the latter area is a polished feather design on a dull surface.

Rosalie Aguilar is credited with the development of carved pottery at San Ildefonso. In this ware the potter often confines the carved design to a band (Fig. 4.11). The raised portion of the design, all in bas-relief, is polished as is the rest of the vessel outside the band. The cut area is painted with a dull or matte slip, thereby offering contrast to and setting out the design. The same comments made relative to matte and polished wares apply to the carved styles in design elements, designs, and all-

over simplicity. Carving is also done on the same shapes used for the polished styles.

Santa Clara

Santa Clara pottery resembles that from San Ildefonso, yet in certain respects it has distinctive qualities. Two outstanding shapes are distinctly Santa Claran, one a double-necked jar (Fig. 4.12) with a strap handle joining the inner lips of the two necks (often called a "wedding jar"), the second a fairly high-necked and wide-mouthed jar with a squat body. Often the latter piece has a decorative raised ring of clay with a depression just below and paralleling it (Fig. 4.12), or a "pressed in" repeated design, the latter commonly a human hand or bear paw. These designs appear on the upper body. Other types of simple depressions may appear on the plain or double-necked jar. Santa Clara potters make the depressions before slipping and polishing; hence this is a subtle type of decoration. Often, and especially in the older pieces, the polishing is not as high as that of the San Ildefonso wares and the surface is rougher.

Older than the above two shapes are very large black or red storage vessels. One was a bulbous jar which often stood as much as 4 feet in height and was equally wide; it had a small short neck. A second jar had a wider mouth, a shorter neck, and was of wider proportions. Both had very simple and pleasing lines and generally no decoration. Mixing

FIGURE 4.10 Matte and polished black ware made and signed by María of San Ildefonso. The very fine painting of feathers and lines and the extremely high and even polish of this piece make it outstanding. The low dish is 11 1/4″ in diameter.

and other utility bowls were like the second jar but with still wider mouths.

By the early 1930's Santa Clara had not only acquired the highly burnished and the polished-matte decorative techniques of San Ildefonso but also was producing a variety of forms in these two styles. There were small versions of some of the above forms; there were vases with tall necks and handles (totally non-Indian!); and there was a variety of modeled life forms including dogs, deer, pigs, mountain sheep, cows, birds, and a few others (Fig. 4.13). Life forms tended to become smaller as the years went by; most of them were and are very simply modeled. Some have considerable charm. Then, of course, there are the inevitable commercial pieces, often quite small and quite non-descript in form. A small percentage of Santa Clara work is done in pale red on darker red, matte and polished red, or with some white added to such combinations.

That creativity in puebloan pottery form is still possible is indicated by a very beautiful Santa Clara piece exhibited at the Scottsdale International Show of 1964. This was a squat bowl with a flat, incurving top which terminated in a small orifice minus a neck. Deep and intricate carving added distinction to this piece. Pieces in this same show, of 1966, again featured the deep carving, with designs more exaggerated in size and simpler in motifs than in previous examples.

Santa Clara has made many pieces of matte-polished and carved wares in black so much like

the ordinary San Ildefonso piece that it is almost impossible to tell one from the other. On the other hand, there are individuals at Santa Clara — Ligoria, Margaret Tafoya, Flora Naranjo, and others — who produce ceramics as distinctive as those of the better potters at San Ildefonso. Several beautiful pieces by Margaret Tafoya observed in 1962 were gracefully formed and their simple designs were effectively placed in relation to shape. Three of these pieces were large, with two wedding jars over 18 inches high and a long-necked jar over 15 inches tall. The carving was deep, the lines of pattern even and sure.

A few years ago, two people at Santa Clara, Lela and Van Gutiérrez, began an interesting style of decoration. They used light colors, almost-pastel greens, blues, and yellows on a buff ground. The designs were extremely small geometric themes, all carefully and well-executed (Fig. 4.14). When Van died, Lela's son Luther took over decorating the pieces. A lovely tall vase decorated in this manner was exhibited at the 1964 Scottsdale show. In 1966, pieces of this type are signed Luther/Margaret.

San Juan

San Juan produces plain black- and plain red-wares or the polished and matte combination, the latter usually in red. Some of the redwares are painted this color in upper portions only, leaving a brown or tan base of natural clay.

About 1930 or 1931 the women of this village, led by Regina Cata, began a revival of an ancient type of decoration — incising (Fig. 4.15). This has been developed by Regina and several others to a high degree. In many instances a jar form without a neck is divided into an upper and lower band, the break coming at an angular turn in the body or below center in a more rounded form. The upper band is often left in the natural buff clay color and is incised. The lower portion is slipped in red or natural and is then polished; this and a narrow band in a similar finish about the rim add definition to the decorated area. In this ware simple or more complex designs are composed of lines of varying lengths. Parallel verticals or horizontals, oblique lines, and short "gouges" are used in various ways to produce repetitious bands, triangles, chevrons, squares, oblongs, and a few other geometric motifs. Lines may be used also as filler or to outline such areas. Sophisticated work results in simple but artistically formed and decorated pieces.

San Juan potters also produce the carved wares described for Santa Clara and San Ildefonso. Sometimes they may combine the techniques of incising and carving in a single vessel. It is often difficult to differentiate the smaller carved pieces

FIGURE 4.11 San Ildefonso matte-polished and carved red jar of small size. The simple triangles and stepped theme are carved within an encircling band and highly polished to stand out against a dull background of the same color. Rim and lower part of the jar are also polished.

of these three pueblos for the shapes are similar. This is also true of the black- and redwares. However, San Juan alone produces the distinctive incised styles. In addition to Regina Cata, Tomacita Montoya is one of the best San Juan potters.

New ideas have developed in San Juan pottery in recent years. One is the use of red in the incised lines. In another ware, incising is used to outline painted design. Many of the smaller modern pieces combine carving and/or a matte and dark red, tan, and white (or lighter tan) on a polished red or plain tan base (Fig. 4.14). When carved also, designs tend to be simpler; they run the gamut from limited geometric elements to simplified kachina heads.

Santo Domingo

For many years Santo Domingo potters made a rather conservative type of black on white (or cream) ware (Fig. 4.16). In more recent times they have added slight touches of red. A good polish was given the surface of their vessels. Both bowls

FIGURE 4.12 Santa Clara blackware vases or jars. Both (a) and (b) are typical in shape and decoration. Many of the large storage jars featured the low and wide neck and the rounded body of (a) — this jar is 12″ high and 12″ in diameter — while water jars not infrequently had long tapering necks and shorter, more squat bodies (b). The so-called "wedding jar" is characteristically bi-lobed (c) and may be plain, as in this more-than-thirty-year-old example, or it may be exaggerated in form and elaborately carved. The use of the ever-popular horned snake theme in highly polished black on a dull black ground (d) exemplifies the early method of producing the matte-polished ware.

FIGURE 4.13 Miniature ceramic animals from Santa Clara. These delightful creatures may be casually modeled or formed with greater detail. Several of these are recognizable, as — from left to right — a turtle, dog, and duck, but the others are rather generalized.

and jars were made, with a hemispherical shape characterizing the former and a globular body typical of the latter. Earlier designs were largely simple and geometric with little variety in the use of bands, squares, or rectangles, However, these forms had their corners cut off by angular or curving lines and the cut-off section was filled in with black. More recently large plant and animal themes in red combined with black have been added. Other color combinations include black on red or black on tan. San Ildefonso blackware has quite recently inspired these potters. In this style both flowers and geometric motifs have been used for decoration. Older vessels are larger, while contemporary pieces fall into the usual commercial category of diminished sizes.

In older Santo Domingo bowls, designs occur inside, outside, or both. Often there is an exterior band with a simple design which may be pendant from the rim or paneled, spotted, or integrated. Interior design is centered or rim-paneled. Although the basic black design elements feature varied triangles, leaf-like themes, and lines, these are combined in such varied ways as to create circles, ovals, triangles, and other shapes in the white background slip.

Jars are usually decorated in a band of simple geometric elements. The latter may be pendant from the rim, paneled, repeated, alternate, or continuous in arrangement. Spotted designs also occur on jars. Painting on older bowls and jars is usually better, for through the years the Santo Domingo potter became more careless as reflected in sloppy work in general.

One of the least attractive consequences of commercialization of pottery is a current style at Santo Domingo. Small pieces are decorated in patterns vaguely reminiscent of classic styles and in a most unattractive glaze-like paint — oil paints from the dime store — in black, brown, gray, and white. It is hoped that this style will be short-lived.

Zía

Zía pottery is made of a coarse and heavy clay. For years these potters have used a white slip, but more recently some of the Zía women have turned to a buff slip. The base of the vessel is red. Decoration is in black alone or in red and black. Although bowls were made formerly, today the jar is more common.

Flow of line in jar outline from neck onto body may be gentle or there may be a more abrupt turn between the two: the former is typical of recent pieces, the latter of earlier styles. On some jars design is continuous from neck to body, while on

FIGURE 4.14 Contemporary Santa Clara polychrome vase made by Lela and decorated by Van. On a very pale tan ground is painted a most elaborate feathered and horned serpent in the pale tones typical of this ware: yellow, green, red, blue gray, and black. The lower part of the vessel is a very soft red. The very small details used throughout the figure are meticulously executed, and, in spite of adhering to native types, appear rather different in their almost-minute size.

FIGURE 4.15 San Juan incised and painted vessels. The simple rounded jar with a slight neck (a) or without (b) is a typical modern piece — like older styles but smaller in size. Various geometrics are cut into the clay and the incisions are painted. Neck and the lower part of the vessel are painted a soft tan (a) or a dull red (b). Typical San Juan pottery motifs are arranged in a scattered fashion on an open, almost-flat dish (c); the base color is tan, the decoration colors are white and brown.

others there is not only a break but also a separate design for each area. Often when the latter prevails, the two patterns are comparable, or there may be a smaller version of the body motif on the neck.

There is considerable variety of design in Zía pottery (Fig. 4.17). Perhaps the most distinctive is a lively bird which has a great single or double wing coming out of its back and three sweeping tail feathers. Two of these birds may appear on a jar, sometimes with a wide band curving over each one. At other times large floral themes appear between the birds; or four deer are used in place of the two birds, with lesser floral motifs between them. Birds are highly conventionalized while the deer may be naturalistic; plant sprays and leaves also have a tendency to be more conventional. Again it may be mentioned that New Mexican Colonial embroidery may have inspired these motifs.[13] Geometric themes are used exclusively on some Zía vessels; these may combine unusual forms such as broad-banded chevrons.

In design layout, single or double bands prevail on both Zía forms. Design elements include varied leaves, crescents, triangles, lines and bands, deer, and birds. In the use of the two life forms and in some geometric styles, the banded layout gives way to more allover integrated arrangement. Painting is often good, with carefully drawn narrow black lines outlining red designs or fine white lines (slip) showing between patterns. Design elements are painted solid. Balance is found more often in design than color.

It is claimed by some that Zía was at one time a great style center for ceramic decoration, and that this village affected other groups. Thus it is thought that Acoma was so influenced, particularly in its bird motif.

Acoma

Technically, the pottery of Acoma is the best made in the Rio Grande drainage. The paste is fine, hard, and light. Walls of Acoma jars are the thinnest of all Southwestern Indian pottery — they give a distinct ring when thumped with the finger. A white to cream slip is applied as background for the black and orange decoration. The "orange," incidentally, ranges from yellow through orange to red to a brownish tone. The deep base area is usually in any of these several colors. Some earlier wares were painted in black on a white slip and had a red base.

In the Acoma jar there is a smooth curve from rim onto the body; this results in the predominance of a continuous rather than a broken design (Figs. 3.7 and 4.18). It is rare when the Acoma potter does not use the area as a single decorative field and then only in the few cases where there is a

FIGURE 4.16 Santo Domingo polychrome (a and c) and black-on-red (b) jars. Typical Domingo designs appear on all these vessels: black triangles with one or two curved sides or other simple geometrics are combined in such ways as to create other forms in the lighter background color. These occur in bands in continuous and joined fashion (a and b) or as separate motifs (c).

more abrupt turn which forms a shoulder. Reputedly, no utility bowls have been made since 1870. Within the past few years there has been a tendency here, as in so many other pueblos, to make a variety of small-sized vessels, including bowls as well as jars, plates, and several other shapes.

Two styles of decoration characterize Acoma pottery, naturalistic and geometric. The naturalistic, simpler and less versatile, features a great and proud bird which is often nibbling on a branch full of "berries." The bird is characterized by a massive curved beak and several feathers; often one of the latter emerges from the back (wing?) and one comes out of the neck, then there are three or four large, separate tail feathers. This creature is quite distinctive compared to the smaller-beaked Zía bird. Generally there are two such birds on an Acoma jar, each with a large arch overhead. Sprigs of flowers may appear on the inside or outside of the arch. Red or yellow is effectively combined with the dominant black.

The Acoma geometric style is intricate, ornamental, and generally allover (except for the base). For the most part, the design fills the entire jar without a break, except for the few shouldered forms in which there are two banded patterns, a narrower top one and a wider one on the body. Bands may be repeated continuous, paneled, or integrated. In the allover patterns, triangles, squares, diamonds, rounded elements, and steps are combined into rather dynamic themes. The geometric forms may be solid or filled with parallel lines; both treatments used together give a lighter touch to Acoma pottery decoration. Other design elements include frets — simple and complex — flowers, birds, feathers, and lines.

Some years ago the potters at Acoma produced allover designs in lines — for example, repeated, concentric, and joined squares (Fig. 4.19). These designs have been revived and, when done by an expert like Lucy Lewis, result in a most effective style of decoration. It takes ability to paint these allover lines in perfect repetition.

Generally, black is dominant in Acoma pottery decoration. There is partial balance in color, more in design. Solids and hatched areas are often balanced. Even though design is characteristically allover, it is not burdensome; this reflects the predominance of lines over solids or the use of small solids. Painting is usually very good, although in old vessels it is not as well done as in some of the later work. Also in older pieces designs are simpler and do not cover as much of the vessel as they do later. Characteristic of Acoma ware is a "spalling" or chipping of tiny fragments from the surfaces of vessels.

FIGURE 4.17 Jars from the Pueblo of Zía. Birds, arches, and leaves are typical of the decoration of these vessels. Other motifs also tend to be curvilinear although some angular themes are used (center). Decoration is continuous, joined, and has a "flowing" feeling. Birds are dynamic; plants are sometimes fruiting (left). Deer are less commonly used for decoration (center). Colors are black and red on a white band with a red inner lip and base.

Laguna

Laguna pottery is similar to that of Acoma in some respects but by no means as fine nor as well decorated. Walls are heavier, paste is not as good, and forms are not as refined. Designs are in the same color as Acoma, namely, a white base on which are painted geometric designs in black and one other color, the latter having the same yellow-to-brown range as at Acoma. On the other hand, designs lack the Acoman vitality and verve, and for the most part are small geometric elements in rather elaborate arrangements. Life designs, so pleasingly done at Acoma, are not common at Laguna; some floral patterns are used. Vessel forms tend to be more like those of Zía.

More specifically, Laguna designs are banded or allover. Often there is a feeling of vertical alignment of design due to the continuation of a pattern from the neck onto the body; such decorations are alternate-repeated and made up of geometric and/or floral themes. Quite different is a Laguna piece with a triple band arrangement. A wide neck band has alternating bird and floral motifs. Resting above and on the abrupt shoulder is a narrow band with a repeated diagonal rectangle. The wide body band contains an elaborate, integrated geometric pattern.

Santa Ana

Although they were still making some utility wares as late as the 1930's, the villagers of Santa Ana do not produce much pottery today. Their native wares were simply but pleasingly shaped: in general, they were similar to those of Zía. Jars were rounded, with short straight necks and wide mouths (Fig. 4.20). Bowls had a generous and outflaring rim. A white or grayish slip was used as a base for the design, while the lower part of the vessel was

FIGURE 4.18 Acoma jar decorative styles. One specialty of the Acoma pottery decorator was the use of a "rainbow" or arch which undulated alternately over and under four great birds (left). Conventionalized leaves, flowers, and berries were also used. Colors include two on a white ground and a darker base: black and either red or yellow, or orange on white. A second style (center) combines geometric and floral themes or strictly geometric motifs (right), both in the same color combinations as the first. Acoma decoration is characteristically allover and unified although in some instances separate motifs are but touching (right).

covered with a soft red slip. Heavy lines defined the band for decoration of bowls; the design was often a simple, running geometric theme. Jars were sometimes decorated from rim to base color with heavy and continuous designs, while at other times there might be separate neck and body panels. In the latter style, neck designs were simpler and of repeated motifs in unbroken bands. Body patterns were also large and generally simple, alternate-repeated motifs. In one example, repetition of four stepped motifs is varied by turning two of them upside down.

Design elements in Santa Ana pottery are limited: in addition to steps there are broad bands, scallops, and a few other odd geometric forms. Often the bold, crude, and large figures are in red outlined in black. Design tends to be continuous and integrated. Painting is often sloppy; the overall effect is bold. In general, vessels are small to medium.

Cochití

The pottery of Cochití is basically a poorly decorated ware. Bowls and jars are simply formed; many modeled animals are crude (Fig. 4.21). A white slip, which has turned a yellowish color in older pieces but is more on the pink side in later examples, is carried almost to or even onto the base, thus making for a large decorative area. Designs are commonly in outline and in black. Both geometric and life designs are used, often on the same piece. Particularly popular are heavenly phenomena, such as clouds, lightning, and rain. Sometimes angular stepped clouds have their corners filled in, as at Santo Domingo. Also, a set of angu-

FIGURE 4.19 Acoma geometric style. Recently this geometric style has been revived by the pottery decorators at Acoma. Diamonds, squares, and other simple geometrics are repeated in fine-line nested outlines, joining at corners or on sides to make an allover pattern. This work is done in black paint on a white ground. This vessel is 8 1/4″ high and 10 3/4″ in diameter. It is beautifully executed.

FIGURE 4.20 Santa Ana black- and red-on-white jar. Rather long lines typify this form, and the geometric themes tend to be simple, allover, and confined to a band. Inner rim and base are of red. The pot is 9 3/4″ high.

lar clouds may be combined with a set of curvilinear ones, the latter below and upside down. Lightning shoots forth where the two meet. Human, animal, and bird subjects are also used. One vessel may be decorated with alternating sets of conventional geometric elements or clouds and birds. Cochití design might be characterized in terms of scattered organization of elements.

Painting on Cochití pottery is careless or even sloppy, although there is some individual variation. Design is often widespaced, leaving large areas of white slip in between the black motifs. Small and simple pendant or band designs at the necks of jars or bowls may be continuous or broken.

Large figures, which include humans, birds, mountain sheep, and fish, combine modeling with painting to make them more realistic. Modeling of life forms is not new at Cochití for it has been done for a century or two. Most of the earlier figures were large in size, while more recently they have become greatly diminished. One women in particular, Terecita Romero, models a great variety of life forms — birds, deer, cows and horses, fish, and mountain sheep (Fig. 4.22). Sizes vary considerably, ranging from under one inch to about 5 inches in length. No matter how small these figurines may be, they have a charm all their own.

Taos and Pícuris

Ceramic wares at Taos and Pícuris are very much alike. With the exception of a bit of rim ornament in the self clay or indentations, the vessels are undecorated. Paste has a high mica content which often shows on the surface (the Taos potter goes to Pícuris for clay); the ware bakes to a golden tan or dark gray. Because the potters desired the effect of the bright bits of mica these wares are never slipped nor, apparently, are they ever painted.

Walls of the Taos vessel tend to be thicker than those from Pícuris. Shapes include tall and thin-proportioned jars or more globular ones, a well-formed low and open bowl, and bean pots (Fig. 4.23). The latter copy the jar forms and often have lids plus lugs at the sides.

Like the Hopis, the potters of Taos and Pícuris often produce a mottled effect in the baking of their wares. This is pleasing, particularly where the base is more golden and the spots turn a darker shade; sometimes the latter are bluish in cast. A fillet of clay about the neck forms an undulating line or some other simple theme. Occasionally the rim of the vessel may be scalloped, or simple indentations or raised designs are made by pressing the clay while it is still damp.

FIGURE 4.21 Cochití black-on-white, red-based jars. The decorators of this ware favored angular and/or rounded clouds usually enlivened with lightning shooting out of the corners and rain dripping from them (top left). Other simple geometric forms are thrown in for good measure. Jars with the same type of decoration often have a modeled head and sometimes a handle (right). Another style of decoration has creatures, such as these birds (bottom left), virtually chasing each other around a band on the jar. Dimensions of this jar are: height, 6 1/2", and 8 3/4" widest diameter.

FIGURE 4.22 Tiny figures made by Terecita Romero of Cochití. Here are turkey, dog, striped lizard, elephant, duck, skunk, pig, and a prehistoric animal. Modeling is simple and a bit of paint adds to the realism of the creatures.

Because the form of the Taos and Pícuris jar is non-pueblo in its leaner lines, many are of the opinion that it is of Apache origin. Tradition at Taos points to early trade relations with the Jicarillas which would account for this influence.[14] Even the clay has been called "Apache clay" by such experts as Guthe.[15] Also, like the Navajos and unlike other puebloans, the Taos and Pícuris potters scrape their vessels with a corn cob. Many evidences, then, point to some influences from Apaches and Navajos in certain aspects of the ceramic art at these two villages.

Changes are occurring today in these Taos-Pícuris wares as in other Indian pottery. One new form is a very shallow and almost straight-edged, flat-bottomed dish; another is similar in general form but has scalloped edges and a modeled bird's head at one point on the rim with a suggestion of a tail opposite it.

Tesuque

The older pottery of Tesuque, although it could not compare with the better wares of the Rio Grande, was far superior to its modern counterpart. Earlier products were cream-slipped, with black decoration and a red base; rarely, red was added to the design. Many of the pieces showed crackling of the slip. Designs were in outline, often nothing more than a meandering line or key or other simple and continuous patterns. Small curvilinear flourishes might project from the main motif. A few life themes were used. Designs were confined to a single band on bowl forms, frequently with two parallel lines marking the panel both above and below, but sometimes the designs were centered. Commonly the rounded jar had two bands marked by parallel lines, or a simple or complex design repeated three or more times at wide intervals. This style of decoration goes back to about

FIGURE 4.23 Taos bean pot and bowl. The bean pot (top) is in the natural tan clay surface; when it is burned, smudges or dark clouds often occur on the vessel. The coarse nature of the clay used, particularly for culinary pots, shows in this piece. The clay is not so coarse in the decorative bowl (bottom). There is a great deal of mica in this clay, adding a sheen to the surface of the bowl.

1700; rarely has it been used since the introduction of poster paints in the 1920's.

In contrast to the soft and appealing shades used by most of the Rio Grande potters, commercial poster paints are garish, hard, and clashing when used together. The only explanation for their increased popularity has been that pieces decorated with them sell. Perhaps it is the best illustration of the feeling on the part of many white people that to be Indian a piece must be garish. Nothing, of course, could be further from the truth, particularly where pottery is concerned. These bright colored paints are added after the vessel is fired and thus will wear off as they are handled. Poster-paint colors are all straight-from-the-bottle purples, pinks, blues, oranges, greens, reds, yellows, and chartreuse.

In poster-paint wares, designs are often borrowed from the traditional styles, such as clouds, feathers, frets, and various geometric shapes (Fig. 4.24). These wares feature solids while the native style was more a design of line. As most of these poster-paint decorated pieces are small, designs are greatly diminished in size. Many new shapes have been added in the poster paint pottery, such as a variety of life forms (including circus animals), hatchets, and other odd forms.

Other Rio Grande Pueblos

A few other pueblos need to be mentioned in relation to pottery. No pottery has been made at Sandía for a long time, and the last potter died at Nambé in the early 1950's.[16] Formerly Nambé made a full-bodied, undecorated olla with an out-turned lip; all observed pieces were black in color.

One family at Jémez is currently making a tan background ware, with traditional designs in black and red.[17] The old style was in black on a white ground and utilized both geometric and life themes. Also there is one person at Jémez who is producing an unusual ware; he, too, is using a light tan base, but on this he paints traditional or non-traditional designs in black, white, brown, and, on some vessels, a pale green. Bases of these pieces are almost terra cotta in color. Traditional motifs include clouds, feathers, rain, and simple masks. Non-traditional indeed are the representations of a pueblo village, or Egyptian palm and pyramid! All of these pieces are small jars.

Like these other villages, Isleta today produces a variety of small curio ceramics. Ashtrays, small bowls, and jars are decorated rather sloppily in simple geometric designs.

Non-Pueblo Tribes

Looking broadly at the picture of ceramic production by non-pueblo tribes, the following generalizations can be made. Among the Yuman peoples there is practically no production except for the Maricopas; a few pieces are made now and then by Yumans proper or Mohaves. Papagos produce a few vessels for their own use and some commercial pieces; the latter trend has been encouraged by several white individuals. Pimas no longer make pottery. Apaches rarely produced ceramics in the past, and they produce none today. Navajos have continued to make pottery drums through the years; recently, there has been a slight revival in the way of a few individuals making occasional commercial pieces. Utes made some pottery, Paiutes made little; neither makes any today. It is the puebloan, as discussed above, who has kept this craft alive in the Southwest down to the present.

Yuma and Mohave

During historic years, the Yumans have never been famous for their ceramic productions. Yumas and Mohaves have continued their aboriginal tradition of plain buff or red-on-buff unslipped ware, with few deviations from this color style. One of the interesting forms made natively by the Mohaves, but abandoned as the craft became unimportant to

FIGURE 4.24 Tesuque polychrome poster paint bi-lobed jar. This small 4" high piece is typical of recent and modern developments in the brilliant shades of poster colors, and in the simple geometric elements, such as triangles, steps, and lines. In this piece colors include black, white, blue, red, yellow, and orange on a buff base.

everyday life, was a shallow tray with "ears" at the sides, used for parching corn, wheat, and seeds. Otherwise, the usual bowls and jars were made for everyday service — as a rule in very simple forms. Types which have lingered through the years have been single- or double-spouted jars in traditional style but in smaller sizes. In time a tendency developed to make these jars more "gadgety" as they were sold for curios (Fig. 4.25). Multiple spouts or other projections became popular in both Mohave and Yuma pieces. Some of the Mohave pieces had human heads modeled on them, even in earlier years. Later these were decorated with vari-colored commercial beads which served as necklaces and earrings.

Decoration of Mohave and Yuma pottery was, and is, generally in line patterns; thus the vessels have a light quality to them. Designs are allover in most cases, featuring repeated deep zigzags with small angles filled in solid; hexagons in outline; groups of concentric oblongs; solid squares with or without T-shaped additions; solid triangles and hexagons; and heavy-line swastikas. Common are multiple outlines for solid figures, or dots filling the inner space of open figures, or spaces between a number of figures. Sometimes the outside of a bowl is decorated with parallel lines. Drawing is careless, with irregularities in line thickness and pattern edges and poor junctions of lines. Where modeling is done, it, too, is crude. Mohaves still model a delightful toad, complete with red dots over his buff-colored body (Fig. 4.26).

Cocopa

Cocopa pottery is extremely crude, and has been for many years. A basic buff- or grayware has been made, with very primitive designing in black or red. Vessels are poorly formed and painting is sloppy.

Havasupai, Walapai, and Yavapai

Havasupai, Walapai, and Yavapai tribes have produced even less pottery than the three preceding Yuman tribes, and today they make none. A very crude, plain cooking pot was the usual clay piece of former years.

Maricopa

The best pottery of historic years made by a Yuman tribe has been that of the Maricopa Indians. In earlier years and into this century, they continued some of the aboriginal forms, such as undecorated cooking pots, plain red water jars, and ladles. More recently they have featured smaller sizes which include simple rounded jars without necks, tall to exceedingly tall-necked jars with small bodies, rounded and slightly incurved-mouthed bowls, and bowls with two or four large and deep rim crenulations. Occasional other forms have been revived or developed, particularly as the craft has been commercialized. However, the work of the Maricopas has remained surprisingly simple after a flurry of "gingerbread" back in the early 1900's. This flurry saw much in the way of scalloped edges, footed wares (which never were developed natively in the Southwest), and odd forms such as cups with handles.

Some of the recent and modern Maricopa wares are quite sophisticated in their simplicity, particularly those pieces made by Ida Redbird and several other potters. Practically all of these pieces carry a very high polish of the deep red slip. Fortunately many pieces are left undecorated. However, some

FIGURE 4.25 Mohave red-on-buff jars and bowl. Simple lines are characteristic of most of the Mohave wares (left and right) but many additions have been made to them, such as multiple spouts, and human heads. Typical elements include hexagons (almost too sloppy to recognize on the large jar), triangles, and lines. Often the triangles result from filling in the corners of V-shaped lines. On headed forms, beads often appear in ears and about necks. This ware is not polished.

FIGURE 4.26 Mohave toad with a cigarette (?) in his mouth. These vital little fellows are modeled rather frequently by Mohave potters. One story relative to the object in this toad's mouth is that a bystander suggested that the potter add a cigarette; another story is that the toad brought fire to the Mohaves.

have a few simple black designs (Fig. 4.27) which feature lines, triangles, and stepped squares. All three of these may appear on one vessel, although lines and triangles alone are more popular. Drawing is indifferent, none of it deserving particular comment.

In addition to the basic red or black-on-red decorated wares, the Maricopas also produce a black on a highly polished white or gray ground. Forms and decoration are like the black-on-red styles. Rarely, the two color styles will be combined in a single piece. These decorative styles and color combinations were borrowed by the Maricopas, apparently, from their near neighbors, the Pimas.

Some interesting comments were made by Breazeale in 1923 regarding Maricopa pottery. First he mentioned an outstanding potter, one Lena Mesquerre. He noted the use of a piece of gourd over which the pot was started; he referred to thick coils for building up the piece; the use of a stone for polishing; and burning over a mesquite fire. He also said that the black paint was a mesquite derivative, that kaolin was the source of white, and that ochre produced the "reddish-yellow." A second burning followed the painting.[18] The shapes Breazeale illustrated are the same as those made in the 1960's, except that necks were not as long as they became in the 1940's and thereafter.

Apache

Apache Indians have never made much pottery, although formerly all three main Southwestern groups, the Arizona tribes and the New Mexican Jicarillas and Mescaleros, made some crude cooking wares and a few bottles. Most of the pieces were of a dull gray or brownish tone and were unpainted. The round-bottomed, open-mouthed cooking vessel sometimes carried a slight decoration in the form of a raised and simple pattern, a fillet of clay around the rim (Fig. 4.28). Today the Apache tribes of Arizona and New Mexico do not make any pottery.

Ute and Paiute

In the past, the Utes and Paiutes used conical or bullet-bottomed cooking vessels; the former also used pottery drums[19] which resembled the Apache pieces in color and finish, and seldom were decorated. No pottery is made today by the Arizona Paiutes.

Navajo

Around the year 1700, when living in the Governador country of New Mexico, the Navajos produced a color-decorated pottery with black, or black and red designs on a buff ground (Fig. 4.29). Designs were simple and geometric. They also made bullet-bottomed cooking pots. For years they continued the latter form, sometimes decorating it with a fillet about the rim (Fig. 4.30). Occasional other forms were introduced, such as a coffee pot! Through the years they also made a small open-mouthed jar for a drum. In the early 1950's a slight revival took place with the making of small versions of the drum and cooking-pot forms; a few are still

FIGURE 4.27 Maricopa black-on-red bowl made by Ida Redbird. The simple black triangles, plain or with volute tails, and line patterns are common on this ware. More attractive than the painted decoration are the simple forms and the high polish. This low bowl is 3 1/2" high and 8" in diameter.

FIGURE 4.28 Western Apache cooking vessel. Strictly utilitarian, these pots feature wide mouths and bullet bottoms. They are usually of a dark gray clay, unpolished and undecorated except for a crenulated rim, as in this example, or a fillet of clay about the neck. This pot is 12" high.

made today. Some of the pots were heavily coated with piñon gum.

Pima and Papago

Except for a few utility and commercial pieces, the production of pottery by Pima and Papago Indians has ceased in recent years. Today the Pimas rarely work in clay. The more direct and intensive contacts of the Pimas with the non-Indian world, and their better economic status, relatively speaking, again account for this loss of another craft.

Although both inherited a healthy tradition from the Hohokams — the Piman being far richer than that of the Papagos — it is not fully known when this background ceased to influence these two tribes. Somewhere along the way the free and happy style of their ancestors was lost. Historic pottery shows none of the variety and beauty of the earlier style. From the first historic records, the pottery of the Pimas and Papagos has been described as simple in form, undecorated buff- or redware, and very slightly decorated red-on-buff styles. Some red on black was made. As wares were commercialized, the latter color combination became more popular (Fig. 4.31), or even a plain redware, or sometimes a black-on-white or gray ground ware. The earlier light polish became a high gloss in time. As in the case of other tribes, the

Pima and Papago potter reduced the sizes of her vessels as she made more and more of them for sale to white men.

Some of the Papago forms which are native and which have survived to the present time include water and cooking ollas or jars (Fig. 4.32). The former are rounded or, sometimes, more elongate-bodied, with fairly small necks. For years ollas have hung under the Papago ramada for everyday use, the mouth enlarged so that water might be dipped out of the vessel. Water is more plentiful and easier to come by today, but in earlier years jars needed very small and long necks to avoid evaporation, and also because vessels were often buried in the ground as a water source to wandering groups.

A slightly smaller version of the wide-mouthed Papago jar is also made today for boiling sahuaro fruit and for cooking beans. A wider-mouthed style is used for frying beans; it has two lugs or "ears" on the lip. Many of the natives maintain that a better taste in foods results from the use of the earthen pot. Fontana illustrates an interesting duck-shaped piece, a child's drinking vessel.[20] Few other household utensils of clay are made today by the Papagos.

On the other hand, Papagos have been making curio items for a number of years and in varying quantities. Variety of objects has changed, too. One year at their annual arts and crafts show they had a large quantity of straight- and shallow-sided, flat-

FIGURE 4.29 Old Navajo polychrome bowl. Some years ago the Navajos made a greater variety of pottery including decorated wares. This bowl has a design in red outlined in gray (or faded black?) on a tan ground. Typically, designs are geometric, simple, and poorly executed. The rim diameter is about 9".

FIGURE 4.30 Navajo plainware cooking pot. These elongate-bodied pieces have very wide mouths and bullet bottoms. Quite often there is a fillet of clay about the neck.

FIGURE 4.31 Contemporary Papago bowls. These two small pieces are of a highly polished surface; the painted piece (a) has a carelessly executed black design on the upper part of a slight shoulder, while the other (b) has only a black line at the rim.

tery was decorated in the following manner. The slip, which was a thinned clay or ochre derivative, was applied with a cloth and polished with a smooth stone. Red paint was derived from ochre. For the black, mesquite chips were collected from areas on the tree where gum had gathered and were boiled.

Decoration on the Papago vessels, whether for native use or for sale, is simple. Large water jars occasionally have a bit of neck decoration in the form of lines or triangles and lines. Often one tip of the triangle takes off and ends up as a spiral. Cooking pots are usually plain. Curio pieces may

bottomed, undecorated pieces of highly polished redware. Another year they had a few grotesquely modeled cows and other unidentifiable animals in dull red clay. Through the years, however, the Papagos have made the following small forms, either in plain buff, or red (usually polished), or red decorated in black: jars which are round-bodied and slightly incurved at the rim; saucer-like ashtrays; either square or rectangular boxes; flat-bottomed and straight-sided round containers; and bowls.

Pottery among the Pima Indians paralleled, in some respects, the Papago developments for native use. Ollas were the largest and best-made pieces; they were plain or sometimes simply decorated. Cooking pots were smaller, undecorated, smoothed, and polished. For both tribes, lesser pieces such as dippers, shallow trays, and canteens may also be listed. If decorated, lines and small solids were used by the Pima as among the Papago. Pimas did make some small trinket items; these, too, resembled those described for the Papagos.

With few exceptions, both Pima and Papago pot-

FIGURE 4.32 A typical Papago bean pot. These soft-red vessels have appealing lines, with generous mouths, are undecorated, and are still preferred for native cooking. The vessel rests on a "head ring" or "pot ring" plaited by the Papago women. The pot is 12 1/2″ high and 14 1/4″ in its broadest diameter.

bear the same design as mentioned for the water jars or some others; generally the pattern covers more of the surface of the small piece. A few other geometric elements and units may be added to the above, such as scrolls, wavy lines, rectangles, zigzags, interlocking scrolls, fringed lines, and in recent years, very crudely drawn floral themes. A few equally crude life forms are painted on some pieces of Papago pottery.

Summary

Ceramics among the Southwest Indians today present a varied picture as far as individual tribes are concerned. Some have lost the art completely, some carry on in a halfhearted manner, while among a few tribes pottery is a flourishing craft. In the last category most important are the Hopi Indians, the Pueblo of San Ildefonso, and to a lesser degree, Santa Clara and San Juan.

From the standpoint of artistry there is also varied development. The Hopis have retained many of their native forms and certainly the traditional colors and designs. They have branched out a little in the area of shapes. The three Rio Grande villages mentioned above, on the other hand, have displayed a great interest in the development of surface finish — especially in the blackware of San Ildefonso, the deep carving of Santa Clara, and the incised styles of San Juan.

Since very few individuals have learned the use of the potter's wheel, it is too early to predict what this may hold for the Indians of the Southwest. What has been done by several puebloans gives promise of a possible future in this unexplored area of expression. As in the other crafts, it will take time to see any results. The terrific change from group-dominated styles to individual production is certainly a factor here as it will be in other areas of the craft arts.

Silver & Jewelry

Chapter V

ONE OF THE OLDEST of the craft arts, the making of items for personal adornment, has combined with one of the newest techniques, silversmithing, to produce one of the best-known of Southwest Indian expressions, silver and turquoise jewelry. There are, of course, many ramifications in the whole field of silver and jewelry, for the former has been productive of more than jewelry, and the latter involves the utilization of several materials in addition to silver.

It has been said, and with good reason, that man would rather be fine than clothed; in other words, personal adornment has long been important to man. This is true worldwide. Man may lack other things in his life, but he will stick a bit of bone through his nose, a sprig of growth in his ear lobe, or tie a bit of sinew about his wrist. There is no known group so lacking in this desire that they do not utilize something from their environment with which to bedeck themselves.

Prehistoric Background

The prehistoric Southwesterners were no exception to this. They too, in their earlier and culturally more poverty stricken days, picked up bits of turquoise, seeds, shell, or other small pieces of odd materials and attached them to their bodies in some crude fashion. Civilized man, who is so surfeited with material possessions, could not possibly understand the joy of wearing a tiny piece of blue stone fastened about the neck with a fiber cord. But this was the beginning, and it expressed a love for adornment which through the years waxed rather than waned.

From his ancestors the historic Indian inherited some variety in materials and a vast array of forms of jewelry. Turquoise, shell, red and black stone, bone, horn, and occasional other materials were used by prehistoric puebloans and other tribes. Objects which were made through the years included, among others, pendants; beads which were used in necklaces, armlets, anklets, and earrings; bracelets; buttons; and hair ornaments. Overlay,

mosaic, incising, carving, and cutting were some of the elaborate techniques developed through the years. The puebloans became quite adept in the use of most of these techniques, all of which continued into the historic period with some additions of both materials and methods.

Although the Hohokams were exceedingly clever at working shell and stone, their presumed descendants of historic years did not follow in their footsteps. Rather there is a dearth of jewelry and little artistry in what the Pimas and Papagos used. This statement can be repeated for the Yuman tribes and, until later years, for the Apaches and Navajos as well. It was the puebloan peoples who carried on the traditions of their ancestors, the Anasazi, in most of the specific forms, materials, and technologies mentioned above.

Historic Development

The dawning of the historic period did not immediately alter traditional native forms of ornamentation. To be sure, the Indians gradually acquired from the white man new materials to add to those already used, and new tools with which to work them. Then, sometime in the early 1800's, came metals. A limited knowledge of working brass and copper preceded the introduction of silver. The latter opened up new avenues of development which have been explored more deeply by the Navajos and Zuñis than by any other Southwest tribe. But the introduction of silver working did not bring an end to the manufacture of other kinds and styles of jewelry. Indeed, shell, turquoise, and certain other materials are still used today, and the techniques used to work them are, in many cases, only slight modifications of those used in prehistoric times.

Shell, Turquoise, and Other Stones

Throughout the years, shell has continued to be popular. It is made into disc beads, used as a backing for and as a part of mosaic, and set in silver. The greater part of shell work today, particularly in the first two uses, is done at Santo Domingo and Zuñi.

Santo Domingo is particularly well known for its fine beads. Today the artisans use abalone, clam, or olivella shell. Small pieces are broken off and drilled by hand from each end, thus producing a hole which is constricted in the center. The worker uses the traditional hand-pump drill (Fig. 5.1), but he may fit it with the point of a nail or the end of a steel file because of its greater hardness. Many Zuñi Indians use an electrically driven drill. After drilling holes in a number of small bits of shell, the craftsman strings the shells and runs them over a piece of sandstone. Water and grit are employed as aids in this process of rounding the beads. There is considerable variation in the finished products: some of the beads are regular, even, and thin, while others have irregular edges and are thicker. Shell beads are commonly called "heshi."

In general, turquoise disc beads are made in the same manner as those of shell. However, since the stone is harder, it takes longer to grind and pierce the turquoise beads, and they break more readily. Furthermore, the two faces as well as the edges are polished, a step which is unnecessary with shell. All in all, the production of turquoise beads is a more tedious and longer process.

Beads vary greatly in size, with those of shell almost always smaller than those of turquoise. In recent years, some very small beads have been made. One string of shell observed at Taos, in 1963, averaged 26 beads to the inch and each bead was less than 2 mm. in diameter.

Shell beads are strung and used in several different ways. A single or multiple strand of plain shell beads alone is more common today than in the past. Often chunks of turquoise, red shell, or coral may be interspersed at more or less regular intervals between groups of shell beads; this type of necklace may or may not have a pendant. A common pendant worn by puebloans is a large rounded piece of shell with mosaic of turquoise over one half of the piece, around the edge in rays, or in some other arrangement.

An extremely popular Navajo style, especially among the old "longhairs" (a Navajo man, usually older, who wears his hair long), is a disc-shell bead and chunk-turquoise necklace with a "jaclah" (or jacla) pendant (Fig. 5.2). The latter is formed of

FIGURE 5.1 A pump drill for making holes in beads of turquoise or shell. This drill is used extensively by the Indians of Santo Domingo and to a lesser degree by the Zuñis and other Indians. This example has a stone point while others may use a piece of metal in its place. The fingers are placed on the small crossbar of wood and the drill is pumped up and down; the stone wheel near the point helps to keep the instrument in motion.

FIGURE 5.2 Above — the Tuba City Trading Post on the Navajo Reservation, showing a typical post vault. Note the paw: tags on all objects; these give the owner's name, date, and amount of money involved in the transaction. (*Courtesy Museum of Northern Arizona*) Below — an all-turquoise necklace (left) has a few pieces of chunk stones on the bottom of the secondar pendant, or jacla. Coral was introduced into the Southwest early in the 1800's and eventually became very popular among th Navajos. Necklaces were made of the new material; sometimes the Navajos added a bit of turquoise for more color (center) Shell disc bead and turquoise chunk necklaces (right) are perhaps the oldest style in the Southwest. Navajos favor this piece with many of the old "longhair" men still wearing them. The jaclas are all turquoise or turquoise and shell. The plain turquoi: and coral strands are also favorites of the Navajos. (*Photo by Ray Manley*)

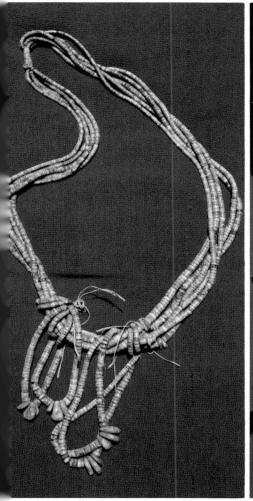

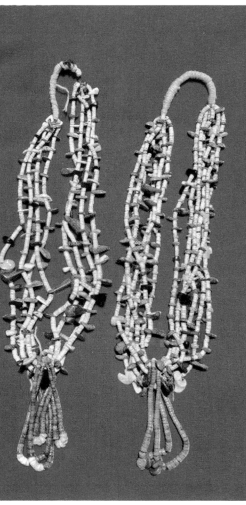

turquoise beads in two short loops. Other materials or objects may appear in the main necklace, such as silver beads, teeth, or at Zuñi, small carved birds or other life figures. The life forms are often carved from mother-of-pearl.

Turquoise disc beads are sometimes made into single or multiple-strand necklaces. Some very lovely chokers of ten strands each have been made in recent years, all the tiny disc beads being carefully formed and matched. Turquoise and shell disc beads are now made into more sophisticated pieces of jewelry; these sometimes have more white shell beads and fewer turquoise ones interspersed in regular rhythms. Both shell and turquoise vary in color and quality. Shell colors run the gamut from dead white through various grays and browns into light and dark pink tones. It was some of the dark red shells which were mistaken for coral in early years. Turquoise varies from pale light blues to deep greens. Good necklaces today have well-matched colors.

Much of the shell and turquoise jewelry is worn in certain ceremonies of the pueblo people. One of the most interesting variations of the several pendant styles described above was observed at a kachina dance at a Hopi village in the spring of 1960. Down alternate and radiating natural troughs of large shells were set pieces of turquoise. These pendants were suspended on the backs of the dancers.

Shell inlay is made into earrings and hair ornaments as well as pendants. The pendant type referred to here is made basically of aboriginal materials which include shell, wood, or jet for the base and shell, turquoise, coral (in place of native red stone), and jet as the design materials. Small fragments are glued into cut-out sections of the base piece. During the 1930-40 period, pieces of phonograph records were commonly substituted for the jet.

The origins of these materials are many. Jet in the form of lignite or cannel coal is found in several parts of the Southwest; some is imported from England. One trader says that some of the best jet comes from the Hopi country. Shell has been traded into the Southwest for centuries. Most of it is from the Gulf of California, a little is from the West Coast, less comes from the Gulf of Mexico. In recent years much wider sources have been exploited; some of the lovely pink shell used in Zuñi channel work comes from the Mississippi Valley.

Coral was introduced into the Southwest early in the nineteenth century. The first reliable reference to this material was made by General Thomas James who was in Santa Fe in 1822.[1] He reported that Indians from the village of San Felipe came into Santa Fe wearing coral beads of bright red color. Research into the subject of coral has revealed that most if not all of it came and still comes from off the coast of Sciacca, Sicily, and from Sardinia, and is worked in Italy.[2] It is shipped to importers in the eastern United States from the Italian manufacturers. Some of this Italian coral is sent to Mexico, and from there finds its way to the Southwest Indian. Quite a bit of Japanese coral now reaches the Indians.

Colors of coral vary from deep pink to red to red-orange. Since shell may be of similar coloration, it is little wonder that the latter was often referred to as coral or "coral-like." No coral has been located in any prehistoric Southwestern sites, nor has any been established at any historic village prior to the above date.[3] Coral has been and is imported into the Southwest in tubular or round bead forms, usually polished, or in the raw pieces of the material. The consensus is that the Indian could not have drilled the long and narrow bead of coral, which is the more common shape, for he did not have the equipment to do so.

Coral has come to be greatly favored by Southwest Indians, and especially by the Navajos. In years past it was said that individuals would spend long periods of time trading for beads that matched until they had a perfect or nearly perfect multiple-strand necklace. Of course, in addition to the coral used in necklaces, it has become popular in recent years to combine coral in several different ways with silver.

When the Navajos borrowed some of their ceremonies from the puebloans, probably back in Governador days, it is likely that they acquired legends and myths along with all else. Some of these legends were recorded by Washington Matthews in 1897.[4] In them he refers to "coral" and "red stone" interchangeably; this would seem to indicate that the former may have been substituted for the latter as time passed. And this in turn may explain, in part at least, why coral has become so precious to the Navajos. To its ritual significance can be added its intrinsic beauty.

Carving, another age-old method of working shell and turquoise, remains popular to this day. Life forms are greatly favored. Although Zuñi is the chief village where such work is done, it is also found elsewhere. From Zuñi come small or medium-sized figures of birds, turtles, lizards, frogs, and such. They average about half an inch to an inch in length. These must not be confused with the fetishes which are carved of stone; the shell and turquoise pieces referred to here were and are made as articles of personal adornment. Such a shell bird with outspread wings and head straight forward, has two small round turquoise eyes and eight pieces of the same material over the back and wings. Slight incising on the rather flat carving is used to suggest wing and tail feathers. The Zuñi craftsman is very clever in carving shell, using its pink or other colors and iridescence to emphasize form. Sometimes the entire figure is in one color or in the iridescent material.

One necklace style is formed of tiny figures of birds interspersed between shell disc beads. In one example each of the many bird effigies is carved in such a way as to utilize most effectively the natural brown markings of the shell for eyes and wing and tail-feather detail. Another necklace is composed of turquoise, shell, and mother-of-pearl mammals (including bears and a mountain lion), and birds interspersed between shell disc beads.

Silversmithing

A variety of techniques and forms in silver working exists today in the pieces produced by Navajos, Zuñis, and Hopis. As in the case of textiles, it is the Navajo who is best and most widely known of all Southwest tribes for the craft of silversmithing. Except for a rare individual here and there, Pimas, Papagos, Yumans, and Apaches do not work silver. For years a few men in many of the Rio Grande pueblos have done some silvercrafting, while in other villages no smiths have ever done any work in this medium.

Blacksmithing, and the working of copper and brass, preceded any knowledge of silversmithing. According to Adair, these crafts existed among the Zuñis and possibly the Navajos as early as 1830-40. Mexicans had a superstition, it seems, that a piece of either of these metals worn on one's person would prevent ill effects from rheumatism. Therefore, they would bring vessels of copper or brass to the Zuñis and have them make crosses, buttons, bracelets, and rings. Navajos also wore some of these objects as ornaments, plus bowguard mountings of brass or copper, and continued to do so for many years thereafter, gradually replacing the baser metals with silver.

Copper and brass were crudely worked. Old pots and pans were melted down, made into ingots, and from them the object was pounded into shape. Little decoration appeared on these early pieces — usually no more than simple geometric designs scratched on with a file. Heavy copper wires replaced the pots and pans in later years; this was often twisted into a bracelet which had no further decoration. These early pieces are important to keep in mind for undoubtedly they had some influence on the beginnings of the silver craft.

Another influence which may have been contemporaneous with the above early developments, and one which certainly was significant in later years, was the use of brass, copper, and German silver by Utes and adjacent Plains tribes. Through other Indians or traders these people acquired the metal or, in some cases, the finished product. One such piece, a wide brass bracelet (Fig. 5.3), bore the metal manufacturer's mark on the back. A rubbing reveals what appears to be, "The American Brass Kettle Manufactory." Parallel incised lines run from end to end of the bracelet, leaving a plain edge slightly wider than the space between incisions. The bracelet was obtained in trade with a Ute Indian of southern Colorado in the 1930's.

At the village of Pecos, New Mexico, which was abandoned in 1838, a cross of silver and several crosses of copper were found. They are described as of European manufacture, or, it is suggested, they are reworked pieces. The silver cross is described as "of a type sometimes seen attached to the necklace worn today by the Pueblo Indians of the Río Grande."[5]

Mexican metal craftsmen were responsible for the first silversmithing among the Navajos. For years these two ethnic groups had been warring with each other, particularly as the Navajos raided the settlements of the Mexicans. However, about the middle of the nineteenth century, one Atsidi Sani, a Navajo of Crystal, New Mexico, learned blacksmithing from a Mexican near Mt. Taylor, east of Zuñi, New Mexico. Since Navajos traded with Mexicans for bridles and horses, Atsidi thought that he could make bridles and sell them to his tribesmen. He visited the Mexican called Nakai Tsosi (Thin Man) by the Navajos, and in turn Nakai visited Atsidi. They became good friends, and in time Atsidi learned the difficult craft of silversmithing.[6] The consensus is that this occurred

FIGURE 5.3 This old bracelet was made from a piece of commercial brass. Although this piece came from a Ute Indian, the same style was probably made in very early years by the Navajos. Some silver bracelets have copied this form.

some time between 1853 and 1868; Adair maintains that it was not until after the Navajos returned from Ft. Sumner (1868) that Atsidi learned silversmithing.

Atsidi Sani first taught his four sons the craft of iron working and later silversmithing. Other Navajos learned from him, too, for through the years he built up quite a reputation as a smith. Another early smith was Atsidi Chon; he is credited with teaching a Zuñi this craft about the year 1873[7] when he established a shop in this pueblo village. In turn, a Zuñi taught a Hopi, and thus the craft spread.

It is as difficult to separate technology, form, designs, and materials when referring to the history of Southwest Indian silver work as it is in relation to other crafts. So interrelated are all of these expressions that mention of one will, of necessity, bring others into focus.

Both hammering (wrought) and casting were developed early by Navajo smiths. Seemingly, American coins were first used. Lesser methods, more a reshaping than a true technique of working silver, were also employed in the early years of this craft. For example, a quarter, a dime, or a Mexican coin would be pounded into a cone-shaped or round hole in a log or piece of iron, the worker using an old scrap of iron which had been ground at one end to press the silver into the hole (Fig. 5.4). In this manner a bell or button would be shaped. Such a method of forming pieces of silver continued to be used for years. Sometimes the imprint on the coin was left on the underside, but the outer surface might be smoothed and decorated in simple fashion.

Hammering is accomplished by heating the metal slightly and pounding it into the desired shape and thickness. This technique results in a soft sheen in the finished silver which some think they can detect; however, certain expert craftsmen say this is not so.

About 1890, when the law which made it illegal to deface American coins was enforced, traders obtained Mexican coins for the Indians. The Mexican "dobe dollar" was greatly favored for it had little alloy and therefore was easier to melt or hammer. Then, as the Mexican pieces became more and more

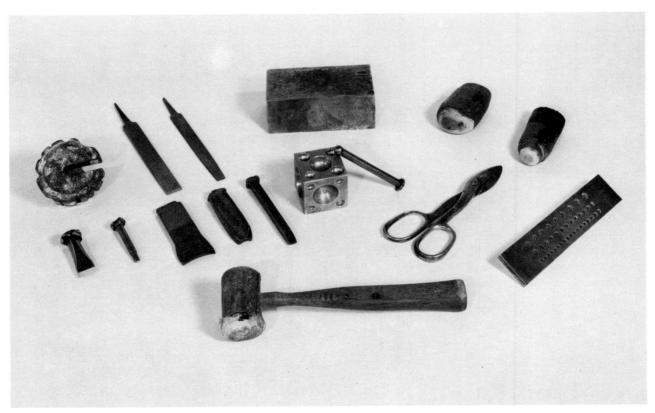

FIGURE 5.4 Some of the equipment used by Southwest Indians in their silver craft. Top row, left to right, the pieces are: An old weight from scales into which wedges or grooved sections were cut so that silver wire could be hammered into them to make triangular or rounded bracelets; files of different grades for finishing silver; a bar of solid metal used as an anvil (a railroad tie formerly served this purpose); an oval and a round "domer" used in the making of bosses or raised areas on spoons (oval one) or other pieces of silver. Second row, left to right, are five dies. Objects from which they were made and designs which they produce: two chisels, one to make a straight line, and a concavity on a second one to make lines on "rope" on concha belts; file, large gentle curves (old die); chisel, half moon with dots; railroad spike, three small depressions, to make tiny bosses; mold for dapper die, with one such next to the hole it fits — used for making buttons or beads of various sizes; metal shears; template for drawing wire of different sizes: these holes are for round wire and there are others for making square wire. Foreground: a wooden maul for pounding silver. (*Courtesy Frank Patania, Thunderbird Shop, Tucson, Arizona*).

difficult to obtain, silver "slugs" about one and one-half inches square and one-eighth of an inch in thickness were made available through commercial sources; these originated in a refinery in San Francisco. Again, the trader usually provided these slugs for the Indian smith. In the 1930's, sheet silver first came into use, but slugs remained popular into the 1940's. The term "wrought" is commonly employed for objects in sheet silver; this term will be used in the following discussion.

Almost any form and size of object could be produced in wrought workmanship. From early years, conchas, medium and wide bracelets, bridle trappings, and many other pieces were made in this manner. Plain forms and wide plain surfaces resulted from the hammering process; thus, wrought silver invited some additional types of decoration. It is quite likely, since this was a favorite method of production among the Navajos, that hammered silver styles encouraged stamping and other decorative techniques. As traders became more common among the Navajos in the late 1870's and into the 1880's and 1890's, they introduced files which made it possible to produce dies. Navajos used these fine files to work a design on the end of old bolts, cold chisels, nail sets, or rivets (Fig. 5.4). The first designs produced on these makeshift dies were copied from contemporary Mexican leather work, a foreshadowing of the borrowing of designs from many sources. This fact negates the idea of "symbolism" of Indian silver patterns.

Casting of silver was developed early by the Navajos. Adair gives the date 1875 as a time when they were doing this type of work. The Mexicans, from whom the Navajos learned the technique, used clay molds for casting. Early Navajo molds were made in a dark stone, probably some kind of sandstone. Later a white or light-colored stone, much softer than sandstone, was used. Today the mold is often of sandstone, a material found widely on the reservation, or of tuff. A few Indians make concrete molds; these will produce more pieces than a mold of stone.

To cast silver, two pieces of the desired stone (Fig. 5.5) are roughly shaped into a square or rectangle, then they are rubbed together so as to smooth one face on each piece. The shape of the object to be cast is cut into the surface of one piece. Formerly all of this work was done freehand; today a smith may first draw the design on the stone in pencil. A few use a ruler, a compass, or some other aid in the drawing process.

Often the outline is cut in a V-shaped or rounded groove; several air vents and a larger channel to receive the molten silver are cut from the design to the edge of the stone. Mutton tallow or soot is spread over the cut area of the mold to keep the

silver from sticking. The two stones are then tied together, the smooth face of one against the cut face of the other.

The mold is then placed on the ground or work bench with the large channel up. Molten silver is poured into the channel and spreads through the cut-out areas. When the metal is set and before it is completely cooled, the mold is opened. The object which greets the eye of the worker is a blackened, rough-edged, and unattractive piece. It is now that some of the most tedious work begins. Projecting spicules of silver on the cast object must be cut away; for this, heavy shears are used. Some pieces come out with a rough surface because of the nature of the casting process; great patience is required in the use of progressively finer files and emery paper to rub these out and to give to the piece a lovely smoothness and sheen. This technique certainly appealed to the Navajo for he is particularly fond of masses of smooth silver.

Throughout the history of this craft, there has been a tremendous variation in the amount and kind of equipment used, especially among the widely scattered Navajos. Smiths in out-of-the-way corners often made their own equipment; some still do. A piece of railroad rail or any large fragment of iron can serve as an anvil, or a commercial anvil may be purchased. Early bellows were made from buffalo hide or goatskins; later a heart-shaped type could be purchased at the trading post. Often a forge was constructed of sticks and mud, with the bellows attached in an equally crude manner. With the introduction of the tin bucket the homemade forge went out; a hole in the front of the bucket received the nozzle of the commercial bellows; then charcoal was added to make a forge which was more efficient than the previous type. A gasoline blowtorch has been in common use for years.

At first the Navajo produced his own crucibles of clay, but these were too porous and too easily broken. Then some fellow discovered that a fragment of prehistoric pottery served well; some contemporary pueblo pottery was also used for crucibles. Commercial types are obtained now from trading posts. Ingot molds were made of sandstone. In early years scissors, shears, pliers, tongs, and hammers came from the trading post; a greater variety of all of these items is available today. Formerly the smith made his own blowpipe by flattening a length of brass wire, then folding it into a pipe. Blowpipes can now be purchased through the trader or in towns about the reservation. Sandpaper and emery paper were and are obtained at the trading post.

As Zuñi jewelry took a very different direction in its development, the equipment also became dif-

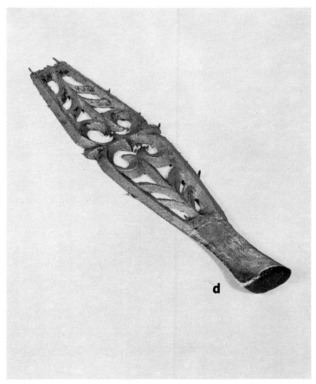

FIGURE 5.5 Mold for silver casting. Two pieces of soft stone of the same shape are smoothed face to face (a and b). In (b) the design and a channel to the end are cut out — this one has the casting in place. The two are rubbed with soot and tied together (c). Molten silver is poured in the channel end; when it is set, the mold is opened. Again (b) shows how the silver followed the cut-out pattern. The silver is removed (d); this shows the spicules and the heavy channel end which must be removed. Shears cut away the excess; files and emery paper are then used in smoothing the surfaces, and the bracelet is bent into shape. (*Courtesy Thunderbird Shop, Tucson*)

ferent. Fine and abundant stone working preceded silver crafting and has remained popular; therefore the tools of the lapidary have been more important than those of the silversmith. To be sure, stones are set in silver and a little stamping is done, but a minimum of silver-working equipment is needed. Added to it, however, are the lapidary wheel and stick, and related devices. Since World War II, there has been electricity at Zuñi, so many of these Indians have power-driven tools. Some Navajos working under other than out-of-the-way reservation conditions have up-to-date equipment also, such as prestolite torches, power-driven buffers, and other such modern aids.

It is not known and may never be known when the first turquoise was set in silver; nor is it known if this was the first material used for settings. Some claim that experimentation with garnets and shell may have preceded the use of turquoise; Adair implies that these were used later.[8] Stevenson, who worked among the Zuñis, claims that she was given the first Navajo piece with a turquoise setting in it, and that it dated around 1880.[9] Several Navajos told Adair that Atsidi Chon was the first to set turquoise in silver when he so decorated a ring about 1878.[10] Adair also calls attention to the fact that the Navajo reservation is a large one, and that this incident may apply to only one portion of it.

When first used in Navajo and other Southwest Indian silver, turquoises were hand cut and hand polished. It is quite likely that Santo Domingo Indians, well known for their beads, cut turquoises also and traded their settings for silver made by the Navajos. Today all turquoise is commercially cut and polished except that done by Zuñis and Domingans.

Commercialization of the craft began when the Fred Harvey Company farmed out silver and turquoise to traders on the reservation in 1899. Significant changes resulted from this. Orders were left for certain designs — swastikas and arrows for example — and for the stamping of many elements on a single piece. The machined stone was established. Today it is a rare thing to see a hand-cut and hand-polished stone, and then it is usually in an old piece.

In setting a stone, a thin strip of silver is first soldered onto the main object to form a box-like enclosure called a "bezel." The stone is then set within this bezel, cushioned on a bit of cardboard or other soft substance. The Navajo bezel is usually plain, although in earlier work it was often notched. The silver equals or exceeds the height of the edges of the stone and is brought up over the turquoise to secure it in position.

The overlay method of working silver appeared among Southwest Indians just before World War

II. A small amount of overlay work was produced at this early date at Santo Domingo, among the Hopis at the instigation of the Museum of Northern Arizona, and by the Navajos. Overlay is done in this manner: two identical pieces of silver are cut out — for example, two circles. One circle is left plain; in the second a pattern is cut out in silhouette with a tiny jeweler's saw. Using a flux, the two pieces are then "sweated" together. The piece is next oxidized, which turns it black. When the polishing is completed the cut-out area is allowed to remain black. Thus there is a contrast between the lower background and the higher silver areas. There is also a greater depth in the background than is found ordinarily in stamped work.

It is in the individual forms of jewelry and other silver objects that further developments in this craft are to be seen. In a broad overall view, the first silver work was done by Navajos for Navajos and other Indians. Forms featured were those used or worn by the Indians, such as bridles, bracelets, beads, earrings, concha belts, and a few other pieces. Decoration was basically simple — few or no stones were used during this period. This kind of production continued well into the 1880's. Although a small bit of production for whites took place before 1899, it was the farming out of silver and turquoise by the Fred Harvey Company in that year which inaugurated the real beginning of commercialization of the silversmithing craft. Indian traders in Gallup and elsewhere furthered the growing popularity of Indian silver. By the time the craft was fifty years old — around 1910 to 1920 — it had undergone rapid development, was widely known throughout the United States, and was pursued by a large number of Indians.

With commercialization the same forms were retained but became more varied, decoration was stamped and often allover, and much of the work was done carelessly and in thin silver. Contributing further to these trends were factories run by white men for the rapid production of the same types of jewelry. The first such factory was set up in Denver, Colorado, in 1910. It was followed by similar establishments in Albuquerque and Gallup, New Mexico, Santa Barbara, California, and other places. The latest such venture is in southern Colorado where several white men are producing jewelry in imitation of Zuñi channel work by centrifugal casting of silver.

If all of these commercial establishments sold their wares honestly as white man's products, and did not attempt to dupe the public with "Indian Maid" and other such labels, the situation would be slightly better. These products, and other efforts to copy the Indians' silver craft, have been detrimental and unfair to the native Southwesterners.

Sometimes the design is a little "off" to imply that it is handmade. Even if an Indian pulls the lever of the master stamp, the machine-made piece costs less than a handmade product. Handmade Indian silver cannot meet such unfair competition.

Navajo Silver

Much of the history of silver given above has pertained to the Navajos — for several reasons. One is that there is more documentation regarding this tribe and, secondly, Navajos have been the leaders in the overall development of this craft among Southwestern Indians. The forms originated by the Navajos have carried over to other tribes; decorative styles began among the Navajos, even though other tribes may have veered in different directions at later times; and certainly Navajo silver has become more widely known, thus paving the way for the reception of other styles.

Interestingly, in the creation of jewelry and silver craft items in general, the Navajos have adhered to their original styles of workmanship. Their first pieces were plain, then one or a few stones were added; cast silver often had no stamping; when stamping was used, it employed a few elements attractively arranged. Above all, these Indians started out with and have retained a preference for mass in design and perfection in the surface finish of silver. These standards have improved as the total picture is viewed. Today a fine piece of Navajo silver combines these qualities at their best to compare favorably with any handcrafted jewelry.

When he wrote his book on Southwest Indian silver, H. P. Mera ended his discussion as of the late 1930's for, he said, "after that time the evils of commercialism may be seen to be adversely affecting the art."[11] Quite the contrary has been true; commercialization has caused some deterioration, surely, but advancement in many phases of the silver craft has continued since the late 1930's. Intelligent and understanding traders have urged the production of better work, and the Indian has responded with some of the finest silver in the history of the craft.

Some whites are attracted by certain elements of a lingering primitiveness and a charm in design in old pieces of Navajo work. But the craft would strangle itself if there were no development beyond the points of accomplishment of the late 1800's and early 1900's. Better equipment, greater knowledge, and longer training of individuals in more recent years have resulted in more finished, more sophisticated, and better designed silver work.

Because of the great variety within each, the different forms of Navajo silver are discussed separately below.

Concha Belts

Concha belts (Fig. 5.6) were among the first pieces made by the Navajos. Although considerable controversy has centered about this form, the consensus is that the concha is of Plains' origin. Eastern United States smiths produced German silver discs for Indians east of the Mississippi who in turn carried them to the Plains Indians. The latter wore them as brooches or hair ornaments. Eventually these discs found their way to Ute, Comanche, and other western tribes which used them also as belt ornaments. The loot of war or trade with other tribes probably brought these discs, now called conchas, to the Navajos.

The Plains' concha was circular in form (rarely oval), undecorated or very simply engraved, plain edged, and with or without holes in the center for attachment to the belt or hair. Some of the earliest Navajo pieces are quite similar to the Plains' conchas; Woodward says some are identical. Although silver discs appear on early Spanish-Mexican bridles, they are smaller in size, scalloped-edged, and much more ornately decorated. Thus both Adair and Woodward conclude that the Navajo concha came from the southern Plains Indians rather than through Mexican channels.[12] However, Adair maintains, and with good reason, that the Mexican concha influenced that of the Navajo, for some of the earliest pieces made by the latter have scalloped borders, a feature rarely seen in the Plains examples.

FIGURE 5.6   Old-style Navajo concha belt of the finest craftsmanship.

Thus large, thin, circular, plain or simply decorated, and scalloped or smooth-edged conchas with an opening in the center for lacing to the belt are characteristic of the earliest Navajo work. Shortly after making these first pieces, Navajos began to experiment and produced some oval conchas. Then they produced a solid disc and soldered a loop on the back for lacing the conchas to the belt. The next change came with the development of dies in the 1880's; these brought about greater ornamentation of the concha (Fig. 5.7). Smiths who made the solid concha often used a male and female die to strike a raised pattern in the center, usually diamond shaped, and then decorated this with lines made with a cold chisel. Stamped decoration was added about the diamond and scalloped border. A rope-like pattern usually separated the two areas.

Turquoise settings were not used in Navajo conchas until around 1900, and they did not become common in such pieces until after 1920. Even now a good Navajo belt seldom has more than a single round or oval setting in a concha, and that one in the center. Adair reports the beginning of the use of a ring of small sets about the edge of the concha much later than 1920.[13] Since that time, and particularly after World War II, there has been a great variety of uses of turquoise in belts. Today as in the past the plain concha is more common.

About the time of the beginning of stamping, the Navajo also started using a small separate piece of silver between conchas. Commonly called a "butterfly," the piece is roughly hourglass in shape. Stamping or other decoration of this piece is often in keeping with the ornamentation of the conchas in the belt, although this is not always true.

The decoration of these conchas reflects the innate versatility of the Navajos. From the late 1930's the Navajos have varied the shape and size of the concha itself: they are large or small, round or oval, rectangular or square, all of these in the usual wrought (and sheet) workmanship. Varied forms are cast. Stones are sometimes not used at all, sometimes they appear singly or in great abundance. The cast piece may be minus any further decoration except for its own overall outline; often the conchas of this workmanship resemble cast brooches or buckles.

In wrought or sheet-silver conchas, there is today quite a variety of decoration (Fig. 5.8). The center section may be cut out in the usual diamond or lozenge shape, or occasionally in some other form, as an oval. If not cut out, it may be plain or perhaps in the shape of a very small, medium-sized, or very large raised diamond or circle. Sometimes the central theme deviates completely, becoming a flower-like pattern. Stamping may be added beyond the central motif in the form of a simple bordering pattern, or it may be much more elaborate and extend to the rope-like design separating center and edge of the concha. Seldom are two or more elements used in this central pattern.

The raised rope element parallels the edge of the concha, cutting off a narrow border. Into the rope are stamped short and usually diagonal parallel lines, or these lines may be straight or wavy zig-zags with a single pointed edge, or in some other simple geometric variation.

The typical Navajo concha today has a scalloped edge. Within this outline is usually a stamped scallop, although this feature may be omitted. There may or may not be stamped circles at the inner points of the scallop. Emanating from the rope and extending into or toward the scallop are three stamped lines, and between each set of lines is a small circular hole. There is some variation in these arrangements.

Bracelets

The most common and most varied piece made throughout the years by Navajo smiths has been the bracelet. This form may well have been inspired by types worn by northern Plains people and Indians of the Eastern United States. Of course there were also the early copper bracelets worn by Navajos, as mentioned above. These included pieces of heavy copper wire which were round or oval in cross section, bent to fit the wrist, and with little or no decoration. Others were the broad flat copper

FIGURE 5.7 Sketch of a typical concha used in belts. In the center is a raised boss (round, oval, diamond-shaped or a cut-out area of the same shape, plain or decorated). Then there is a wider or more limited smooth area. Next is the rope, a ridge with straight or diagonal lines cut into it. Last is the rim: alternating triple lines and circles — generally all the way through the silver — and scalloped at the rim. A stamped scallop is done inside the cut one and a stamped circle at the tip of each of the scallops. Large conchas are round or oval.

styles. Both were copied by the first workers in silver, the first in silver wire and the second in hammered or wrought technique (today in sheet silver). Another form which has been persistently popular is triangular in cross-section; from its inception, it has been decorated on its flat faces, with straight lines of the cold chisel in earliest times and with stamping in succeeding years. Another bracelet was made in quite early years, one in which heavy round wires of silver were twisted together. Triangular bracelets were combined sometimes with other forms to make composite styles.

These were the basic bracelet forms. Additions to, elaborations of, and use of new techniques in making these forms account for the tremendous variation which is common today.

Since most decoration on bracelets up to the 1880's was done with the cold chisel, file, or awl point, it was limited in quantity and the majority of it was straight lined. But the flat surface of the wide wrought or hammered bracelet invited stamped patterns, so after the acquisition of dies several elements were combined to produce varied designs. In time, curvilinear elements appeared and were used alone or in combination with straight lines. Decoration on the wrought bracelet was generally simple; often it was the repetition of a single element. Common themes for decoration included plain and complex crescents, triangles, chevrons, lines and bands, circles, dots, diamonds, and radiating elements.

After turquoise was first set in rings in the 1880's —or late 1870's — it became popular for bracelets (Fig. 5.8). The Navajo smith favors large oval or round forms but also uses square or rectangular pieces. A single stone, or a central turquoise with a smaller at each side, or a row of larger or graduated medium-sized stones have been and are the three most popular arrangements of settings in Navajo bracelets. When stones are used, there is less stamping, but seldom none at all.

Cast bracelets appeared about 1875 (Fig. 5.9). Generally, stamping was not and is not done on the better cast bracelet. Some of the most graceful of silver designing occurs in this technique and in bracelets. Forms run the gamut from a simple band with effective constrictions at regular points, to narrow or wide arrangements of simple or more elaborate, straight and/or curving openwork bands. A delicately curved S-figure is a basic motif; many cast bracelets are but simplifications or elaborations of this theme.

Wire bracelets, which appeared early in the history of Southwest Indian silver, have been revived on several occasions. One such revival occurred around the opening of the twentieth century. Some are still made today. The simplest wire bracelet is of heavy, round or square wire, with simple straight-lined patterns cut on with a file or cold chisel. Some of these were revived in the late 1930's in several of the Indian schools, and in the style of the earliest bracelet of this type.

Other variations of wire bracelets are made also. For example, two wires of lighter or heavier weights may be twisted together, or a lighter and a heavier wire are so joined. One wire may be twisted first, then joined with a plain one. A single twist of very heavy wire may support a single stone, or two or three such wires may be laid side by side and joined by soldering at the ends, with a stone or row of them set along a center strip. Other openwork arrangements are done with plain or twisted wire, to make for an endless array of bracelets of this type. Although some are heavy, many of them have the feeling of lightness of the cast bracelet but lack the delicacy and simplicity of design so characteristic of the latter.

Bracelets today are so numerous, so varied in form and decoration, that it would be impossible to do more than mention a few of them. There is the endless variety of thin, heavily stamped, and generally less artistic curio pieces. Widths vary from about one-half inch to several inches. To the basic stamped elements listed above may be added many ideas of white men, such as snakes, arrows, swastikas, and such. The chief differences between the curio bracelet and one of good quality can be summarized easily: The latter bracelet is heavier and well crafted; there is less stamping, with fewer elements on a single piece; and there is better total design.

Rings

Rings represent another early form of Navajo jewelry. The first ones were of plain silver, similar to those of the Plains tribes who, in turn, wore rings like those of the Indians of the eastern states. Plain bands of silver were made by the Navajos with low self-bezels which after a time were marked with simple designs scratched on with an awl. Still later the rings were stamped with dies. The first designs were copies of the same on brass and German silver rings received from the Plains Indians.

Although the first settings in rings appeared about 1880, these did not become common until around 1900. At first, high and crude bezels enclosed them, and small balls or drops of silver, often called "raindrops," were added in rows or

FIGURE 5.8 Some of the variety of forms in silver, with workmanship well represented also, by Navajos, Zuñis, Hopis, and Santo Domingans. (*Courtesy Read Mullan Gallery of Western Art, photo by Herb McLaughlin*)

FIGURE 5.9 Examples of Navajo necklaces, bracelets, brooches, buckles, and rings. Note the variety in techniques — wrought, cast, overlay — and in design. (*Photo by Ray Manley*)

clusters on either side of or around the stone. This general style has persisted to the present moment.

Before turquoise became popular as a setting — according to some beliefs — several other materials was used, among them glass, garnets, malachite, and cannel coal. The latter two materials were familiar to the natives, for they had been used in jewelry for centuries. Petrified wood became fairly popular in the 1930's; it was cut and polished by white men, for it was too hard for the native to work with his crude equipment.

As in other pieces of Navajo jewelry, stone was used sparingly in the earliest rings. Navajos have always favored one large stone (Figs. 5.8 and 5.9), preferably oval, although sometimes a square, a rectangular, or a round stone is used. A Zuñi cluster style has been more popular in recent years, particularly among Navajo women. Three or four stones in a vertical row is another popular arrangement in rings.

From simple beginnings the Navajo has expanded his work into a wide variety of ring forms. All of the styles of the past are made today, some with greater sophistication and technically much better.

Some of the plain rings are deeply stamped; many of them are cast. The Navajo sense of design asserts itself in the greater simplicity of the ring, for the smaller size of this piece denies the elaboration found in bracelets, brooches, and other larger forms.

Other varieties of modern rings include many with stones and some in new techniques of manufacture. Observed at the Navajo Arts and Crafts Guild in 1963 were many single-stone rings, with stones cut in all conceivable geometric shapes and some in free form. Some stones were surrounded by silver drops, some by rope. Bezels tended to be lower than in earlier work; stones were thinner in cross section. A dozen or more rings were done in the channel technique.

Earrings

Some interesting changes have occurred in the earrings of the Navajos. After the introduction of silver, the earliest types produced were reflections of eastern American Indian styles. Among them were plain wire loops, sometimes with one to three silver beads at the bottom; a crescent-shaped piece of silver to which was hinged a center drop or section; and flattened crescent-shaped pieces of wire with or without engraving or stamping. Another type was a long slender teardrop from which was suspended a tiny "squash blossom" with very short prongs. This last earring seems to have been inspired by the same shape which appeared as an ornament on Mexican clothing. These teardrops and blossoms have been found in California and in Mexico in association with capes and trousers. Woodward identifies them as pomegranates rather than squash blossoms.[14]

The large loop earring with one or several silver balls or beads at the bottom was a style popular among Navajo men until about the turn of the century. The style has been revived several times since then.

Navajo men, and the old longhairs in particular, turned to turquoise drops alone (Fig. 5.10) when this stone became more available. A large chunk was suspended from the pierced ear by a cotton string. These are still popular among the old men. Women, on the other hand, wore long strands or loops of small turquoise beads with bits of red shell at the bottom; some of these were five inches long. These did not last, however, for Navajo women took to the silver-turquoise combination and never have abandoned it. After the turn of the century, they wore the then-current Navajo earrings de-

scribed above, but with the growing popularity of Zuñi styles in the late 1920's and into the 1930's they came to favor the latter (Fig. 5.11). Popular among Zuñi-style earrings worn by Navajos are: single stones of oval, rounded, or square form surrounded by other stones and fancy wire work; one or two vertical or horizontal rows of stones surrounded by wire work, often with tiny pieces of vari-shaped, flattened silver suspended at the bottom; an exaggeration of the last style, with more and smaller

FIGURE 5.11 Sketch of Zuñi earring. Many small stones are used, in rows or clusters, and many dangles appear, in the form of rings, tiny squash blossoms, or rod-like pieces of silver. Navajo women wear these as well as Zuñis.

stones and with each horizontal row linked to the one above; and variations on any of these styles.

Commercialization of the earring has brought about a great many changes. One of the most important occurred in the late 1930's — the shift to a button-type earring. This catered to the taste of the white woman, and its popularity has never waned. Quite naturally, the first such earrings copied the old style or contemporary buttons made by the Navajos.

Then traders encouraged the smith in new directions in earrings. One of the most beautiful of the old styles, particularly when well-made, is the so-called "hogan" button (Fig. 5.18). It is a cone-shaped piece with wide or narrow and shallower or deeper depressions from the top of the cone to the outer rim. This earring and all other button types

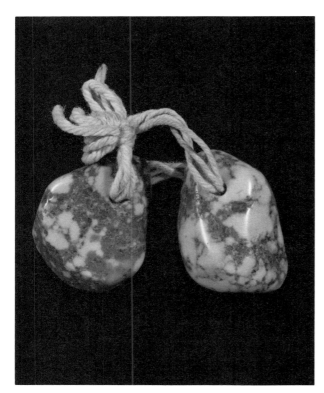

FIGURE 5.10 Navajo old-style turquoise earrings. These are merely chunks of choice stone which are drilled, and then a piece of cord is run through the hole. They are still favorites of the "longhairs."

have plain pieces of silver soldered to the back, and the findings, whether screw or clip, are attached to this plain surface.

Stamping occurred early on buttons, thus it was natural that it should appear on the button earring. This was one of the styles which the traders encouraged. Of course there is a great variation in craftsmanship and designing, and this earring type runs the gamut from very crude to extremely sophisticated, and from very small to quite large sizes. Designs vary from plain surfaces with but a single row of stamping near the edge to almost all-over stamping.

Charming life figures which the Navajos have borrowed from petroglyphs (Fig. 5.12) have been adapted to earrings. They are particularly appealing in the small sizes demanded of this piece. All forms adapted to silver are found in the earrings including deer, rabbits, men with elaborate head pieces, goats, the hunchbacked flute player, and the rainbow goddess.

Necklaces

Necklaces present an interesting and unusual chapter in Navajo silversmithing. The first beads were round, quite large in size, and plain. In time some plain beads were fluted, or the round form was depressed, or the bead was made in the form of a squash blossom. However, the plain round bead never lost its popularity, and to this day forms a fair part of the total squash-blossom necklace. Still another shape which has been popular from time to time, and particularly in more recent years, is the so-called "piñon" bead, an elongate style with four almost-flat faces.

Various bead shapes have been used in a variety of ways in necklaces worn by Navajos. Some of the oldest necklaces used plain beads alone in long strands. Through the years the Navajos have continued to make fine round or more oval beads. Coins, particularly dimes, had a shank soldered on the back or at the edge so that they could be strung with plain beads (or sewed onto garments). Some of the simple plain bead necklaces had a "naja," a crescent of silver, attached to the bottom. These are to be noted in early sketches and photographs of Navajo men and women. Then a few squash-blossom beads were added and later a few more. The squash-blossom necklace (Figs. 5.9 and 5.13) with its unusual beads and naja pendant has long been associated with this tribe, and certainly is most distinctive of them. It has become a popular commercial item.

The so-called "squash blossom" bead, as indicated above, is really a pomegranate blossom. This is evident in many of the old forms where the extremities of the bead are short and more out-flaring and the adjoining seed portion more bulbous. As time passed and artistic license played its role, many variations of the bead form developed. Originally symbolic to the Spanish, the blossom lost meaning as it passed through the Mexicans to the Navajo Indian. The stories told about the squash blossom necklace, particularly those pertaining to fertility, are strictly figments of the white man's imagination.

When first introduced to the Navajos, the naja was used as a decorative drop from the center of the horse's bridle. Navajos acquired it from the Mexicans who obtained it from the Spanish,[15] who, in turn, borrowed it from the Moors. The last two groups used this crescent as protection for horse and rider against the "Evil Eye." Apparently, the Navajos acquired no such symbolism along with the naja. Actually, "najahe" or "naja" means crescent in the Navajo language, and no doubt refers to the shape of the piece. The comments relative to lack of symbolism in the squash blossom necklace also apply to the naja.

Woodward claims a Plains origin for the Navajo silver headstall and the naja. However, his arguments for the latter, premised on the use of silver pendants on bridles by the Kiowa-Comanche in the early decades of the nineteenth century, are defeated by his statement, "The bridle trappings of the *conquistadores* no doubt carried these same traditional ornaments."[16]

The najas (Fig. 5.14) made by Navajos at first had a wide or narrow crescent form, and were usually plain, single, and without benefit of any stone. In time, however, they became elaborated in various ways. In some instances the single crescent became a wide band slightly rounded on the upper surface and with little or no taper towards the ends, or the single form was replaced by double or even triple crescents usually joined at the ends. These terminations are of interest, too, for some are undecorated points, some are blunted and stamped, others are hands, while some are covered with button-like pieces or set with turquoise. Sometimes from the interior center top of the naja a turquoise, a cross in silver, or some other small decorative feature is suspended. Above this, and on top of the naja, is a loop for suspension from the bridle or necklace; this loop is generally quite wide, plain, and fairly heavy. Rarely is it ornamented.

Mera feels that the najas which were used on bridles were simpler than those suspended from necklaces.[17] However, since many originally used on bridles were later used for necklaces, this would seem to be a questionable point. Furthermore, bridles are rarely made today, yet many of the necklace najas are extremely simple in design,

FIGURE 5.12 Navajo silver jewelry. Top left and right are rather typical brooches. The far-left pin in the second row is an old style; in the same row are two petroglyph pieces, a pendant representing a dancer in an elaborate head-piece (center) and a bird (parrot?) with his head turned back. Below, typical examples of good Navajo silver. (*Photos by Tad Nichols*)

FIGURE 5.13 A variety of silver work crafted by Navajos. The small ash trays and the box represent later developments in the overlay technique. All forms in the righthand group are older styles of concha belt, squash blossom necklace, buckle, bow guard, bracelet, and brooch. (*Photos by Ray Manley*)

particularly those from the Navajo Arts and Crafts Guild.

Many najas, both in the past and today, are cast, usually in a single piece. Some wider and thinner pieces are hammered or made from sheet silver. Stamping tends to be more common on the wrought type; if decorated, the cast pieces usually have filed patterns on them, although occasionally they may be stamped. In recent years, separate najas have been sold alone or on short strings of globular beads. They may have a pin attached on the back so that they can be worn as brooches, a further adaptation to make them more saleable.

In the main part of the squash blossom necklace, size and shape of the blossom vary from time to time and from one smith to another — early examples were often large and had short petals on the blossom. A round or nearly round bead is soldered to a flat shank which has a hole in it for stringing. Opposite the bead are the petals, soldered to the bead. Some of the short petals turn outward almost immediately beyond the bead, while others extend twice the length of the bead's size before flaring. There is considerable variation in the grace of proportions and degree of turning of the petals,

which sometimes are barely open and other times wide-spaced. There may be three or four petals. The bead of the blossom and the stem of the petals may be decorated, the former with flutings and the latter with filing. Rarely, a turquoise is subtly placed on the inner side of one of the petals.

One of the variations on the theme of the squash blossom is the fleur-de-lis (Fig. 5.9) which will be described later. A less attractive variation is a flat version occasionally made by the Navajos; this is commonly three-petaled and decorated with stamping. Crosses appear in necklaces (Fig. 5.8) in this same arrangement, but, since they were made for or by puebloans, they too will be discussed below. Another old style which has been revived in recent years is a horseshoe-shaped or tiny naja form of bead.

Buckles

When Navajos first made concha belts, they did not ornament them with a fine buckle as they do so often today. Rather, the first buckles were "very simple in form, small circular loops of silver with a crossbar holding the tongue in place."[18] As the Navajo smith developed his craft, he retained the

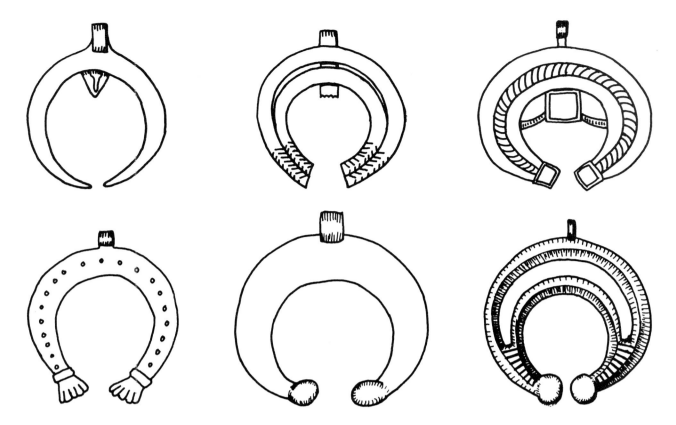

FIGURE 5.14 Sketches of a variety of naja types. In order they are: (a) plain, with pointed ends; (b) double, with blunt ends; (c) flat, with "rcpe" in the center and turquoises at the ends; (d) hand endings; (e) wide and plain; (f) a recent, double style. Today many plain silver najas are produced, and are worn as pendants or brooches.

functional character of the buckle but explored widely its decorative potentials. Buckles became larger or smaller circles, ovals, squares, and rectangles, solid except for the insertion of the tongue. Some resemble the conchas of the belt, with the same or different decoration, while others are entirely unrelated to it in shape or ornamentation. The central opening for the tongue varies from one just large enough to accommodate the fixture to very large ones which allow much of the leather strap to show.

Both wrought and cast techniques have long been popular in the making of buckles, with occasional repoussé fcr added decorative effect (Figs. 5.8, 5.9, and 5.13). The raised "bosses" in the repoussé style of work are usually rounded or oval. The buckle was always symmetrical in outline until the introduction of the white man's style. Hammered pieces usually carry stamped decoration, from simple to complex in nature, often resembling that of conchas and bracelets. Cast buckles generally feature the leaf pattern, again in simple or complex arrangements and open styles. Although both styles are often in plain silver, either may add a large single stone or several smaller ones. Like the Navajo concha, the buckle with many stones is a later product.

Ketohs

Perhaps one of the most interesting of the Navajo silver pieces is the bowguard or "gatoh" or "ketoh." After a guard was no longer needed to protect the wrist in shooting the bow, some ingenious fellow thought of converting the leather strap to an ornament. Here again copper fragments on the guard preceded the use of silver. Then to the wide leather band was secured a large piece of silver.

The first ketohs were rectangles bent to fit the wrist and with limited filed or stamped decoration (Fig. 5.13). Then cast pieces were made (Fig. 5.8); often these again repeated the corn leaf or S-shaped theme. One of the most popular cast styles of ketohs has four of these leaves emanating from a central motif and moving toward the corners of the piece. Supplemental and usually straight bars of silver take off from the center and terminate in the middles of the sides and ends. There may be additional straight or curling motifs, but, generally speaking, the design in ketohs is quite clean. A turquoise may be centrally placed, or there may be one at the center and one in each of the corners. This is one piece the Navajo has made for himself or for other Indians through the years; in fact, the bowguard, the canteen, and bridles are the pieces which have not been commercialized.

SILVER & JEWELRY 133

Brooches

In many respects, brooches or pins have resembled several other forms, especially the ketoh and some of the buttons, buckles, and conchas. Actually the first brooches were nothing more than enlarged buttons; this is particularly true of the simple conical style, plain, stamped, or fluted. Some of these large pieces had a loop soldered far up the under side. They were tied on the garment as were the buttons. It was not until about the end of the 1930's that the findings, the sharp-pointed pin and its necessary attachments, were made available in quantity to the Navajo; this transformed the large buttons into true brooches. In his summary of Southwestern Indian silver, Mera uses "Buttons and Small Conchas" as one of his headings.[19] This, of course, indicates the close connection between these forms — the button, small concha, and brooch. Also, in his 1944 publication, Adair refers to "Buttons and Pins" in one section on Navajo silver; however, he talks about buttons alone throughout his discussion except for one reference to brooches. This, too, reflects the close relationship between these two forms.

In addition to the simpler wrought types, and styles formed with the male and female dies, some cast buttons have been enlarged to become brooches. One of the most favored of this style is a spoke-wheel form. There are quite a few variations on this theme: some are closed smooth-edged wheels, while others have a scalloped edge. Some are open, with each spoke terminating in a circular blob. Others are star-shaped (Fig. 5.12). A central turquoise may be added. This brooch style, in the scalloped and the open-wheel versions, is still popular today.

Since the development of the Navajo Arts and Crafts Guild, cast brooches have become popular. These vary in size but average around 2 to 2½ inches in length. The favored ketoh theme, the corn leaf (Fig. 5.9), is extremely common in this brooch. There are, of course, many deviations from the basically simpler ketoh pattern.

Some wrought brooches are still made, and many of the more popular ones have quite a bit of stamping on them. Turquoise is more commonly used in this style today. One venture in cast brooches should be mentioned because it has become popular among some of the smiths for the Navajo Arts and Crafts Guild. It began in the 1940's, at Wide Ruins and Pine Springs, with some smiths making small silver copies of petroglyphs (Fig. 5.12). Delightful and active little characters they are, with a fair variety of subjects. Among them are dancing men, some with what appear to be tall ceremonial headpieces; dancing rabbits — or men with rabbit headdresses; birds of several varieties; and mountain sheep. As cast pieces, they are done in outline form. Although predominantly plain, a few have a well-placed, small turquoise added, for example, as an eye. This petroglyph pin style has been made into earrings, rings, pendants, and a few other pieces.

Buttons

Next to bracelets, buttons are one of the most numerous of the products of the Navajo smith. They have been popular as worn by the Navajos since they were first made in the early days of this craft. From the beginning, buttons have been decorative to the Navajo (Fig. 5.15). Buttons are sewed up and down the front of the blouse, outlining the collar, and up and down sleeves, but not a one serves any utilitarian purpose. In fact, topping those at the front of the woman's blouse might be a large and sturdy safety pin! Buttons do not commonly appear on men's shirts. However, they are used on their moccasins, on their shoulder straps and pouches, and on their bowguards.

Buttons are extremely varied in form, size, and decoration (Fig. 5.18). At first they were fairly large, slightly convex, and with two holes in the center for attachment to the garment. Used in early years for buttons were Mexican and American coins; of the latter, dimes and quarters were — and still are — most popular. Occasionally half dollars might be used. In 1962, dollars were observed being used to fasten and decorate the sides of a Zuñi dress. In these instances the coin is left in its natural state, with a loop soldered to the back.

From the beginning to the present, the two most popular shapes of buttons have been rounded and conical, with a number of variations of each type. They run the gamut from perfectly plain, unstamped examples to elaborately stamped pieces. Cast buttons, wheel-like and with radiating spokes and round or oval in form, have enjoyed continued popularity.

Conical and hemispherical buttons are made by pounding the silver into molds of wood or metal. Through the years decoration followed contemporary trends, with a few special developments here and there. Early decoration was etched, scratched, filed on, or made by striking with a cold chisel. Many later buttons simulated some of this earlier decoration. In some cases buttons were made

FIGURE 5.15   Variation in quality of turquoise is well illustrated in this woman's selection of jewelry. She wears one necklace of a clear blue and a second that is much greener in color. The same applies to the bracelets on her right wrist. The blanket she wears is a Pendleton — these women do not wear the products of their own loom. (*Photo by J. H. McGibbeny*)

in conical form from a coin; the inscription on the under side was left, but on the upper side it was obliterated and some simple decoration was added.

Adair notes that the button had not been commercialized as of the date of his research in 1938.[20] However, in the early 1940's some traders became interested in this piece. Perhaps one reason the button had never been popular among whites was because the shank for fastening was buried far up under the cone or rounded portion of the piece. Several traders urged the Indian to bring the shank out beyond the rim of the button so that it could be sewed to a garment without all the circumvention practiced by the Navajo woman. The Indian woman ran a piece of cloth through the high shank and secured the cloth to the garment, or she sewed it to her blouse through a tedious process of threading and unthreading a needle.

Although the origin of buttons is uncertain, Woodward is convinced that they are derived from Spanish-Mexican sources. He sees this derivation in comparable shapes, such as flat, domed, and conical pieces. Moreover, Woodward finds comparisons in decoration; in fact, he says that the Navajo used "every single one of these types" — referring to Mexican styles.[21] Of particular interest are fluted and punched styles.

Bridles

A rather unusual development took place among the Navajos in the making of silver bridles. Perhaps this can be explained in the fact that the horse had great prestige value for the men of this tribe — silver trappings augmented this value. If a fellow could not afford a headstall with silver he might use conchas alone.

Woodward and Adair disagree as to the origin of the bridle, the former attributing it to the Southern Plains Indians, and the latter to the Spanish-Mexican. The second idea seems more logical in the face of the origin of other pieces, particularly the naja. Since the naja was early attached to the bridle, it would seem illogical that one was adopted and not the other. Of course, there is the possibility of influences from both directions.

In general, the bridle (Fig. 5.8) is composed of seven to thirteen parts.[22] A number of wide bands of silver are mounted on the leather by bending the metal edges over, by the use of bars soldered on the backs of the silver pieces, or by loops which run through a slit in the leather and are held in place by a small fragment of the same. There is slight variation in the form of these pieces. The center top bar may be perfectly rectangular or it may have a projection on its lower side with a hole through it from which hangs the naja (Fig. 5.16). At either side of this ornament there may be one or

two pieces; if two, the one closer to the center is quite small. The end pieces are part of or soldered to the topmost vertical cheekstrap decoration. The second cheekstrap piece is almost invariably a concha. Below the concha are two leather straps, the front one ornamented with a bar of silver which tapers at its lower end, while a second piece, partially under the first, is covered with a rectangular bar of silver. The latter has a loop at the end for the attachment of the bit.

Variations in the bridle occur in many details. Sometimes there are extra units, such as a small, elongate or oval piece between the concha and the tapering unit below. Decoration of each piece presents the greatest variation. In general it follows the usual styles through the years of etched, filed, and stamped designs. However, the bridle rarely is ornate in its decoration. Simple stamping at the ends and/or edges of the silver bars is the most common decorative device; occasionally the ends of some of the pieces are scalloped. Bridle conchas and naja also reflect the design styles of their particular time. The tip of the tapered bar carries some type of decoration, often a single or multiple rounded unit with filed or stamped decoration.

Stones are used sparingly in bridles. One example shows turquoise in the center top and at the ends of the naja, in the centers of the conchas, and in the tip of the tapered unit.

Today bridles are rarely made, and then only for sale. The horse is losing — if it has not lost — its

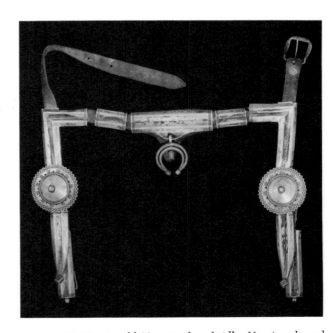

FIGURE 5.16 An old Navajo silver bridle. Varying-shaped pieces were crafted to fit the long leather straps, yet each was designed to fit into the whole. A hole was made in the center piece for suspension of the naja (probably the place where this piece was first used). A concha on each side strap is typical.

prestige value to the pickup truck. Moreover, the bridle involves a great amount of work, and therefore has to sell for a high price; thus it has never proved to be a popular commercial item. For the most part the contemporary bridle lacks the beauty of design and craftsmanship of the old piece.

Miscellaneous

A great variety of silver items fit into this miscellaneous category. This applies to earlier years as well as to today. Among the pieces made in past years were canteens, mother-in-law bells, tweezers, pouches, hatbands, gunpowder chargers, and decorative pieces for garments. None of these objects was made in abundance except the last — some are no longer made. Recent and contemporary pieces will be discussed later.

Leather pouches (Fig. 5.17) were worn by Navajo men, but gradually have been abandoned except for ceremonial use. A leather strap, decorated usually with buttons along its length, was suspended diagonally from shoulder to opposite hip, and the pouch was fastened to the strap. The flap of the pouch was ornamented with a central small or large button, a "butterfly," or a concha; a row of smaller buttons might then be attached on the face of the bag all the way around, on only three edges, or at the bottom alone. Again there was considerable variation in this decoration. These pouches are rarely made today; when they are, it is in the old style.

FIGURE 5.17 Navajo medicine man's pouches. On the right is an old one with a plain strap and the pocket flap decorated with two large matched buttons, one medium-sized and different, and six matched small ones. The new pouch (left) has sixty-two "hogan" buttons on the strap, and matched buttons (in two sizes) on the W-shaped pocket flap. Both are made of leather.

A small bell (Fig. 5.18) was formerly made, and sometimes worn by older women to warn their sons-in-law of their whereabouts, a reflection of the Navajo taboo against a woman and her son-in-law looking directly at or speaking to each other. The bells were of simple, open form and usually had a bit of stamping about the rim of the piece. Reputedly they were worn at the women's waist.

Canteens (Figs. 5.8 and 5.18) are thought to be either copies of the American soldiers' water containers,[23] or replicas of the Mexican tobacco case of leather, copper, or brass.[24] They represent one of the most attractive pieces of Navajo silver craft work and were early prized by the Indian for tobacco.[25] It is possible that they were made for the soldiers at army camps on the reservation; thus they may represent, along with powder chargers and buttons, the first "curio" items in silver made by the Indians of the Southwest. They are rarely produced today, for they are not only difficult to make but also they serve no particular purpose except as a collector's item. The canteen is generally about 3 inches in diameter; some may be larger, some smaller. It is difficult to solder the two domed pieces together; where they are joined, the binding line is covered with a twist or braid of wire. A short neck is soldered to the top of the piece; into this fits a lid which is a ring of silver with a button top. The lid is secured by means of a chain; in turn, the chain is fastened through a loop high on the canteen edge.

Designs on canteens vary greatly, ranging from quite simple to fairly elaborate. One old piece has a deer etched on one domed surface, and a rabbit on the other;[26] some have centered flower-like patterns or scalloped themes. An interesting deviation from the more typical Navajo styles of design just mentioned are radiating lines and bands, these emanating from a central boss or round stone. One example of this style has two equidistant, deep and plain lines alternating with adjacent double bands filled with chevrons. A second has a more elaborate alternation of comparable themes.

Because the Navajo is predominantly Mongoloid, he has little facial hair, and tweezers suffice to care for the removal of this scanty growth. Makeshift devices were used for years, but when metal was introduced to this tribe they began to make some of their tweezers of this more efficient material. Technically, these were very simple — just a flat piece of silver, about an inch in width, bent back against itself, and with the usual stamped patterns for decoration (Fig. 5.19). More popular than silver for these pieces was brass, for it was a sturdier metal, particularly for this special use. Tweezers are still made and used by the Navajos.

Hatbands (Fig. 5.18) were early made of silver.

FIGURE 5.18 Miscellaneous Navajo silver pieces. An old necklace (a) with even-armed crosses and a naja decorated with hands. A silver hatband (b) decorated with three bands of repeated diagonal lines. The miniature canteen (c) (3″ in diameter) is set with a stone and has a radiating pattern and removable lid. Several styles of buttons (d) are illustrated here; smooth-surfaced, domed, dime, hogan (crenulated), and stamped. The mother-in-law-bell (e) is small and decorated; it was worn by a Navajo woman to warn her son-in-law of her whereabouts.

Although their origin is unknown, it is probable that they were inspired by the beaded or horsehair bands which came into the Southwest from the Plains and Mexico. Thin strips of silver about an inch in width are bent to fit the hat; they are stamped with simple geometric designs the length of the piece. A slide in the form of a butterfly or decorative button holds them in place. Hatbands have found slight favor as commercial items; a few have been sold as belts for slim-waisted girls! Adjustment of size is possible in a few of these bands as they have several holes at one end through which a small tongue on the opposite end may be inserted.

Reputedly, quite a few gunpowder measures (Fig. 5.19) were made in early days; they became obsolete with the development of better guns and have not been made in later years. An elongate piece, tapering toward a constricted middle, had a scoop-like opening at the end of one half, while the other half was stamped and terminated in a bit of decoration. These measures were attached to silver chains by loops soldered near the mid-point. Adair reports that after they were no longer used many of them were melted and made into other pieces; this may explain their scarcity today, even in museum collections.

Ornamental pieces have been made through the years to be attached to the woman's blouse for decoration (Fig. 5.19). Although the majority may be described as roughly rectangular, there is a great deal of variation in the shapes of these pieces. The butterfly, often inserted between conchas in belts, is a favorite form. Plain rectangles with stamped patterns, oblongs with one straight and one scalloped edge and with dangling pieces suspended from the latter, rectangles which are scalloped all around — all with stamping or other decoration

over the surface — these are but a few of the variations on this popular piece. Sometimes a row of dimes is soldered to a wire base to serve as a decorative piece. Other dress ornaments resemble brooches in their form and decoration. Generally, all of these pieces are made in pairs, one to be worn on each side of the blouse. Triangular-shaped pieces, with a cut-out inner corner, are crafted to fit the tips of collars. In decoration, these pieces reflect the style of the day. Turquoise is added sometimes, but the majority of the garment ornaments are devoid of stones.

There is such a variety of miscellaneous pieces made today by Navajo silversmiths that it would be impossible to even list all of them. It should be kept in mind that not only are craftsmen plying their trade on the reservation but also quite a few members of this tribe now live and work in various Southwestern cities — in Phoenix, Tucson, Scottsdale, Albuquerque, Santa Fe, and others. Often they are subject to the whims of their clientele and the smith may produce a sophisticated free-form choker necklace as quickly as a squash blossom type. As a matter of fact, no one person could know all the varieties and kinds of objects produced by the Indian smith today; certainly this does not make the pieces any less "Indian." This is especially true of Navajo work, for the imagination and versatility of this tribesman in his craft expressions make possible almost any deviation from the old styles as well as a variety of new inventions.

Since the commercialization of Indian silver, boxes have been very popular, those with hinged lids being favored (Fig. 5.13). They vary in size from tiny pill boxes, through stamp sizes, to cigarette and jewelry varieties. Smaller boxes have been more popular with the Navajos, while larger ones have more commonly been made by the Zuñis. Forms vary, including square, long or short oblong, round, and oval. Decoration is also quite varied, ranging from a beautifully finished plain surface to heavily stamped top and sides. Stones may or may not be used, and if they are, the rule is a single one. Some of the most attractive of these boxes have a single band of well-executed design close to the edge. Although this form is foreign to the Navajo background, the decorative motifs on boxes are the same as those found on typical Navajo styles, such as belts, bracelets, and others.

Flatware was produced in small quantities during the 1930's although some individual pieces — baby spoons and forks, for example — go back to earlier years. Most authors dismiss the subject of these and comparable forms with a stigmatic "curio piece;" therefore there is all too little documentation regarding flatware. Flatware is still not too popular, although baby spoon and fork sets, salad

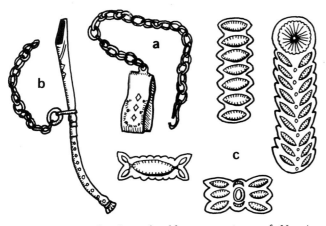

FIGURE 5.19 Sketches of seldom-seen pieces of Navajo silver. A wide piece of silver was bent back against itself to form tweezers (a) with which to pull out the scant facial hair of the Navajo. In the early days, a gunpowder measure (b) was used by the Navajos; some were made of silver and ornamented in this fashion. In place of buttons, pieces of silver of various forms (c) were stamped and attached to the woman's blouses for added decoration.

forks and spoons, letter openers, iced tea spoons, and other individual pieces are made today in considerable abundance. The best of the salad servers (Fig. 5.20) are decorated in a simple but sophisticated manner, usually with stamped patterns.

Quite naturally a complete service in flatware would represent too much of an investment for any but the most interested clientele; therefore such sets are rarely produced. Here, as in most costly ventures, trader sponsorship and financial backing are essential. A handsome flatware service for twelve was exhibited at the Gallup Ceremonials in 1963. Both design and craftsmanship were outstanding. Except for baby sets, stones are rarely used in flatware, and then it is typically a single turquoise at the end of the fork or iced tea spoon. Since the development of channel, more stones have been used in flatware; this is discussed under Zuñi silversmithing.

Navajos have employed the overlay technique

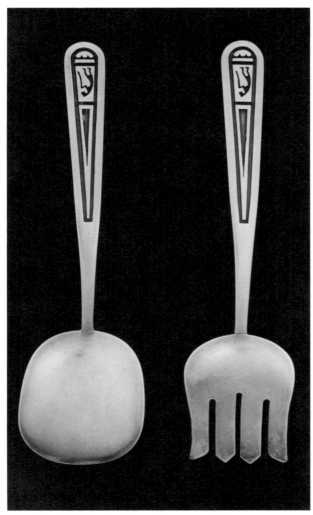

FIGURE 5.20 Navajo flatware silver. A salad fork and spoon are worked in overlay technique. Geometric themes are combined with a prehistoric subject, the hunched-back flute player.

in quite a bit of flat silver. A salad set (Fig. 5.20) is illustrative of this style of decoration. A simple line follows the oval of the fork and spoon ends and tapers to a cut-off point about two-thirds of the way down the handle. This black line is set in a quarter of an inch from the edge and encloses a combination of a single life element and several geometrics. The technique lends sophistication to the pleasing design.

The silver craft is a healthy one among the Navajos today. Much fine work comes into the Navajo Arts and Crafts Guild at Window Rock. Too, there are traders who employ Navajos of their respective locales in the production of jewelry and other silver. Some of these Indians are employed in off-reservation towns and cities, largely in Arizona and New Mexico. Adair estimated that there were 600 Navajo smiths in 1940;[27] the number today could well be the same or more.

Pawn Jewelry

"Pawn" is a subject which holds a great deal of interest for a number of people. Among the Navajos pawn is primarily jewelry which is left with the trader as "credit." For many years these Indians have put their wealth in silver rather than converting it into money; indeed, they call silver, turquoise, and shell "hard goods." Under the pawn system a man leaves an item, a silver belt, for example, at the trader's and borrows large or small amounts against it, once or many times; or he may use it for trading for food, clothing, or other items. He may redeem the pawn in a single deal or in many small "payments." This redemption may be in the form of a check for labor, a rug, sheep's wool, or anything else of value that the trader will accept. The trader is required by law to keep pawn for a designated period of time before it becomes "dead" and can be sold.

Some individuals have the mistaken idea that "old" pawn (roughly of twenty-five or more years ago) is better than "new" pawn, and that all old pawn is valuable. But in the past, poor as well as good jewelry was pawned; by the same token, not all new pawn is poor. Perhaps far less pawn goes dead today, for the economic situation of the Navajo is much better than it was in the past. Furthermore, although there was much lovely jewelry to be bought in pawn, work of equally fine craftsmanship and artistry is made specifically to sell to the trader.

Zuñi

A Zuñi by the name of Lanyade learned smithing from a Navajo. As a result of this contact and teaching, early forms, design styles, and settings were all similar to those of contemporary Navajo work. It should be mentioned particularly that the Zuñis first produced plain silver, then used large stones in their work, two situations which contrast quite vividly with present trends. It seems natural, however, that the change to and preoccupation with varied and small stones rather than emphasis on silver work eventually occurred at Zuñi, for much of their designing in other lines is not only varicolored but also patterned in many small repeated units.

From about 1830-1840, the Zuñis did metal crafting in copper and brass; then in the year 1872, according to their first smith Lanyade, they began the use of silver.[28] Around 1890, turquoise was added. Although they have changed the details of their craft several times, the Zuñis have favored the use of this stone in most of their work. In a limited number of pieces they have used nothing but shell or coral; but to this day they still employ large quantities of turquoise in most of their silver.

Some of the Zuñi craftsmen do good metal work, but to a majority of them it is the stone that counts, the metal serving only to hold the pieces in position; yet their best metalsmiths are as capable as any in this work. To illustrate their lack of interest in the process of working silver it might be mentioned that for many years Navajos have done some or all of the metal work for certain pieces, while the Zuñis set the stones in the same. Years ago it was not uncommon for a Navajo to make a box and the Zuñi to then do the elaborate mosaic for the top of it; more recently in one situation, Navajos did quite a bit of channel silver and Zuñis cut and set the stones in these same pieces.

In the overall history of this craft among the Zuñis, the dominant technique has been and still is wrought silver with stones set in bezels, although, of course, there have been changes through the years. In the beginning there were large stones in high bezels, for this was the current style in the early days of contact between Navajo and Zuñi smiths. Some shift to smaller stones was made about the turn of the century; by 1910 every piece was set with turquoise.[29] But it was not until the twenties and thirties that the Zuñis used more and more really small stones; also, by this time the bezels were not quite so high. Where a Navajo would use one or three turquoises, the Zuñi would employ a dozen or more; where the Navajo was satisfied with a single row of stones, the Zuñi might have three or more rows. The Navajo often favored a single large stone, while the Zuñi would cluster a group of smaller ones around the larger piece. Earlier Navajo eardrops were all silver; Zuñis often elaborated the earring with rows or clusters of stones.

Then came World War II and the assignment to Indians of a priority to acquire silver and to produce jewelry because it was a source of their livelihood. This, plus electricity, plus other influences encouraged the Zuñis to accelerate production. From a technical viewpoint, the coming of electricity may also have inspired some of these smiths to do finer work. Be that as it may, it was about this same time that the Zuñis produced the first needlepoint — slender stones pointed at each end (Figs. 5.21 and 5.22) — and other very small stone work.[30] The beauty of the best Zuñi work today is reflected in perfectly cut stones which may be equally flawless in size and color in a single fine piece of jewelry.

Stones, coral, and shell are the center of interest of the Zuñi smith, and they are handled in a number of ways. In addition to the needlepoint technique, turquoise is also used in equally small or even smaller sizes of various shapes — round, oval, square, rectangular, triangular, and a few others. All of these pieces are mounted in a plain or crenulated bezel, with a separate thin silver frame for each fragment of stone or shell. All bezels, including the tiniest, must be hand crenulated. There is more variety in the shape of turquoise than that of any other material. With this emphasis on the individual stone, it is rather natural that channel work found favor in the eyes of the Zuñi smith.

Related to the use of small stones — and many of them — is the Zuñi penchant for the addition of drops of silver, tiny silver dangles (on earrings), and fine plain or twisted wire surrounding stones. Dangles take the form of squares or rectangles, round or oval pieces, long thin pieces with a round end, or in some cases, miniature squash blossoms. Plain wire is commonly looped in various ways about a central stone, often giving a Mexican filigree effect to much of this Zuñi silver.

A late technique which has become a favorite at Zuñi for commercial developments has been named channel (Figs. 5.21 and 5.22). Starting in a simple and limited manner about 1940, the Zuñis have developed this technique to a point of perfection. This work is characterized by a number of features. A solid or hollow silver base has arranged on its top or within it a number of thin strips of silver, each standing on edge, and all of them forming honeycomb-like boxes or pockets. These vary in shape according to the pattern designed by the smith. Into each box he places a thin piece of turquoise, or other material, each cushioned and imbedded in an adhesive. Every piece of turquoise, other stone, or shell is completely surrounded by metal, thus giving an intricate and definitive appearance to the relationship of silver and stones in the finished piece. Channel materials may be set in one or more rows of square, rectangular, triangular, or varied geometric shapes. Bracelets, rings, and earrings are the favored forms for this work.

Generally, the casting of silver has never been popular with the Zuñis. One evidence of this disinterest is the fact that a Zuñi smith commonly will sell filings and scrap silver in Gallup, there to be bought by Navajos who will use the materials in casting. However, Zuñis have always done some work in this technique, and in recent years several smiths have produced fine cast work and a fair quantity of it. Zuñi cast pieces include bracelets, necklaces, belts and brooches.

Certainly the Navajo and Zuñi smiths each struck their own stride in silver work early in the nineteenth century. Thereafter each directed his major efforts toward the refinement of his particular interest, with some experimentation along the way. Up to about 1920, Zuñi silver was made primarily for Zuñis, Navajos, and other Indians. Beginning about this time, a little white trade started, and after 1930, this became one of the strongest influences on the Zuñi craftsman, for he designed much of his work for sale to white customers.

One major difference still exists in the silver craft at Zuñi as illustrated at their December, 1962, Shalako Ceremonial. It is customary for the people, both ceremonialists and other villagers, to wear quantities of jewelry at this time and also to display it in the ceremonial rooms. The preponderance of turquoise or turquoise and silver in large pieces with many settings indicates the Zuñis' personal preferences along these lines (Fig. 3.8). Outstanding pieces seen at this ritual were bowguards (often two were worn by one man), many jaclahs suspended from a single turquoise necklace (more than twelve on one Shalako dancer!), loop earrings of turquoise or turquoise with a little shell, squash blossom necklaces, and cluster bracelets. Always the silver was ornamented with turquoise — even the belts were decorated with multiple stones. Greatly refined and tiny stone work was not in evidence; this supports the idea that small stone work is one of the chief avenues of commercialization at Zuñi. Even the Zuñi work most popular among the Navajos is seldom of the very finest and smallest type, for Navajos prefer more abundant stones and a slightly heavier treatment of them.

Two examples of the finest work well illustrate the Zuñi trend in small stone work. One, a ring less than an inch in width and just an inch in length, has ninety tiny round turquoises on its surface. Incidentally, there is a gentle curve in the form of the ring so that it would better fit the finger. Another is a bracelet with the area for settings

just under 1½ inches wide and 2 inches long, including silver drops at the sides. Within these dimensions are five rows of needlepoint stones, each row containing 24 stones for a total of 120 in the piece. Stones are well matched for color and shape; bezels are perfectly cut; there are tiny silver drops at each side of every stone, slightly larger ones between rows and at the outer edges, and large silver drops at the ends of each row of stones. Simple but well-executed stamping appears on the silver bands extending from each row of turquoise to the end of the bracelet. Both of these pieces represent the best of silver and lapidary craftsmanship. Today Zuñi women smiths are responsible for some of the finest of this work.

Mosaic (Figs. 5.21, 5.22, and 5.23) has long been favored by the Zuñis; in fact, when excavating their prehistoric ancestral home of Hawikuh, Hodge found shell, turquoise, and jet pieces in this technique. An important phase of revival occurred in mosaic in 1935 when Hodge asked Teddy Weake (also Meahke), a Zuñi smith, to make some mosaic pieces.[31] Mosaic is important not just for itself but also because it surely had some influence on the development of channel and, perhaps, on other styles. Much of the Zuñi mosaic is nothing more than overlay; erroneously it is called inlay.

In mosaic, small fragments of various shapes are stuck in an adhesive on a flat surface. For the shell, bone, or other bases of prehistoric times, the Zuñi now substitutes silver in most cases, although some mosaic on shell is still made. In the metal work there is an outer band encasing the entire pattern. The obvious difference between mosaic and channel is that in the former the stones are juxtaposed while in the latter, as described above, each stone is separated from every adjoining stone by a silver band.

Outlines of mosaic pieces today are in simple geometric or life forms. In the former, circles and ovals are common. In the latter category are real-life figures and also those from mythology. The dragon-fly is recognizable among the few real-life forms; the double cross is thought to simulate the conventional form of this dragon-fly. Much more popular are ceremonial dancers — buffalo and antelope figures, among others — or mythical subjects, such as Knife-wing god and any of the kachinas, Fire god, Big Horn, Shalako, and Mud Heads, for example. Other subjects include pueblo boys and girls, horses, eagles, and mountain sheep. The head or the full figure of any of these may be repre-

FIGURE 5.21 A variety of Zuñi silver techniques and forms. Cluster arrangements of stones are represented in the upper right and central (middle row) necklaces, lower-left bracelet, and the middle of the three belts. The bracelet in the center of the top row is channel and the two brooches immediately below it are in mosaic style; in all three pieces, shell, turquoise, coral, and jet are used. (*Photo by Joseph Muench*)

sented. Three or four colors and materials are often used in this work — white, pink, or red shell, turquoise, jet, and coral. Very recently a trader in Gallup introduced tortoise shell to the Zuñis, and they are using it as background for the mosaic or within the figure. It offers additional texture, quality, and color, and its pleasing opaqueness adds depth.

It is amazing how small some of the parts of these mosaics can be. The tiny eye of a figure may measure one-thirty-second of an inch in diameter! This means the Indian lapidary must cut the stone to this size on his wheel. Often mask decoration or costume detail must be cut in irregular pieces. Perhaps the best of these mosaics attest to the skill of the Zuñi lapidary more than anything else. Not only are the pieces perfectly cut but also the careful workmanship makes it possible to fit each piece smoothly and flawlessly against the others.

Another artistic expression of pre-Columbian days which has been significant in Zuñi jewelry is that of carving small figures in turquoise or other materials. Fetishes were and still are carved in stone and sometimes decorated with tiny insets of turquoise or other colored materials. When the figure is not to be set in silver the carving may be either flat or in the round; when it is to be set in metal it may be flat or, at least, it has a flat back to facilitate mounting. In earlier years, a dragon fly or other simple form was carved of turquoise, then set on silver with a metal bezel holding the single piece of stone, and with decorative metal work beyond the bezel and outlining the figure's form. Another style involved making a figure in silver and then setting several stones on its body. From these simpler beginnings, in stone and silver, the Zuñi turned more and more to the true mosaic types described above. Very few carved stone and silver combinations have been produced through the years.

It is obvious that the forms of Zuñi silver, in general, would follow those made by Navajos, first because the craft was learned from them, and secondly because the Zuñi has long produced much of the silver worn by the Navajos.

In early years, bracelets, buttons, earrings, and belts were popular. Zuñis wore bowguards before they did silvercrafting; some of these were decorated with bits of tin or brass just as were those of the Navajos. After Zuñis learned to work in silver, they applied this material to the wrist guard. Beautiful and large manta pins, used to fasten the woman's blanket dress down the sides, were made in fairly early times but are rarely produced today. The squash blossom necklace was borrowed from

the Navajo but after turquoise was used, the Zuñi so completely buried it under the stone that it is hardly recognizable as such (Figs. 5.21, 5.22, and 5.23). Somewhere along the way the fleur-de-lis was substituted for the squash blossom, and in time it became something of a favorite. On some old Zuñi pots there is a pattern which resembles this French motif, and it is quite possible that such was its source for silver design.

Although the Zuñi has "invented" only a few new forms, such as the cluster, he has demonstrated great originality in the variety of styles which he has produced. This is reflected in the head and figure forms in mosaic, in the development of brooches, particularly the manta pin, and in the application of all techniques to each form and in new uses (i.e., for necklaces), or old carved forms (Fig. 5.24). Beautiful buckles are made today in channel; dainty pins are executed in the fine, small stone work not done by any other tribe. Large and small crosses are crafted in all Zuñi techniques. Although the general concept of a necklace may have been borrowed, the Zuñi has again demonstrated originality in delicate choker styles of leaves, flowers, and other creations in small stone work (Fig. 5.8).

Hopi

Two differing stories tell how the Hopis acquired silversmithing. One story has it that a Zuñi Indian, the previously mentioned Lanyade, went to visit his Hopi friend Sikyatala in the village of Sichomovi on First Mesa and taught him the silver craft.[32] A second version credits the same Hopi with trotting over the well-worn trail to Zuñi where he learned this craft.[33] But wherever he learned, the consensus is that a Zuñi taught a Hopi the craft of silver working in the year 1898. Sikyatala first made jewelry and sold it to a nearby trader or to his tribesmen. He is also credited with teaching several other Hopis how to do this work. By 1904 the craft was being practiced on Second Mesa at Shongopovi, and by 1907 at Old Oraibi on Third Mesa.[34]

Early silver styles and technology among the Hopis followed the Navajo tradition. The Hopis continued this style for years, and still produce some work more like the Navajo than that of any other tribe. In the late 1930's, the Museum of Northern Arizona attempted to inspire Hopi smiths with designs which had been adapted from their other tribal crafts. Not too much change resulted from this experiment but enough to reveal potentials along these lines.

FIGURE 5.22 All varieties of Zuñi jewelry are illustrated here: plain and chunk bead work in shell, coral, and turquoise (top right); channel in turquoise (middle right); mosaic in turquoise, jet, shell, and coral (top left and center, bottom center); needlepoint in necklace, bracelets, and brooches (bottom right). (Photo by Ray Manley)

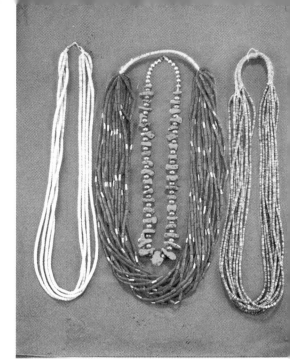
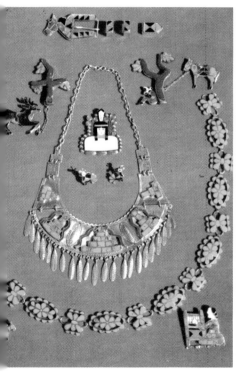
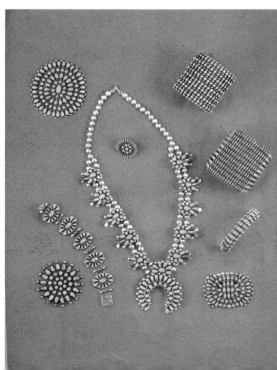

It was not surprising, then, that early in 1947 a similar experiment was inaugurated, this time in the hands of the Hopis themselves. First the high school was used as a shop, then a quonset hut was set up in New Oraibi. Paul Saufki, a fine smith, was in charge of teaching young Hopi veterans in an on-the-job-training program. Fred Kabotie, the outstanding Hopi artist for years, served as designer at least long enough to get the trainees started. Several such groups of ex-service men went through the training program, and some of them have continued the production of silver. Some new techniques were developed and fresh and vital designing characterized their work.

In 1944, Adair reported that there were about twelve Hopi silversmiths. This number did not change much until the post-World War II venture when a larger number of men took part in the training program. Nineteen men graduated from the first class while a few more were in the second class. Not all of these smiths have kept up with the craft, so the number of silver workers again decreased; actually the number fluctuates from year to year.

Through trade with the Navajos and Zuñis, the Hopis have obtained much of the silver which they have worn through the years, even though some of their tribesmen have pursued the craft. This, coupled with the fact that silver never became the economic factor among the Hopis that it did among both Navajos and Zuñis, contributed to their limited development of silver work. Most of the traders among the Hopis are native tribesmen who do not have the finances to back such an expensive venture as silver working. The largest white trader, Lorenzo Hubbell, ceased to handle silver in the second decade of this century. Thus there were few or no ready sources of raw materials and only limited outlets for the finished products of the Hopi smith.

This problem was not alleviated until the establishment of the Hopi Silvercraft Guild right after the graduation of the first class of G. I. trainees. The Guild made possible the purchase of materials at wholesale prices; with this, advantages accrued to the smiths. Moreover, the craftsman did not have to pay for his materials until his silver work was sold.

Although influenced to some degree by the Zuñis, the Hopis have never used the very small-stone style of jewelry production. Small silver forms (Fig. 5.25) have prevailed through the years, particularly bracelets, buttons, and rings; apparently these had copper and brass prototypes. Even before the G. I. training program, belts, bowguards, and other larger pieces were rarely made. Bracelets have been and remain the featured article, perhaps because they are the best-selling item. Now buckles and brooches have become more popular; necklaces, particularly choker types, are made in fair numbers; some rings and earrings are crafted; belts with small and varied conchas are more abundantly produced than formerly; and a few other items, such as hollow ware and pendants for necklaces, have been added.

Interesting techniques were and are featured by the Hopis in their school and in the Guild products. Foremost among these is overlay (Fig. 5.26). Several young Hopi men on Second Mesa have developed a craft enterprise where they feature a sophisticated adaptation of their native designs executed largely in the overlay technique. Not only does the craftsmanship reflect great skill but also the finish on the silver is superior. By using a brush technique, that is, polishing with fine steel wool, they attain a pleasing soft sheen on all pieces. This overlay and the Hopi Guild work have both been well received.

In a pamphlet which he issued in 1950, Fred Kabotie describes copper inlay, another technique used by the Hopi smiths. In this the same steps are followed as for overlay through the cutting of the design in one piece. Then a piece of copper is cut to fit perfectly into this space. Kabotie says that the "copper is placed in the cutout design of the overlay and the whole is soldered together. The medium is difficult to handle because of the difference in melting points of the metals."[35]

"Cut-out" is another category in the Hopi silver techniques listed by Kabotie. This is done with a single piece of silver; the design is simply cut out, as for the top overlay piece, and this is the finished object. Many necklaces, some brooches, and earrings are made in this technique.

Although little or no casting was done in earlier years by Hopi smiths, this has become a popular technique with the advent of the school and Guild developments. The entire procedure is the same as described for the Navajos. Buckles are often made in this way, as well as some brooches, a few bracelets, and some rings (Fig. 5.25).

Turquoise and stamping are both employed by the Hopis for decoration of some pieces of jewelry. Stamping usually appears on plain pieces. Dies are made by each smith. There is not the variety of designs commonly found among the Navajos. Many

FIGURE 5.23 Zuñi jewelry, including a variety of mosaic (upper and middle left and lower right); note particularly the ceremonial head and figure in the middle left panel. Excellent cluster work is illustrated in the upper- and middle-right panels. (*Photo by Joseph Muench*)

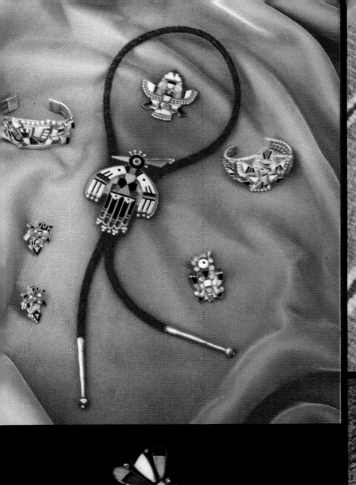

Sand Cast

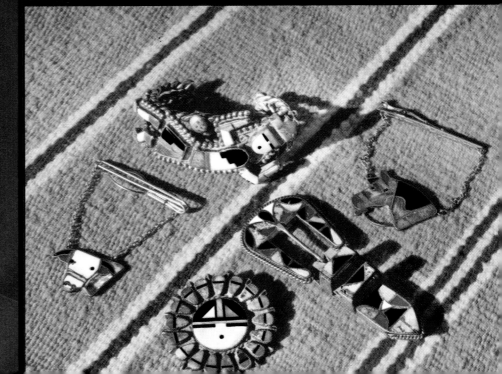

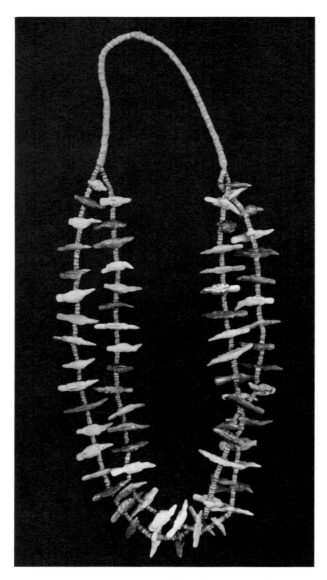

FIGURE 5.24 Zuñi necklace of disc beads and tiny carved figures of birds, also of shell. Many colors are used, from white through pale pinks into deep browns. More detail is represented on some birds than on others.

them reminiscent of Hopi pottery decorations. Of course, in the silver versions all of the designing is simpler, for technology alone would almost demand this. Then too, the silver object is infinitely smaller than the pottery jar or basket, therefore, of necessity the silver decorative theme is smaller and must be simpler.

Rio Grande Pueblos

The silver and jewelry story in the Rio Grande is very different compared with the pueblos of Zuñi and Hopi and the Navajo tribe. Two points are outstanding: the entire production is much smaller, and no one pueblo has developed a style which is distinctly its own. Santo Domingo made a start in the latter direction around 1940 when it used its pottery designs in overlay pieces (Fig. 5.26), but the smiths did not keep up this individual style. Santo Domingo does produce the best shell disc beads, along with Zuñi, of any Southwestern group. Santo Domingo and Zuñi also have done the best work in inlay, using turquoise, jet, shell, and coral on a shell or wood base. Formerly backings in Santo Domingo work were of shell, wood, or pieces of phonograph records; today it is not uncommon to see plastic used in place of any of these materials.

Silversmithing has been introduced into the pueblos of the Rio Grande at different times according to Adair.[36] Acoma (1870-1890) and Laguna (ca. 1870) were the first two villages to learn the craft, probably from Mexicans. Before silver was worked at Isleta, in 1879, some smithing was done in copper and brass. Santa Clarans learned the craft about 1880, Santa Ana and Jémez some time in the 1890's, and Santo Domingo about 1893. Apparently there were no silversmiths at San Ildefonso until the 1930's.

In the Rio Grande in general the silver craft has been taught to puebloans by Mexicans, other puebloans, possibly some Navajos, or by a few Anglo-Americans. Particularly in recent years, Rio Grande villagers have worked in shops in Santa Fe or Albuquerque, learning this craft art from white men. All of these influences are reflected in pueblo silver: there are fancier touches such as crosses and leather die motifs from the Mexicans; new designs from the white man; cluster styles and other details from Zuñi; and limited stones and stamping from the Navajos.

The Rio Grande puebloans have carried on heavy trade with the Navajos; the Santo Domingans in particular have never missed an opportunity to attend any gathering of Navajos. There they trade

designs could be classified as frets and a few are scroll themes; again, these are derived from Hopi design sources. Turquoise is used sparingly, with rarely more than a single stone in a piece of jewelry. The stone is used more to accent and point up the design and workmanship than for itself.

Designs in Hopi silver of this later period have been adapted from their tribal ceramics, basketry, and textiles. Many of the patterns retain an angular simplicity or, if curvilinear, are simple in a majority of cases. Repetition and balance, so characteristic of most Hopi designing, is seen also in the silver craft. So too are asymmetric themes, many of

FIGURE 5.25 Some of the variety of Hopi silvercraft. In all but the bottom-right panel are shown good examples of overlay work — bracelets, necklaces, earrings and brooches. Excellent examples of wrought or hammered silver appear in the last panel. Note that turquoise is used only sparingly by the Hopis. (*Photos by J. H. McGibbeny*)

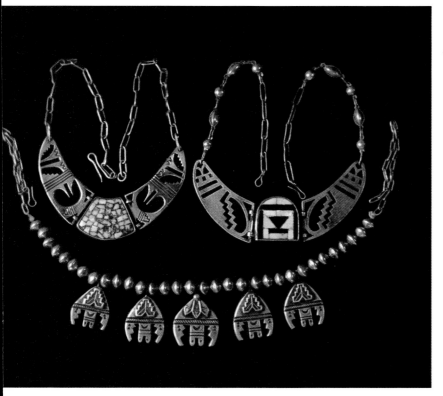

FIGURE 5.26 Two overlay silver bracelets. The upper one is Hopi, while the lower is an early Santo Domingo example; both show the influence of pottery design on the newer craft. Overlay is done by using two pieces of silver of the same shape, cutting out the design in one and "sweating" the two together to form one piece. The piece is put in acid and blackened and the raised part only is polished.

their turquoise and shell beads for Navajo rugs and finished silver. Quite naturally, all of these contact situations influenced to some degree the end products of the Rio Grande puebloans.

The fact that many of the puebloans use much shell and turquoise jewelry for ceremonial wear might also explain their lack of interest in silver. Of course, Hopis and Zuñis, because of their closer contacts with the Navajos, are exceptions to this statement. The Zuñis do both, still featuring much in the way of turquoise and shell alone, and because of several white traders living in their village who have encouraged them to commercialize their silver, they have been greatly influenced in the more extensive development of the craft. Pueblos in the Rio Grande lacked the presence of white traders who could finance silverwork; this has probably contributed to the limited development of the metal craft among them.

Today there are a few silversmiths and many bead makers at Santo Domingo. Ellis says that children — even down to the age of three years! — have their own drills and make beads. Mary and Ray Rosetta are among the better heshi producers.[37] Among the silversmiths is Vidal Aragon, whose uncle is one of the finest heshi workers. Vidal uses a variety of techniques, including overlay, cast work, and wrought with stamping. He is quite creative in his use of modern design. At one time he ornamented silver pins with designs from prehistoric pottery.

Actually the Rio Grande situation does not differ greatly today from what it has been through the years — a few silversmiths in most of the villages but no large number in any one of them. These men may ply their craft in their villages or they may work in Santa Fe, Albuquerque, or occasionally in other towns and cities of white men, as they have in the past. Equipment and techniques differ accordingly, with some men in the native villages or elsewhere better equipped than others. Generally, the Indian employed by a white man has better equipment with which to work; in turn, he is sometimes confined to the whims of his employer, while the smith in his own village can be more creative. There are, of course, many variations in these situations.

Summary

The Southwest Indian has made a great deal of progress within the past one hundred years in the silver craft. Not only has he acquired new and special technologies, but also he has applied a great deal of ingenuity and creativity to the many articles in silver and stone which he has crafted. Too, he has responded to public demand, always trying new forms and new ideas of design. In more recent years he has created fine pieces in cuff links, tie tacks and bars, money clips, watch bracelets, and bolo ties. All techniques are used in the making of these and other pieces, and all tribes have participated in these new ventures.

The future of silver is no easier to predict than that of any other craft. However, since jewelry has long been one of man's — and women's — great interests, it is quite possible that it will remain so for generations to come. Too, as man's taste becomes more universal, Indian silver will grow in favor. The Indian's changing and developing esthetic tastes will be reflected in his jewelry as in other arts.

Kachina Dolls & Carving  *Chapter VI*

THE AMERICAN INDIAN north of the United States-Mexican border never developed sculpture in large pieces. There were, however, splendid attainments in smaller work — for example, in masks and figures. Potentials in the latter have never been realized by many of the Southwest Indians, while some tribes have done commendable sculpture on a small scale. Zuñi stone and shell fetishes are well carved. Zuñi work in wood ranges from extremely crude, as in the war-god images, to very fine, as exemplified in some of their masks or kachinas. The efforts of other tribes vary; each will be treated individually in terms of craft work in carving. Strictly religious pieces will not be discussed here, although there are some objects which are borderline in their significance and use which will be considered.

Kachina Dolls

Without question, the best known work in wood carving in the Southwest is the kachina doll. The story of this development is a complex one. It is best known for the Hopi Indians, and therefore will be told primarily with this tribe in mind.

The kachina doll was and is made for native use by Hopi fathers and uncles to give to their daughters or nieces; primarily the doll is hung on the wall or from the rafters of the house so that it may be seen at all times. The purpose is to teach the child the mask, the costume, and body painting of the kachina. Therefore the doll has to be as perfect as possible, and certainly so in mask features. This may explain in part why the earlier dolls were accurate and detailed in the mask, while the body might be no more than a generalized outline, often with mere suggestions of arms and legs.

The term "kachina" refers primarily to the masked dancer in the pueblo village, or to the spirit which the dancer impersonates. Among the Hopis these spirits are intermediaries between man and the gods; they are spirits of the dead, if not the dead themselves. They are the spirits which bring water, or the clouds from which rain comes. Another tribe pictures the kachinas as gathering above the clouds

and tipping their great jars so that water falls upon the earth below. "Kachina" also refers to a Hopi religious cult. All Hopi boys are introduced to the kachinas at the Powamu Ceremony, and thereafter they may perform in the kachina dances.

Indeed, it is difficult to define "kachina." Although the complex concept and the dancers have to do with the religion of the puebloans, the dolls are not religious objects in the same sense. They are not idols. The Hopis do not worship kachina dolls.

Puebloan groups believe that kachinas live under lakes (Zuñi), or rivers, or on mountain tops (Hopi). The Hopi kachinas live on the San Francisco Peaks of northern Arizona or on other peaks for six months of the year, then they live in the villages of this tribe for the remainder of the year. They appear in dances from the time of their arrival at the end of an initiation ceremony (the Powamu) in late February to their return to the mountains at the Niman Ceremony, or "Home Dance," in July. During their period of residence within the villages, they perform at various times in dance groups. The dancers are, of course, Hopi men wearing masks and impersonating the spirits.

To the kachina personator, the mask is the most important part of his entire dress, although the costume and paraphernalia carried by the kachina are important too. There are, broadly, two types of masks, those of the greater or more sacred spirits, or kachinas, and those of the lesser kachinas. The former do not change; supposedly they were given to the Hopis by the kachinas themselves. On the other hand, the lesser kachina masks not only may, but do, change. The greater kachina mask is simple and generally has no protuberances. Contrarily, the lesser types often have great ears, snouts, beaks, or other dramatic features. It is the latter type represented in the kachina doll which has proved so popular as a commercial craft piece. It should be borne in mind, too, that some doll carvers have refrained quite generally from reproducing the greater kachinas, perhaps in good measure because of their greater sacredness.

Ornamentation has to do with the specific kachina and his special realm — masks of the deer kachinas are topped with the horns of this creature, for example. Quite naturally, since the kachina complex is concerned basically with rain, crop growth, and the fertility of all life, there are painted or carved symbols pertaining to these aspects of pueblo life. Such details are prominent on many parts of the body or costume, or masks, such as clouds, heavenly phenomena, and rain. Also, costume and details aid in the identification of kachinas, as, for example, the velveteen blouse and the "chongo" hairdo of the Navajo kachina.

Prehistoric Background

Insofar as is known, wood carving in the prehistoric past of the Southwest was confined to small utility and religious objects. To be sure, not much of this perishable material has been preserved. Figurine carving in wood is extremely scarce. One small "effigy paho" (sacred figurine), perhaps the "granddaddy" of all kachinas, was found at the ancient site of Double Butte Cave which is located in the Gila Valley of south-central Arizona (Fig. 6.1). Haury dates the material from this ceremonial cave as of the thirteenth or fourteenth century.[1] This

FIGURE 6.1 Sketch of Rio Grande kachina doll and prehistoric Gila Butte Cave figurine. The two figures are presented here to show the similarity between the very simple Rio Grande style and the prehistoric doll.

date is posited on a pueblo occupation of the area prior to the arrival of the Spanish and after the Hohokam Classic Period.

An interesting — and perhaps related — item is a Hopi tradition that in their wanderings after they arrived on this earth they stopped at Casa Grande, an important prehistoric village some 60 miles from the present city of Phoenix, and that the kachinas were with them then.

The Double Butte Cave effigy, simply worked and painted, is more like some simple Rio Grande dolls or the plain flat dolls still made by the Hopis and tied to their baby cradles. In the ancient piece, a fragment of cottonwood was smoothed into a figure 7¾ inches high. There are no indications of limbs; only the head is slightly carved. Haury says, "The face treatment of the Double Butte effigy is unquestionably intended to represent a mask."[2] The figurine is painted as follows: black on the body and back of the head, a diagonal green band across the chest, one half of the face red and the other half blue, and red around the face.

This effigy figure is good evidence in favor of the pre-Columbian development of both masks and the kachina concept. Further support for this theory is given by the painted kiva murals of Awatovi in the Hopi country, illustrated in Watson Smith's *Kiva Mural Decoration at Awatovi and Kawaika-a*.[3] Smith points out prehistoric examples which are not only masks but also, he says, "are so closely similar to modern masks as to make their identification reasonably certain."[4] This analogy is based on forms, colors, and details (Fig. 6.2).

Additional examples of masked figures have been found in kiva murals in the Rio Grande Valley at sites ancestral to historic villages. One site is Kuaua near Bernalillo; the other is Pottery Mound, not far from Albuquerque. On the kiva wall at Kuaua is a "Mudhead" similar to those which today participate in kachina dances. Independent drawings of masks have been found elsewhere, such as the painting on a sandstone slab from Kinishba in east-central Arizona.[5] Pictographs in widespread parts of the Southwest also reveal masks.

Since masks and the kachina cult are so intimately interrelated in Southwest pueblo religion, there thus seems little doubt of the existence of a kachina complex in pre-Columbian days. This, of course, does not prove the great antiquity of kachina dolls. However, the Double Butte Cave example, and possibly several others, and the well-established socio-religious pattern of dolls and doll giving point to a considerable age for kachina dolls.

Historic Development

Dockstader suggests the possibility of kachina doll origin through or at least as an influence from

FIGURE 6.2 Prehistoric Awatovi masks (left) and modern kachina masks (right). The full story of masks in the Southwest is not known, but comparisons of this nature would surely indicate a long history and some possible connection between the mask types of the past and present. (Prehistoric examples from Smith, *Kiva Mural Decorations at Awatovi and Kawaika-a.*)

carvers of Catholic saint statues.[6] Zuñi kachina dolls are more slender than Hopi dolls, have moveable arms, and are costumed in cloth as are the early statues of the introduced religion, but there any similarity between the two art forms ends. Indian masks in no way resemble saints' faces; kachina clothing and trappings are the antithesis of Catholic garb and paraphernalia. Furthermore, even though the friars taught natives the art of carving, kachina dolls reflect the conventionalities and forms of native craft work far more than they reflect any Spanish-Mexican styles of artistic expression.

The kachina is distinctly puebloan, although it is very probable that the Navajo Indians were influenced by this concept and that out of it developed their masked dancers, the yei. Dockstader says that when applied to the doll the name properly should be "tihu," and not kachina, or, more specifically, "kachintihu" — figurine of a kachina.[7] He would also call the earliest kachina, the flat and simply painted dolls made for Hopi cradles, by the name of "puchtihu." However, since the term kachina is so well established by popular usage, it is used in preference to others in this discussion for the regular doll and the cradle piece.

It is not known when the pueblo Indians began the making of kachina dolls as they are carved today. Certainly they were being made in the second half of the nineteenth century. Dockstader notes, "I know of no extant specimens [of kachinas] made during the years 1500-1850, nor are there any certain references to them in the literature of that period."[8] During the 1880's, a number of dolls were collected by Hough. A decade later, Fewkes, who was doing ethnological work among the Hopis and archaeological work in their ancestral homes, also collected dolls and made them better known to white men through Indian paintings of the same.[9]

About the same time, Indian traders — Hubbell and others — sold dolls to collectors and encouraged the distribution of this small figure carved by Hopis. These incidents piqued the curiosity of the white man and prompted his purchase of these strange little figures. Thus commercialization of the kachina doll began before the turn of the twentieth century, although some years passed before the dolls were made in appreciable numbers by the Hopis for sale.

As the doll has become more and more popular with the white man, and as the buyer has grown more and more critical of craftsmanship, further

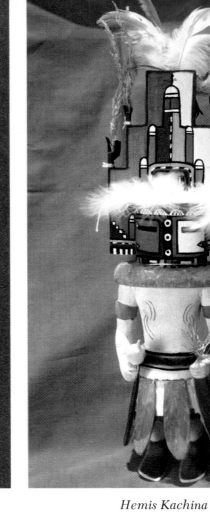

Owl Kachina

Zuñi Warrior God Kachina

Hemis Kachina

Black Ogre Kachina

Polik Mana

changes have taken place in the carved kachina doll. Arms have been separated from the body, "stumps" have become legs, and today both are modeled. In very recent years, the entire figure has been carved in more active positions — dolls carved like this are called "action dolls." Greater and greater attention has been given to detail, also. For years the Zuñi doll could be distinguished from the Hopi by the fact that the former was actually bedecked with pieces of cloth, fur, and such, while the Hopi doll had all features represented in carving and paint. Recently a few Hopi dolls have simulated the Zuñi style in that they have a piece of fur or skin about the shoulders or wear a cloth kilt or shoulder blanket.

A few details of dress are common to the majority of Hopi kachinas (Fig. 6.3). For example, most of them wear the old-style embroidered cotton kilt and one or several belts which might include the wide woven and brocaded one, the braided rain sash, the red belt, or even a concha belt. A fox skin is commonly suspended from the back of the waist, yarn ties are about the arms and legs, and the figure may have a blanket about the upper body. Variations from this common dress are seen in such kachinas as the Navajo, or the Kachin Mana (female impersonation). The latter wears the Hopi woman's native dress. Many objects are carried in the kachina's hands — rattles, a bow and arrow, sprigs of greenery, staffs, or yucca leaves. And the body is painted too, with simpler or more complicated designs.

The kachina doll, like its original counterpart, is painted or bedecked with the proper clothing, jewelry, mask, and ritual objects. Many times the doll will be very simply carved and painted except for the mask, and this may be in larger size, proportionately, with essential details well represented. In the same piece other features may be simplified or omitted. These comments apply to fine kachinas; to be sure, commercialization on a large scale has greatly altered the situation. Perhaps the most significant of the changes has been overall simplification, including the mask. Many of the small dolls, in particular, have few or none of the differentiating characteristics of the original kachina. A definite distinction should be made between the doll required by the discriminating buyer and one made for sale to the uncritical; the two are miles apart in artistry and craftsmanship.

Hopi Kachina Dolls

Actual Hopi kachinas vary in number from time to time; the same variation may or may not be reflected in the dolls. Reasons for the varying numbers are many, including the fact that Hopis add kachinas, as is evident in such historic subjects as Cow and Cat kachinas. Borrowing from other tribes is known, as exemplified by Hemis Kachina which came from the New Mexico pueblo of Jémez (Fig. 6.4). New ones are created, like the Cross Legged Kachina which "is thought to be the spirit of a very kind Mishongnovi man who died about seventy years ago."[10] There is a Mickey Mouse Kachina, too! Furthermore, kachinas are eliminated on occasion. Doll types also fluctuate in number — for example, when popularization favors specific kachinas of a limited number. Or a museum may have all known kachinas carved for its collection by one Indian. In the late 1800's, Fewkes reported that there were about 190 kachinas; Wright and Roat, in 1962, said the number "is probably over 250."[11]

Kachina dolls also vary in size. About 1940, a Hopi man was producing tiny kachinas by the hundreds (Fig. 6.5); although varying slightly, they averaged one inch in height. Rarely have any such small dolls been produced other than the ones made by this old fellow except for those made into earrings or brooches. Not much detail can be represented in these tiny figures, but disproportionately large ears and snouts, body blankets, kilts, sashes, and some mask painting are to be noted. In some cases the specific kachina can be identified in miniatures. The Southwest Museum, Los Angeles, has a collection of small dolls, 1½ to 2 inches high, which are quite well made. Typical commercial kachina dolls are larger in size, with the smallest of these seldom less than 2 inches in height, and some few as large as 30 inches tall. The majority measure less than one foot in height.

To make a kachina doll, the Hopi man searches for the right piece of drift cottonwood root in the nearby washes, or sometimes he trades for such a piece. First a section is sawed off, then the rough form of the desired figure is whittled out, often with no more than a pen knife, sometimes with the aid of a chisel. Smoothing and surfacing may be done with files or wood rasps, or natively with a piece of sandstone, and in more recent years with sandpaper. In general, the Hopis have made parts of the mask, such as snouts, ears, horns, noses, and

FIGURE 6.3 Hopi and Zuñi kachina dolls. These five dolls illustrate typical details of dress for the kachinas, such as breechcloth (top, left), kilt (top, center), shoulder blanket (bottom, right), animal skin about shoulders (top, left), bandolier (top, center), moccasins (top, all), and sashes (top, right and bottom, left). Head pieces vary from a small bundle (top, center) to a great carved and ornately feathered style (bottom, right). Facial detail ranges from simply painted (bottom, right) to large projections (bottom, left). (*Photo by Jack Breed*)

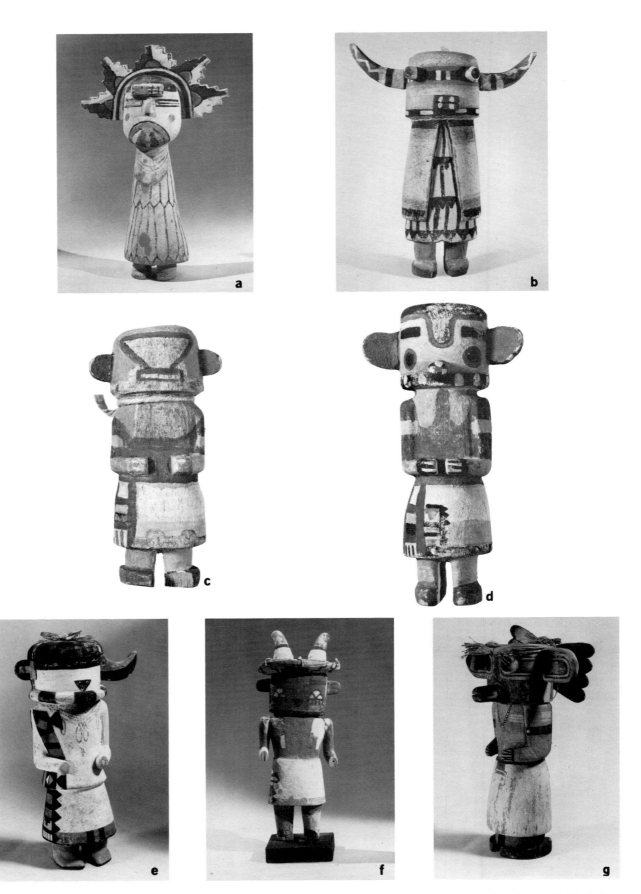

FIGURE 6.4   Old and recent kachina dolls. Old dolls (a through h) are formal, stiff, simply carved and painted. Mask features are generalized. Legs and arms lack form, fingers are not carved at all or very simply, and arms are glued to the sides in all but (f) and (h). There are no additions to the wood and paint except a small detail in (h). The newer dolls are quite the

opposite: most of them show action, and masks and head pieces are depicted in great detail. There are some additions in cloth, buckskin, sticks, "whips," and yarn ties. Some of these kachinas are too generalized to identify, and (h) is not known, but others have been identified as follows: (e) Hututu; (f) Mountain Sheep; (i) Ahote; (j) Humming Bird with Corn Kachina body; (k) Velvet Shirt; (l) Left Handed; (m) Hemis; and (n) Antelope.

FIGURE 6.5 Six miniature kachina dolls carved in 1939. Facial details are painted on, protuberances such as snouts, ears, and horns, are carved and painted. Feathers are appropriately placed. Backs of dolls are finished, as seen in the fifth from the left. All dolls are less than one inch in height, exclusive of feathers.

headpieces separately, then attached them to the doll. Certainly such an ornate stepped superstructure as that of the Butterfly Kachina must be carved as a separate piece.

After all is carved and put together, the entire figure is covered with a base coating of white paint made from kaolin. Over this are applied the proper bright colors straight from poster-paint containers — the reds, blues, greens, yellows, and other shades required for each individual doll. In the dancer's mask and body paint, color has great symbolism. Although there may be some variation, there is also a certain rigidity as to which colors may be used. Before the acquisition of poster paints, and occasionally thereafter, colors for dolls were derived from the same sources as for painting the dancer — blue and green from malachite, black from corn smut or soot, red from hematite, and yellow from limonite.

After the doll is painted, the Hopi man adds whatever he deems necessary to complete a specific kachina (Fig. 6.3). Feathers are most commonly used; for example, they appear at the tip of each cloud in the Butterfly Kachina. Sometimes these too are carved, although real feathers give an attractive finishing touch to the doll and have become popular as further commercialization of the piece has occurred. If the kachina maker plans a fur wrap, cotton kilt, greenbough for the neck, tin and glass beads to simulate concha belt and jewelry, or other such additions, they are added last of all.

Several points mentioned above are illustrated in examples of Hopi kachinas. A group of twenty-nine dolls made in the 1920's will serve as "early" types while a variety of post-1950 dolls will exemplify "later" or "recent" styles (Figs. 6.3, 6.4, and 6.6). Early dolls are often made in a single piece, such as a rooster complete with a large comb; later types are more apt to have additions, such as a modern Butterfly Kachina which has separate headpiece and hands pegged to the body. In an early Hemis Kachina the arms are carved in low relief, the legs are heavy, formless, and just slightly apart; a recent owl kachina has arms and legs not only free but almost fully modeled. Hands in the early dolls are mere "blobs" in some cases, and at best the fingers are painted on; today hands tend to be too large but are crudely or better worked, sometimes with each finger carved and then painted.

Modeling in the early kachina body is limited and usually confined to a constricted waist and a rounded or oval form; late kachinas are often modeled throughout, some to a point of exaggeration of chest, leg, and arm muscles. Of the twenty-nine early dolls, only one is represented in bent-body action; today action is to be seen in arms, body, and legs in varied motions of the dance. Older kachinas often resemble a cylinder with a masked head attached, while recent ones are often fully modeled, well-proportioned human bodies with esoteric mask-heads.

Carving of the kachina doll gives it a basic form; painting gives the piece its full character. It is in the colors and the designs that identification becomes complete. This is particularly true in the greater or Mong Kachinas, for all of their masks are basically simple. Additions are also revealing, such as ears, horns, snouts. Feathers are significant to the dancer as to color, from what bird, and from what part of the bird they come; sometimes the doll maker attempts to follow these dictates.

The list of design elements which are symbolic is

FIGURE 6.6 Hopi and Zuñi kachina dolls. Colton identifies the left doll as Powamu kachina. The most prominent character in the Hopi Bean Dance in February. The doll on the right is the Zuñi Chakwaina kachina, associated with creation; this one appears at the Pamuya Dance on Hopi First Mesa. (*Photo by Jack Breed*)

endless — heavenly phenomena such as sun, moon, stars, lightning, clouds; plants such as corn; animals or parts of them or their tracks; geometric elements including lines, dots, circles, squares, rectangles, steps, and crescents. These are but a few of the designs which may be painted on kachina mask, body, or costume, or be carved on the headpiece, or appear on some piece of paraphernalia. They are common on the better dolls.

The Hopi "cradle doll" is a flat slab of cotton-wood about 3 inches in width and 6 to 8 inches in height; it is only slightly carved and then painted (Fig. 6.7). Generally the rectangular shape is broken by a slight indentation to indicate separate body and head (mask) areas. Rarely there is a suggestion of a chin or a very simply modeled lower part of the face and a rounded top to the mask. Sometimes fairly elaborate and stepped headpieces, slab ears, noses, horns, and feathers may be added.

Painting on the flat doll varies. Basically the figure is covered with white and then red, blue, yellow, and black are added. Sometimes the blue is more turquoise, or green is substituted, particularly in several older examples. There is much outlining in black. Mask features vary: they are conventional and simpler or more complex depending in part on the specific kachina represented; or they are made up of more realistic down-cast and lashed eyes, a dot for a nose, and an upturned-line smiling mouth. In the conventional style, black rectangles for eyes and a square for a mouth are painted on a blue or white mask-face, or the mouth is replaced by vari-colored bands or lines, and there may or may not be geometric cheek decorations.

Body decorations of these dolls are very conventional. There are no legs; rectangular arms which end in straight-line fingers are painted, one blue, one yellow. The same colors are used for a shawl-like affair over each shoulder. A black line indicates what seems to be a necklace.

The remaining decoration on the typical cradle doll is in the form of vertical red bands, all touching the straight base of the figure. A central band reaches to or goes above the hands, then at either side are one or two bands of equal size which stop below the hands. It is thought that the elaboration of this flat doll, or puchtihu, may have developed into the carved kachina doll as it was known in the later nineteenth century.

Zuñi Kachina Dolls

Currently there are quite a few Zuñi kachinas on the market. When first revived, production was largely by one individual; today more men are carving dolls. Not many dolls have ever been produced at this village, and never has there been the commercialization so common among the Hopis.

FIGURE 6.7 Two Hopi cradle dolls. These dolls are carved to be used on the baby cradles. Both dolls are flat slabs of wood with little carving on them. The one at the top is the simpler, with a slight indication of division between body and mask and the barest essentials throughout. The hands are carved, and there is a projecting snout. The second doll is better made: there is more rounding of the lower face and there is also added a more elaborately carved, stepped super-structure. Painting on body and face is also more elaborate and better executed.

Some years ago examples of very fine Zuñi kachinas were obtained by collectors — the pieces produced today are greatly inferior to the older ones. Because of the numerous and constant contacts between the Hopis and Zuñis, there have been and are today many exchanges of ideas between the two tribes. Kachinas reflect this as much as anything.

In general, the following can be said to aid in distinguishing the dolls of the two tribes (Figs. 6.3 and 6.8). Zuñi dolls are usually taller and thinner than Hopi ones. Typically the arms of the Zuñi kachina dolls are carved separately and nailed on so that they are moveable; this is rarely done by Hopis. The Zuñi doll is not in an action position, while action dolls have been developed recently among the Hopis. Quite typically, the Zuñi carved figure is ornamented with pieces of handwoven or commercial and hand-decorated cloth, fur, lambs' wool, and buckskin; not until recent years have the Hopi dolls been decorated in comparable fashion.

These characteristics can be helpful in identifying the particular tribe which produced a given doll, especially when several traits are used. The development of action dolls by the Hopis has contributed a most important identifying trait, for the Zuñi doll is almost always stiff and wooden in its pose. The legs are particularly stiff in their shapeless form and straight position. Yet allover workmanship is generally careful and precise; details are excellent and reveal the identity of the Zuñi kachina. The moveable arms of the Zuñi doll are not to be confused with the Hopi doll arms-in-action. Moreover, the conception and crafting of the Hopi doll is superior to that of the Zuñi in one other feature: the former will stand alone, while the latter usually must be nailed to a block of wood to maintain its upright position.

Although some older Zuñi kachinas are about the same height as the Hopi, generally 7 to 10 inches

FIGURE 6.8 Zuñi and Hopi dolls. This Zuñi kachina (left) is one of the ogres which aid in disciplining children; the long hair, pop eyes, butcher knife in the right hand, and the cane add to his ominous nature. The garments are textiles, the hair real, the arms moveable — all features peculiar to Zuñi dolls. The second doll is a recently made Hemis kachina. It shows the best in modern Hopi doll carving: modeling in body, arms, and legs, good proportions, action, excellent painting, and the use of cloth, real greenbough, feathers, and other realistic detail.

tall, others are much taller. One Shalako Kachina in the Southwest Museum, Los Angeles, is 37 inches high, and has an additional 7 inches of feathers on top of its head! Blankets on this large doll were made of white commercial cloth with traditional Zuñi designs embroidered on it in red, green, and black. Red and blue glass beads about the neck simulate the turquoise and coral originals of the dancer. Coarse but real hair — possibly horsehair — hangs down the back, while wool serves for the head hair. The skin of a small animal with the head attached is draped about the neck. Many of the Zuñi Shalako kachinas have eyes made of cloth — large, round, bulgy white ones with black centers. It is common for the Zuñi figures to be wearing buckskin moccasins.

In general, older Zuñi kachinas are made of pine. They are not as well carved as the Hopi, perhaps because the carver knew they would be partially covered with cloth, fur, and feathers. Some parts are not painted at all, particularly those which are well concealed by other material. But the general effect of the older Zuñi dolls is that they are magnificent creations. The carving is not as poor as it is today, sizes are larger, the painting is more carefully done, and the additions are more abundant and more imaginative than in the contemporary Zuñi kachina. However, a few of the most recent dolls show improvement.

One example of a modern piece bears out all of the above traits expressive of degeneracy in the late work. The wood is quite soft — not pine. There is a slight bend to the knees, a trait rarely seen in the old pieces (Hopi influence?). Black wool for the hair is reminiscent of the old Zuñi style. Painting is very sloppy. But what really brings this piece up to date is a plastic kilt!

Rio Grande Pueblo Kachina Dolls

The story of kachina dolls in the Rio Grande is incompletely known. Pressures from the Spanish in matters pertaining to religion brought about evergreater secrecy, with the result that little is known about certain aspects of the kachina cult. Changes have also occurred. However the kachina cult has persisted among the tribes of the Rio Grande, with some points comparable to and some contrasting with the same cults among the Hopis and Zuñis. Masks and elaborate costumes are used. Some groups are known to have carved kachina dolls in the past; today these dolls are made by many Rio Grande puebloans.[12]

Although there is the likelihood that some were of more elaborate nature in the past, the consensus is that the majority of the Rio Grande kachina dolls are extremely simple. One reference dismisses the subject by saying, "Among the eastern Pueblos the dolls are but a board or cylinder, painted and given a head feather."[13] This is not a poor description of many of these dolls.

There are certain aspects of the kachina cult in the Rio Grande which would make the doll an object to be carefully guarded, for example, the early recorded practice of giving carved wooden images to pregnant women or to a woman who wanted a child.[14] A small wooden doll and cradle may be presented to a woman by certain kachina dancers at Cochití.[15] There seems to be greater emphasis on the aspect of fertility in the Rio Grande; according to Harvey, even when a doll is given to a child, the latter may be encouraged "to play with it as though with a little sister or brother. Regarded as a person, the New Mexican kachina doll is implicitly or explicitly a child in the mother's house."[16] Harvey thus supports the idea of greater sacredness of the Rio Grande pueblo kachina dolls.

Both the flat and cylindrical kachina dolls made in the Rio Grande pueblos resemble the Hopi cradle doll. One example in a Southwestern museum, from Acoma, is even simpler than the Hopi flat doll; it has a flat back, top, and bottom, and the entire front is rounded. It is 7¾ inches high, which is about average for the dolls from the Rio Grande. Its simplicity is reflected in its having no more than an incised line to indicate the division between neck and body. Wedge-shaped eyes and square mouth are black on a red base. The entire body is white, front and back. The back of the mask is black as are the top and bottom of the piece.

Other Rio Grande dolls may be more colorful, although none bears the ornate carving of the Hopi and Zuñi styles. Some have slightly elaborate headpieces or great horns. Some are painted in bright purples, lime greens, or magentas to give "a gay appearance to the dolls and lend a modern look to and old form."[17] Harvey also reports that the dolls made at Acoma are the most colorful today; they are often decorated with exotic feathers and artificial flowers. Carvers at Laguna, Santo Domingo, and Jémez are more apt to use native mineral paints and prefer fewer additions to the basic figure.

Two kachinas from Jémez, observed in Santa Fe, were each 8½ inches high, cylindrical, and painted in a slightly different manner from the usual Rio Grande Pueblo type. One had a red body with a white blanket about it, the latter decorated in black. The second had a white body with feathers glued all over it.

Several very recent kachina dolls from Acoma are less attractive than the above and less in the Rio Grande tradition. Moveable arms are nailed on; great ruffs about the neck are made of green yarn clipped evenly all about; cloth kilts are crudely painted or decorated with shiny glass fragments (not beads) glued on; and belts are of giddy commercial braid or leather. Mask features are very generalized on these dolls.

Non-Kachina Figurines

Hopi

In addition to kachinas, Hopi Indians carve other dolls. The kachina is masked at Hopi, thus any carved figures without masks are not kachinas. Among other pieces carved by Hopis are the butterfly dancers, eagle dancers, snake dancers, buffalo man and maidens, a woman grinding corn, an old man, a young woman, and a few others (Fig. 6.9). Actually, there is little difference between many of these figures and kachinas from the technical and artistic standpoints.

Individual ability plays its part in the carving of these Hopi figures, whether kachinas or otherwise. Religious tradition served as a control to make

FIGURE 6.9 Figure of a Snake Dancer. The Snake Dancer is not a masked performer, thus this carved figure is not a kachina doll. However, very much the same artistic traits prevail in this piece as in dolls — but the snake is exaggerated in size.

the kachina doll a more conventional figure; only with action pieces have certain of these barriers been broken down. Subject matter plays a part too. For example, quite recently a Hopi Indian has been carving Apache Crown Dancers. These reveal more action than the usual kachina figure. This, of course, is the realistic situation, for most kachina dancing is reserved while the Apache Crown Dancer is very active. Moreover, the Crown Dancer is not Hopi, therefore traditional controls do not need to function in carving the piece. These carved dance figures are fat — many of the Apache Crown performers are too, so why not?

Some of the Hopi non-kachina carvings reveal a carryover of all the kachina traits, presenting stiff and formal figures of corn grinders or dancers, without masks. Others throw over the traces and present human figures full of rhythm and realism. Such is a bent figure of a white-haired old man carved in 1963 by Neal Kayquoptewa (Fig. 6.10). Very realistic are the wrinkles in the fat, naked stomach, the projecting lips, the wide mouth, and heavy jowls. The age of the old fellow is emphasized in his white and simply bobbed hair, the bent posture, the right hand leaning on a twisted stick.

Rather startlingly realistic are twenty-four figures of Hopi Snake Dancers done by one of their tribesmen about 1900. For such an early time they are indeed well executed, for there was little or no previous work of this type to anticipate such an accomplishment. The Snake Dance is put on by the Snake Clan assisted by the Antelope Clan. In these carved figurines the main performers are presented; in their actions is told the story of the dance. Antelope Priests stand ready to receive the snakes after they have been danced four times about the plaza. Snake Priest Carriers are represented with snakes in their mouths, their hands in various positions as they extend the reptiles' bodies. Close to these men are the "Huggers" who place their left hands on the shoulders of the Carriers, and soothe the snakes with a feather in their right hands. Then there are "Gatherers," their bodies bent to pick up the snakes from the ground where the Carriers have placed them.

Realism is expressed not only in the simple and strong carving and life-like postures, but also in many added details. The figurines have cloth kilts around their waists and string ties about the hair. The latter is straight and bobbed, almost covers the eyes, and hangs uncut and long down the back. The real Snake Dancers wear much jewelry; beads appear on many of these carved figures. Body proportions are quite good, and there is a fair amount of modeling. There is considerable variety in posture of figures and positions of arms and legs. It is surprising that more artistry did not develop at an

FIGURE 6.10 Carving of old man, by Neal Kayquoptewa, Hopi. The old fellow has bobbed gray hair, and wears a black breachcloth, black footless stockings, and moccasins. There is a fair amount of modeling in the figure. His cane and fagots are natural pieces of wood.

earlier stage of kachina carving, for this Snake Dance group reveals considerable potential talent.

Another pleasing figurine or doll carved by a Hopi in the late 1940's is representative of an Acoma girl (Fig. 6.11). It is done in the manner of the old style Hopi kachina: an almost cylindrical body, arms in low relief with hands just barely indicated in pencil lines, legs formed by cutting a channel down the center of the cylinder, and rounded and pointed feet. The bobbed hair and a rectangle for a nose are in relief. All other details are painted on — the black dress caught over the right shoulder, the lace-edged and flower-embroidered apron, and the heavily fringed and flower-embroidered shawl which reaches from the head almost to the bottom of the skirt. A base coat of white paint — as well as the total figure style — is also in the old kachina tradition. Not in this style, however, are the realistic eyes, painted eyebrows, and Cupid's-bow mouth.

Other Pueblos

Potentials for further expression of the abilities of these pueblo carvers in wood are aptly illustrated in a créche or Nativity scene made by Pete Aguino of San Juan Pueblo several years ago. Kneeling or

FIGURE 6.11 Carving of an Acoma girl, by a Hopi; done about 1950. It is simple in its carved lines and delicate in painted detail. Yet it is detailed in the lace-edged and embroidered apron, the embroidered manta, the decorated pot on her head, and the painted underblouse, while the native dress and boots are rather simply presented.

FIGURE 6.12   Court scene modeled by Manuel Vigil of Tesuque. Although simply done, the figures are posed to suggest the wicked culprit, the dignified judge, the distraught relative. All of the figures are clothed to add to the realism of the scene.

standing, and carved in an extremely simple manner, the figures convey a feeling of reverence. Rich colors were used for the robes worn by all five figures and for the dress of one of them.

There are, of course, other pieces of non-kachina and non-religious carving being done by puebloans here and there. Exposed to white men as the Indian is, tempted by the potentials of picking up a few dollars here and there, or even encouraged by an outsider to "try his hand" at carving, these efforts are bound to occur. Varied as are the results today, the prediction can well be made that they will be more so in the future.

Some puebloans have also done modeling of figures in clay. Here, too, is a long tradition, for prehistoric and historic vessels alike were ornamented occasionally with heads or figures of humans, animals, or birds. As pottery became commercialized, some of the purely decorative figures became independent craft pieces. The recent and contemporary and very charming animal, bird, and other life

types created by Terecita of Cochití Pueblo fit into this category. So, too, do the owls and frogs from Zuñi, the lovely turkeys from Acoma, the many animals from Santa Clara, Tesuque, and other pueblos. Many of these are mediocre, some are examples of good craftsmanship, and still others display a certain creativity.

A rather different trend has developed in recent years wherein some puebloans have modeled figures which tell a story. Such are the works of Monroe Vigil of Tesuque. Among the many subjects he has created are an old man and burro, the man in old-style dress and chongo hairdo; a woman sitting with her legs straight out and nursing a child; another woman grinding corn; a buffalo and an antelope dancer; a man leaning on a cane with one hand and with a child on his back. One other figure is that of an eagle dancer with winged arms stretched straight out and stiff in the manner of early watercolor painting.

In general, these Vigil figurines are simply

FIGURE 6.13 Two modeled figures of the "Rain God" from Tesuque. The figure on the left is old, one of many made for a commercial venture. The one on the right is a recent product. The old figure is simpler — in that it is devoid of painted design — but it is better modeled. It is more smiling. The newer version has an elaborate cheek decoration, a necklace painted on, a sneer on its face, and is poorly modeled.

modeled, displaying none of the refinements or craftsmanship so commonly exhibited in Hopi kachina dolls today. They are presented in awkward and stiff poses. Characteristic of all mentioned are very large noses which descend straight out of the forehead, mere slits for eyes and mouth, and no details on the hands. Staffs, rattles, and bows are just stuck through a hole in the hand. All but one are wrapped in cloth garments — even the child on the old man's back is suspended in a piece of yellow cloth! The body of the eagle dancer is painted in appropriate colors, black and yellow.

Much more ambitious is the Court Scene created by Manuel Vigil, also from Tesuque, in 1961 (Fig. 6.12). The group is set up about a desk and benches, the latter items crudely made of wood. Modeled in clay, the figures include a judge, bailiff, sheriff, the prisoner, and several women spectators. Simple though the workmanship is in all figures, there is, nonetheless, a subtle suggestion in pose to make one know that this man with his head buried in his hands is the condemned criminal, while another bushy-haired and dignified character is the judge. Appropriate clothing for each person helps to build up this image of identity. Facial features are modeled and details painted on. A general smoothness and simplicity in the modeling and the facial details here and in the above figures resemble a statuette made in this village in quantity many years ago. This was a so-called "Rain God," a seated man with a bowl in his lap (Fig. 6.13). The figure was made for a white man's advertising scheme.

Several years ago, Anna María Vigil of Tesuque created a charming Nativity scene in clay. The figures have no feet, for all are covered with robes which reach to the floor. Arms and bodies are simple, smooth, soft cylinders. Head scarves conceal all but the face — and the face is unmistakably Tesuque in its very large nose, painted, closed eyes and slit of a mouth. There is an uptilt to the heads which gives great dignity to all figures.

Navajo

Some wood carving and clay modeling have been done also by non-pueblo peoples. Outstanding among the former are the products of two Navajo men, Clitso Dedman and Tom Yazzie. Dedman worked during the late 1930's and 1940's, carving a few sets of yeibichai figures — dancers in the Navajo Night Chant. One very fine set (Fig. 6.14) shows the Navajo man at the head of the group, and then the twelve dancers, six with full masks and six with half masks. At the end of the group is a clown. Carving in these pieces is excellent, and the painted details are very fine. Costuming, details of masks, and dress minutiae are as well done as in any other carving by Southwest Indians.

Tom Yazzie, on the other hand, has created a far wider range of subjects, but his artistic ability has not yet surpassed that of Dedman. Yazzie learned to carve from a white man. The material used in his figures varies, since he uses, as he says, "Whatever I can find," — driftwood, a plank, anything handy. Poster paints are used, but Yazzie handles them

FIGURE 6.14 Navajo Yeibichai carved by Clitso Dedman. There is a good representation of the details of costumes and masks and body form in these figures, from their moccasined and stockinged feet, to their short kilts and animal tails at the waist, the bare upper bodies, simple masks, and long hair. Painting of the figures is employed to add further detail.

effectively. A young fellow, Yazzie is not consistent in the pursuit of this craft, sometimes neglecting it for six or more months at a time.

Yeibichai dancers are favored subject matter for Yazzie's carving. In one set the figures are about 9 inches tall, and include the usual man and woman leaders, the twelve yei, and a clown. Clothing and all parts are carved and painted, then a few items are added, such as colored glass beads to simulate turquoise, shell, and coral, and bits of tin to serve

for silver jewelry. Trousers and shirts are of different colors. Each man carries a gourd in one hand and a greenbough in the other. The result is a colorful line of dancers, and one quite true to the actual Navajo ritual group.

One of the most active of Yazzie's groups is that of Navajo Fire Dancers (Fig. 6.15). At this performance men paint their bodies white, wear nothing but moccasins and a breechcloth and a tie about the head; they light cedar bark brands at the

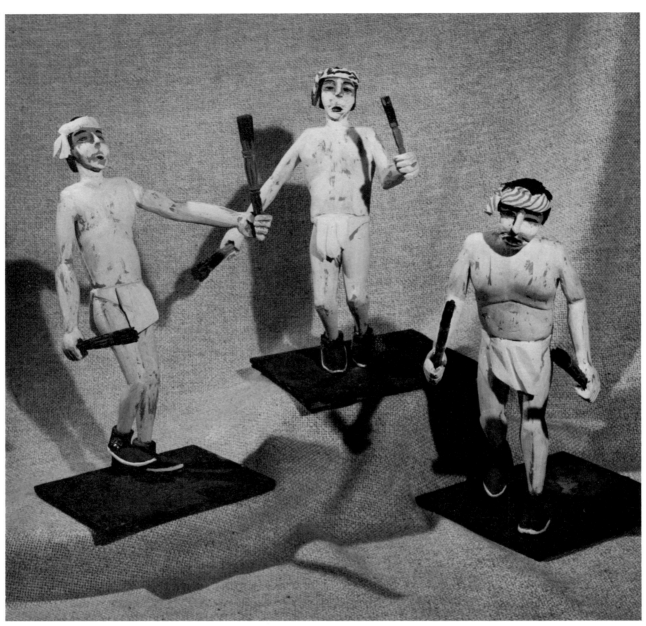

FIGURE 6.15 Fire Dancers carved by the Navajo, Tom Yazzie. All detail is carved, including the breechcloths, headbands, and moccasins; a little paint is added for design in headbands. Body form and muscles are modeled. Some of these figures are very active for this is the nature of the dance.

great fires, and, running and gyrating, brandish and slash each other with these flaming pieces. Yazzie catches the grimaces and laughs on the faces; he reveals the arms, bodies, and legs in a variety of motions and poses. All additions and dress are cut in the wood and painted. Modeling shows muscles, details of anatomy such as rounded buttocks, a suggestion of a waistline, and flying breechcloth ends and hair ties.

Many other subjects have been treated by Yazzie. A corn grinding scene shows two women busy at the metates and seven other figures watching. A squaw dance is very realistic, with much activity in the thirty figures — women dragging men into the dance circle, men at the edges in different

poses, and women sitting or standing around. Fire-making is demonstrated by two men twirling a fire stick while six others watch them. A sandpainting scene is realistic as it portrays two men with sticks in hand smoothing the sand, a sick man with another fellow painting him, and a typical group of three women and five men sitting about. A Feather Dance is made more realistic by the addition of real ribbons, feathers, and beads on the man and woman performers and on the five old men seated on the sidelines.

One Yazzie group, labelled "Yucca Ripener," shows a woman and an old man with bow and arrow in hand; the two are the center of attention of five men seated in a row with their blankets wrapped about their hips. Reflecting the fun of the mud dance is a delightfully gay group of men, naked except for their breechcloths and with bodies muddied, dragging a completely clothed and not unwilling victim to the nearby mudhole where he will be dunked. This scene is also full of action.

In general, the carving in these figures depicts a great many features which are then touched up or given life with a bit of paint. For example, the hair is represented as cut in the chongo style or, in the case of some of the women, hanging down their backs. Anatomy is often quite well represented, especially in the muscles, but also in the fat stomachs, bosoms, high cheek bones — often exaggerated — a wrinkled old face, and details of the hands, usually large. Postures of men and women are well expressed, whether the figures are sitting, crouching on their heels, standing, or dancing. Interesting details of dress are well depicted in carving, such as pleated skirts, or blankets about the shoulders or hips and with folds realistically portrayed.

Painting on the Yazzie figures is effectively handled. Often the poster paint merely emphasizes what has already been carved. Color is pleasingly used, as for example, a different one for every shirt or skirt in a given group, a feature so characteristic of the Navajo Indians in real life. The hairdo may be well carved, but color makes it that of an old man or woman, a middle-aged person, or a young girl. Details are added in paint which would be impossible in cutting, like the small designs on kilts and hair ties, in blankets, or other items of dress.

In individual pieces, Yazzie sometimes approaches the work of Dedman, but in general the latter maintained a high standard in most of his work. Yazzie, on the other hand, fluctuates; particularly in his earlier pieces there is more crude craftsmanship. Yazzie's subject matter is more varied than that of Dedman, the latter featuring the yeibichai dancers. On the other hand, some of the details in Yazzie's work are so similar to Dedman's that they suggest he probably studied the fine examples of the older man's yei figures on display in the Navajo Arts and Crafts Guild at Window Rock.

Other figures have also been carved in wood by Navajos. The majority of these are poorly done, although an occasional example may be well carved and carefully painted. At the one extreme is a yeibichai group of ten figures mounted on a board, the work signed, "Henry." As a whole this group is quite good, but it lacks some of the vitality of better Yazzie pieces: there is a greater feeling of repetition, in some features broken only by color;

the painting is often cruder; and the carving is not up to most of Yazzie's work. Henry's figures are about 6½ inches high, while Yazzie's seated figures are about 4½ inches high, with the standing ones ranging from 7 to 9 inches tall.

Among the cruder pieces of Navajo carving are nine wooden human figures. Seemingly they were meant to be yeis, but the craftsmanship is so poor that one cannot be too sure. Rectangular eyes on several suggest the same on masks; round heads with flat faces might also be an attempt at mask representation. Suggestive of the same is the fact that four of the faces are painted white. In most of these dolls there is the barest indication of a neck line, arms are skinny, far too small, and slightly-modeled affairs on a formless body, buttocks may be very slightly indicated, and legs are rather formless "sticks." These figures appear to be old.

Animals have sometimes been carved by Navajos. In one collection all of the creatures are very generalized in form; three are unquestionably cows, another is more of a skunk in its painted black and white bands than in its carved form, and a fifth looks more like a Navajo legendary reptile than a real-life figure. Carving on all of these is very poor and painting is even poorer, but they have some potential in the direction of variety.

Papago

Another tribe which has done some limited but interesting carving in recent years is the Papago of southern Arizona. On the San Xavier Reservation, near Tucson, a man and his wife, Franco and Chepa Domingo, started carving and dressing dolls a few years ago. In their work they have featured everyday activities from Papago life, some of it traditional. Among the subjects depicted are women performing a variety of tasks — one with a kiaha or carrying basket on her back (Fig. 6.16), another baking bread in an outdoor oven, one grinding mesquite beans, still another drawing water at a well, and a last one making sahuaro jam over an open fire. Some of the carving shows men at various tasks, such as two fellows twisting a horsehair rope (Fig. 6.17), a man at a well, and a Papago ready to fight another Indian.

The carving on all of these figurines is crude, even gross in some ways. Materials contribute to this feeling, for the native sahuaro and cholla which are used have rough surfaces. Carving with a pen knife and a bit of finishing with a rough file or rasp do little to dispel this feeling. Figures are placed on irregular pieces of cholla, and the objects associated with the task at hand are usually carved of wood. The height of the dolls ranges from 8 to 11 inches. Most of the figures are jointed at the waist and elbow so that they may bend to their respective duties. This adds greatly to the illusion of action.

Bodies of these Papago figurines are crudely and simply carved, with little indication of proper proportions; there may be a bit of modeling in the

FIGURE 6.17 Carvings by Franco and Chepa Domingo, Papagos. In (a) two Papago men are twisting a rope in the old manner; they are dressed in old style clothes, too. In (b), a man is ready "to do battle," with a club in one hand and a shield in the other. Proportions are poor, leg size is exaggerated, heads are too large and facial features are gross, yet like the other two, these figures tell a story in the life of these people.

FIGURE 6.16 Carvings by two Papagos, Franco and Chepa Domingo, show a native woman carrying a load in a burden basket or kiaha (above), and a Papago woman making sahuaro cactus fruit jam (below). The late Franco carved the pieces of cholla cactus and sahuaro, Chepa dressed them and put real hair (her own) on them. Although crudely carved, they tell a story of Papago life.

legs, less in the arms. Facial features are exaggerated in size and very coarse. A touch of realism is added in the long and black hair which Chepa has provided from her own combings. Chepa also has dressed the dolls, using scraps of cotton print for dresses and undergarments of the women, and white cloth for the trousers and overblouses of the men. Women's dresses are as formless as the figures.

The many small touches which give greater interest to these figures were added by Franco. He painted facial features, toes, sandals on the feet, or the design on a carved "basket," and he put tiny cut wooden chips in a basket to simulate mesquite beans. A tiny braided kiaha (burden basket) is complete with sticks.

In spite of simplicity and crudeness, these Papago figurines have a great appeal — their action and details tell a story. Heavy and gross though the facial features are, they suggest characteristics of this dark-skinned Indian tribe. Ethnologically, they recall events of the past or tell of current activities far better than words can do. There will be no more of this man's interesting carving, for Franco died in the late spring of 1966.

Yuma

In the realm of clay modeling, much less has been done by non-puebloan than by puebloan tribes. Some tribes have done a bit of modeling, particularly of animals and humans, as part of the ceramic craft. Perhaps the most outstanding examples in the direction of more independent expression were the clay figurines done about the turn of the century by the Yuma tribe of the Lower Colorado River. Now in the Arizona State Museum, Tucson (Fig. 6.18), most of these dolls are from about 5 to a little over 7 inches tall. They are simply and most delicately modeled, painted, baked, and left in the natural buff clay color except for decorations.

Both men and women are represented in these Yuman figurines, generally in the appropriate native dress for their day and time. Body proportions tend to be fair except for rather large heads and eyes. All figures are upright and straight, even dignified; the monotony of this position is broken by placing the arms akimbo, or by putting one or both hands on the chest, or in some other slight variation of details. Fingers are separate and toes nearly so. Modeling is slight but good, with marked bosoms and sometimes a suggestion of knees. The great eyes are gouged out and painted. Slits form thin lips, sometimes with teeth represented in the open mouth.

There is much facial and body painting on the Yuman figurines, most of it in red with small touches in black, such as around the eyes. Designs on faces, arms, bodies, and legs duplicate familiar Yuman patterns of this early day; they include lines, dots, crosses and zigzags — all elements used on pottery or for face or body decoration. Some of the painting suggests a vest-like garment.

Like the carved Papago dolls, the Yuman clay examples have real hair, long and black, attached

a   b   c   d

FIGURE 6.18 Clay figurines modeled by the Yuma Indians. These dolls were made about the turn of the century. Proportions are poor, heads and eyes are much too large, modeling as a whole is only fair, painting is sloppy, yet there are many attributes to these pieces. They give details of dress, hair-do, and body and face paint of this early day (a and c for men, b and d for women). They show how a baby was carried (b), pierced ears for earrings, and necklaces in place. The dolls are modeled in a buff clay, with red and black paint on the unslipped surface.

to their heads. Women are dressed in red flannel skirts with a wide black belt, sometimes with another material tied around the hips. A wide black belt also secures the men's red flannel breechcloth which hangs short in front and quite long in back. White or blue and white commercial glass beads are wound about the necks of both men and women in multiple strands and in choker style, or necklaces are painted on the figures. One of the women has white bead earrings; others have pierced ears. Several women carry pots on their heads, while some of the other figurines (where the hair is missing) show wide depressions on the tops of their heads. Several females carry babies, one over the right arm, another on the back. All in all, these Yuman dolls are quite appealing.

Summary

The preceding pages have presented a few examples of how the Southwest Indian has branched out in directions closely related to the traditional craft arts of carving and modeling. However, with the exception of the kachina doll, none of these ventures has become established as a distinct form of tribal expression. Some distinctive sculpture has been done by several Indians of this region, such as the work of the Apache Allan Houser but such sophisticated art is far removed from the craft arts, and hence not a part of this story. Perhaps it is only a matter of time, though, before many Indians move in this direction in the field of carving.

Minor Crafts  *Chapter VII*

In addition to the basic and very important crafts of basketry, textiles, silver, and pottery which the native Southwesterners developed, these Indians also became adept in the production of a wide variety of other objects. They made clothes and innumerable smaller items from the skins of the animals which they hunted; they provided their infants with cradleboards for their safe keeping; they manufactured endless numbers of tools, weapons, and implements, and a surprising variety of musical instruments.

Out of unfamiliar materials brought to them by the white man they evolved crafts new to them, such as special types of glass beadwork. In the miscellaneous and lesser crafts, these Indians were not without imagination and artistry. Time and again they applied to the smaller or less important expressions the traditional ways of doing things, the age-old art styles, and their high skill in the crafts; too, they adapted new materials and new technologies to their changing needs.

It is by no means possible to cover here all of the minor products of the native craftsman; however, a sufficient sampling is given to show the versatility of the Indian. Furthermore, this discussion again points up and sustains the premise that the expressions of a given tribe show an interrelatedness; it demonstrates once again the tribal nature of the craft arts. The technical efficiency in one craft is reflected in another, the design style of one is carried over to a different or even to a new expression.

Drums

When the drum was first made in the Southwest is not known, nor is it known whether there was an early native type of clay or wood. The two-headed wooden type was introduced by the Spanish. Drums present one of the blank spots in Southwestern prehistory, with the possible exception of the use of some clay vessels for this purpose, for none has been found. Drums have been used by Indians of the Southwest throughout the years, and

quite a variety has been made — of these two facts one can be sure.

Natively, the drum is used primarily for ceremonies, rarely for other purposes. Today a few Indians make drums largely for sale, as for example, several families at Cochití. Some villagers continue to produce them for native use, such as the Zíans and other puebloans. Pueblo peoples have made, and some still make, two basic styles: a large pottery type and a two-headed, wooden drum. Non-pueblo folk, on the other hand, use pottery drums of a small variety, or a shallow wooden ring with a single head, while a few use a basket for this purpose.

The two-headed pueblo drum (Fig. 7.1) is made from a fallen cottonwood or aspen trunk; a section is cut and hollowed out with a knife, and both ends are then covered with skin. Underhill says that the older drums were covered with skin of antelope, deer, mountain sheep, or even buffalo hide; today horsehide or goat skin may be substituted.[1] Skins are cut in a circle with a scalloped edge, soaked overnight, and then secured to the hollowed log. Points of the scallop are pierced with an awl, thongs are inserted in the holes, the two heads are laced together, and a loop handle of rawhide or thongs is attached on one side. The drum may or may not be painted. Beaters for these drums are often nothing more than padded buckskin on the end of a straight stick, or a stick with a circled end.

Types of drums in the Rio Grande vary in size, shape, lacing, and decoration. Many of the Tewa drums are of tall slender proportions, while some at Taos are relatively much broader. Commercialization has greatly decreased the size of the drum. Lacing varies; in one style a single lace goes through each point at each end, creating deep V's, while in the other style two laces hit alternate points at each end, crossing in the center of the drum and forming an X pattern. Cochití uses the first of these techniques while Taos uses both.

Lacing is important not only because it secures the drum heads, but also because it often creates areas for color decoration. The entire area of wood back of the lacings may be painted — a soft blue color being favored for native use. Much more common, however, and particularly in the drum made for sale, is the use of color in the elongate triangles of wood between lacings or in the half circles outlined by the scallops formed by the cut skin. Often there is a line of contrasting color where the half moons and lacing meet. Variations include painting of alternate triangles in one color, alternate triangles in two colors, or the half circles alone or in combination with one of the other schemes. Drums made in large numbers and smaller sizes for sale are apt to be more garish, both in the choice of colors and the number of colors in a single piece. The following are several combinations of colors on the commercial drum for the V's, the half moons, and the line between them, respectively: dark blue, white, orange; brown, white, orange; brown, white, blue; and green, orange, white. All of these are poster-paint colors.

Many of the drums made for native use range from about 17 to 21 inches in height, and from 15 to 19 inches in diameter. One of the "fat" Taos types measures 21 inches in height and 26 in diameter. Elbert Martinez and Adam Trujillo are good drum makers at Taos. Bob Brooks, an Anglo-American, hollows out low and wide trunks, which are then laced by Indians of this same village. In some instances, the latter are 3 or 4 feet in diameter but only about one foot in height.

At Cochití there is a family, the Marcello Quintanas, which produces a great many of the contemporary commercial drums. They make all sizes and decorate them in a variety of colors. Smaller drums measure from 4¼ inches high and 4¾ inches wide to about 6 inches high and a little more or less in width. Medium-sized drums range around 9 inches in diameter and 8 in height. Many of the drums produced for sale by this family are well made, while some are poorly done. This is true of other Cochití drums; commercialization has affected size greatly but it has not destroyed better craftsmanship in all cases.

The Hopi drum (Fig. 7.2) is made of cottonwood, and generally is not as tall as the Tewa type, but proportions vary from shorter and wider to tall and more slender. Drums may be painted or not — one beautiful Hopi drum was decorated alternately with blue and yellow in the deep V areas. Drums are rarely made by the Hopis for sale.

Formerly Hopis also made large pottery drums. Several fine examples of these are in the Indian Arts Fund Collection, Santa Fe. They are 17 to 18 inches high and have very short necks and narrow mouths with outflaring rims for tying on the drum heads. Flat shoulders with an abrupt turn into an almost straight wall are typical. The base is flat. Decoration is confined to the shoulder or extends onto the body.

The Zuñis preserve the use of the large pottery drum to the present. At their Shalako Ceremony

FIGURE 7.1 Cochití drums. The drum on the left is about average in size for those made for use in this village; it is 20″ high and 13 1/2″ in diameter. It is unpainted. The example on the right is painted: green in the long triangles with alternate ones unpainted, and yellow in the two end areas. Aspen trunk is used in both drums and hide is employed for both heads and lacings.

FIGURE 7.2 Hopi drum. The proportions of this drum are low and wide: 23 1/4″ high and 21″ in diameter. Lacing is simple, as in the Cochití type, and is of hide. The drum is made of cottonwood.

in 1962, several such beautiful pieces were in evidence. This type is like an olla; it is of massive size, wide-mouthed, and slightly constricted at the neck with a skin tied in position at the latter point. Water is placed in these drums, giving them a fine bell-like resonance. The pottery drum may be decorated or plain. Zuñis also use a two-headed drum.

Pottery drums (Fig. 7.3) made by Navajos are small in size, often about 8 or 9 inches in height and a little less in diameter. They are wide mouthed, with a slight constriction at the neck, are black or dark gray in color, and are undecorated except for a fillet of clay about the neck; sometimes the fillet is indented. Over the mouth is tied a piece of skin. Adams states that the majority of Navajo families still have these drums.[2]

The basket drum is exemplified by the one used by Papago Indians. Densmore says that any medium-sized household basket is turned upside down and beaten with the open palm of the hand. She cites an example of a basket so used as being 16½ inches in diameter and 5½ inches deep.[3] Navajos use the "wedding basket" as a drum.

Flutes

Although the flute was primarily a ceremonial instrument, it was also used for other occasions, such as when a young man was courting a young lady. The pueblo flute was made from a section of soft wood — cottonwood, for example — about 3 feet in length. Underhill reports that it was hollowed by inserting a hot wire through the length

of the piece.[4] Four holes were cut at one end, and a smooth piece of wood inserted at the other for the mouthpiece. It was decorated by painting — turquoise was favored — or by attaching feathers.

One of the most decorative flutes in the Southwest was that made by the Yuma Indians of the Lower Colorado River about the turn of the century (Fig. 7.4). Thirty-three examples in the Arizona State Museum were examined. These reed flutes range in length from 13 to 24 inches, with most of them being 16 or 17 inches long. The majority have four holes placed slightly closer to one end than the other. All but three of the thirty-three examples are decorated. Generally there are three areas of decoration on these flutes, a central, slightly larger one, and a smaller one at each end. Each area is usually filled with a number of small carved and painted designs; some of these are extremely tiny and delicate. The "carving" is really a simple cutting through the slick surface of the cane so that the paint will adhere. Much of the carving is careless and the painting is not too well done, but the general effect is interesting.

Design elements and their organization in these Yuma flutes are reminiscent of pottery patterns. There are two basic arrangements, one from end to end of the decorative area, and the second an encircling band. Design elements include dots in rows, as outlining, or within geometric forms; triangles which are solid or open and often with hook projections; diamonds, usually with several corners

FIGURE 7.3 Navajo pottery drum. The elongate open-mouth type of pot serves the Navajo well for his drum. The skin head is tied on just below the fillet of clay which is found on most of these pots.

filled in solid and the rest filled with dots; circles; plain lines or bands; squares; and hourglass patterns treated like the diamonds. There is great diversity of design, with exact repetition practically nonexistent. There are many arrangements of these units of design, such as one element used in vertical, horizontal, or diagonal rows; several elements combined in one motif; or one element used alone. Colors include blue, red, yellow, black, and blue-green. All are now pale; they may have been brighter when first painted.

In several examples of more recently made Yuma reed flutes, there are some interesting points of contrast. The workmanship is cruder as a whole, with some painting attempted directly on the surface, that is, without benefit of cut patterns. Colors are not handled as effectively, design elements are more limited, and designs lack the attractive arrangements of the earlier flutes.

FIGURE 7.5 Hopi rattles. Although used basically for ceremonies, sometimes rattles are used for other occasions. Often they are made of gourds with wooden handles inserted at one end. Many are decorated; designs vary from simple line patterns (left) to floral themes (right).

Rattles

Perhaps the most common musical instrument made by Southwest Indians is the rattle (Fig. 7.5). It, too, is used primarily for ceremonial purposes, but occasionally may be utilized otherwise, such as for non-ritual dances; some rattles are made for sale. Gourds grow in abundance in the Southwest, several of which are desirable for the making of the rattle. Some puebloans cultivate gourds.

In making a rattle, this procedure is followed quite often. The two ends are cut off, the gourd is dried, pebbles are inserted and shaken around to loosen the meat and seeds, then all are dumped out. Packed with sand, the gourd is allowed to dry thoroughly. The sand is drained out, then rounded pebbles are added and a long stick is inserted, extending through both ends. At its shorter end the stick is secured with piñon gum, while the longer end serves as a handle. Gourd rattles may be left plain; rarely, they have pricked patterns of the constellations (Navajo); or they may be painted with stars, flowers, or other life or geometric themes (pueblo). Formerly, native red and white mineral paints were used, but today commercial paints, bright turquoise, blue, red, and yellow, are often substituted. One Apache woman is making rattles for sale, decorating some of them with traditional geometric designs in enamel paints.

Fiddles

Although there are other musical instruments made by the Southwest Indians, most of them were

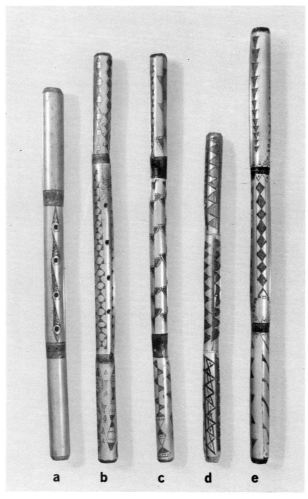

FIGURE 7.4 Yuma cane flutes, made about the turn of the century; designs are cut out and painted. Designs are usually arranged in one (a) or three areas (b through e). They are like those on pottery, such as triangles (a and c) and diamonds (b, c, and e); the treatment of pattern is similar also, such as filling in corners of diamonds (b) and outlining geometrics (c). Colors include blue-green, yellow, black, blue, and red. Length of flutes runs from 13″ to 24″.

or are exclusively for ceremonial usage. One exception is the fiddle made by Apache Indians (Fig. 7.6). This instrument varies in size from one foot to a little over 2 feet in length. Often fiddles are made from the central stalk of the agave; the piece may be straight or slightly curved. Designs are sometimes partly cut out and partly painted, or they may be just painted. One example, made in the late 1920's, shows five bands of decoration in red, green, black, white, blue, and yellow, with generous undecorated areas between bands. Three wider bands ornament the center and ends of the fiddle, with simpler ones between them. Alternating bands of each of the above colors are arranged in full or half circles, diamonds, zigzags, and triangles. Simply painted elements sometimes project from terminal points of the more elaborate motifs, such as a red circle with a blue center at the tip of a triangle.

Ends of the hollow fiddle are plugged, and there are several small holes in the piece. Sticks project from each end to support the horsehair strings. This Apache instrument is definitely post-Spanish in development.

Skin Craft

Quite naturally, the skins of animals were used in great abundance and for a variety of purposes

FIGURE 7.6 Western Apache fiddle. Made of maguey stalk, this example is 25 1/4″ long, 5 1/4″ in diameter at the base and 3 1/4″ at the top (some are much smaller). As this was a later development (post-Spanish), designs were borrowed from other craft sources and are geometric. Colors on this piece include red, blue, white, green, black, and yellow.

in earlier years by Southwest natives. Skin garments, bags, and other objects are found in prehistoric sites. Some tribes, long before the Spanish came, had abandoned skin for cotton garments, as did most of the puebloans. Others, like the Apache, continued to wear clothes made of skins far into the historic period. As a matter of fact, one may still see an Apache maiden wearing a full or partial buckskin dress, the latter over one of commercial cloth, at her "Coming Out" Ceremony. These, no doubt, are family heirlooms. Buckskin dressing is still practiced, though rarely, by some tribes such as the Apaches.

Buckskin was the common material used in skin craft, and although methods of preparation varied somewhat, basically they followed the same general pattern. Puebloans in general kept the skin in damp sand, or in water for a week or so. Havasupais staked the skin in a stream, and in several days the running water had loosened and washed away the hair.[5]

The skin was scraped with a metal blade (formerly stone), then stretched out and rubbed thoroughly on both sides with deer brains which had been boiled. Substitutes, largely commercial, have been tried for this last process but none has proved as successful as the native method. Excess oil was wrung out of the skin, the piece was rubbed between the hands and, in some instances, given a final smoothness by rubbing with a piece of sandstone. An old Walapai man who was blind chewed the skins to soften them. Tanning with vegetable materials, such as canaigre, mormon tea, or white fir, was one substitute method which should be mentioned.

Some coloring was commonly added to the garments, moccasins, or leggings made of buckskin. The white leggings worn by Hopi and other pueblo women are made whiter by rubbing kaolin into them (Figs. 3.7 and 3.13). Navajo and pueblo moccasins are commonly treated with mountain mahogany to give them a rich brownish-red color. Apaches rubbed portions of garments, such as a rounded area about the neck of a blouse, with yellow ochre. Black was occasionally preferred; the Zuñis obtained this color by boiling sumac stems and leaves. All of the skins become hardened by dying with any liquid, therefore they had to be buried and rubbed back to softness. Some ceremonial moccasins are turquoise in color; this shade is produced with copper sulphate.

Some other skins were prepared in the same manner as deer. Coyote, fox, and wildcat skins were treated with brains, then pulled and rubbed with the hands until soft. The hair was left on, so ashes were rubbed in, more or less to keep it from falling out. Buffalo hide was pounded, rolled, pulled, and finally rubbed with a piece of sandstone. This last hide was often used for moccasin soles, with the hair on. Cowhide was later substituted for these soles, and it was treated more like the buckskin. At a later date, cowhide was blackened with a soapweed (*Yucca baccata*) combined with charcoal. This is the typical sole used by Rio Grande puebloans today.[6]

Some pueblo women of the Rio Grande still wear high boots or leggings for daily use; more women and a few men (at Santo Domingo, for example) wear the moccasin in the same way. Others wear the high boots and moccasins only on ceremonial occasions. In the Rio Grande there are subtle differences in the moccasin-legging for each pueblo. For years the heavier the legging, the more prestige a woman had for it meant that her husband was a good hunter and provider. Leggings of pueblo women are of a shaped, single piece or a long strip (puttee) which is wrapped about the leg; Navajo women also wear the latter style. Apache types were ankle or knee length; there was a turned-up toe on these styles of the Western Apache (Fig. 7.7).

Whole and large skins were beautifully tanned and worn as robes. Bowguards were made of any scrap of skin, be it mountain lion, wildcat, antelope, or buffalo; later they were made of cowhide. Apache men made shirts of buckskin; their women wore a one- or two-piece dress (Fig. 7.8) of the same material which was sometimes decorated. The only "sewing" done by puebloans on garments and bags was really tying in some instances or lacing in others; much better work was done on their moccasins.

Southwest Indians made a variety of bags and pouches of skins. Very often the ceremonial pouch and other bags or quivers were made from the whole skin of a small animal or a fragment of buckskin. It was not until late in the nineteenth century that the Apaches beaded their buckskin bags, first for themselves and later to sell. Beaded styles are discussed below.

When the horse was introduced, some of the Indians learned to make saddle bags of buckskin or hide (Fig. 7.9). Once in a great while the Apaches in Arizona still make these. Two long strips of hide were sewed together, and a slit cut in the center. Fringe was attached at the two ends as the bag is sewed. These were often decorated in an interesting manner: one or several patches were arranged at both ends between the tip of the slit and the fringe. Designs, usually stars, crosses, scallops, or simple geometric themes, were cut out in the patches before they were sewed on; black, red, or yellow cloth was placed under the cut-out areas. A red baize-like material was a favorite for

this decorative touch. Incidentally, after buckskin became more and more difficult to come by, the Apaches substituted cotton cloth for these bags. They used a white or off-white material for the bag proper, appliqueing geometric patterns in several colors, such as yellow and black or red and green,

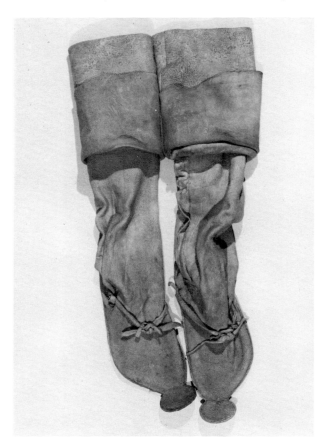

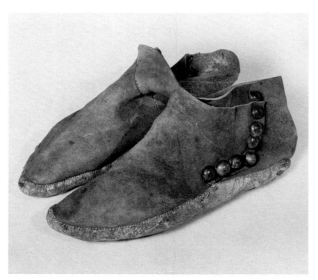

FIGURE 7.7 Western Apache and Hopi — probably — moccasins. Both are made of buckskin with heavier soles of hide. Most interesting is the old-style hip length Apache one (above) with the odd toe protector which is an extension of the sole. The low Hopi moccasin (below) is usually decorated with one or more silver beads.

on a single bag. Fringe, too, was of cloth on these later bags.

Hide shields (Fig. 7.10) were made by several tribes in the Southwest, including some of the Yumans, the Papagos, and several of the Tiwa puebloans. The hair was removed, the hide cut into a large disc, and a handle put on the under side so that it could be held. Underhill reports that the puebloans laid the shield over warm ashes, thus hardening it.[7]

A number of pueblo shields examined in 1952 showed a variety of decorations (Fig. 7.11). One

FIGURE 7.8 Western Apache woman's buckskin blouse and doll which shows full dress. The western Apache woman's dress was two-piece: a fringe-sleeved blouse, and a skirt which was often fringed at sides and bottom. Sometimes decorative additions were made; these included small tin tinklers, commercial beads, or coloring of the buckskin. Buckskin boots completed the costume. The doll shows this complete costume, even to the upturned-toe moccasin.

FIGURE 7.9 Western Apache saddle bags. After the acquisition of the horse the Apaches borrowed the idea of the saddlebag, using hide for its construction, and adapting his own designs for decoration. Cut-out designs were most popular, with red and/or black cloth inserted under the open areas. Plain (above) or decorative fringes finished off the bag.

FIGURE 7.10 Sketch of Papago shield. Shields were made of hide and painted; quite simple patterns were used for decoration. This swastika-like design was created by painting the white theme, outlining it in red, and then allowing the blackening hide to further emphasize the pattern.

favorite theme is a pair of short stubby horns in the upper half rising out of a central transverse band. Rayed or straight lines, or in one case zigzag lines terminating in arrow points, emanate from the same central band and extend into the lower half of the shield. One of the most interesting of these shields has a black lower half separated from the transverse band by a very narrow light line; the central black band has five large circles in the natural color of the hide. In the upper part of the shield is a horned serpent coming out of the central band as though it were emerging from murky waters.

Although geometric patterns seem to prevail in these shields, life designs were sometimes used, as indicated in the serpent. A shield in the Museum of New Mexico, Santa Fe, has crude drawings of two other animals on it, a deer and a buffalo; sufficient realism exists to identify these animals. A geometric form such as a circle may be outlined in color, or it may be both filled in one color and outlined in a second — a red star outlined in black, for example. Considerable variety in color may appear on a single shield, such as blue, green, red, and yellow or black, red, green, and yellow. A single color or two colors may be used, such as red alone or red and black.

Glass Bead Work

Commercial glass beads from Venice were introduced into the Southwest by the Spanish around 1540; later ones came from Czechoslovakia. Later, too, they were popular among the Plains Indians and were used extensively by them. When the Southwest Indian acquired these commercial beads, his innate artistic taste dictated that a few only should appear on a single item. Thus on an Arizona Apache blouse and skirt there might be a single and narrow band of blue and white beads outlining an ochre-colored area. A few beads were used to ornament a small bag or pouch, or a pair of Jicarilla Apache moccasins. It was not until later that the Arizona Apache Indians began to make necklaces and complete bags of beads without benefit of any buckskin.

FIGURE 7.11 Pueblo hide shields. Although there is considerable variety in the decoration of these shields, these three are representative. A simpler decorative type (left) has a central dark band with light circles and edges and a star in the remaining top and bottom sectors. Highly conventionalized buffalo horns combined with curved and straight, vari-colored bands were also popular decorative themes (center). Somewhat more elaborate are the treatments of life subjects — they tend to be realistic. A horned serpent (right) comes out of a dark band decorated with simple circles.

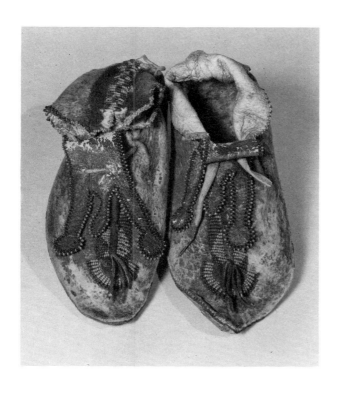

FIGURE 7.13   To the left are two Western Apache beaded bags, both made of buckskin and heavily fringed. Small cones made of tin are attached to the fringed bottoms of these pieces. Note the emphasis on dark-colored beads in one and stress on light colors in the other. To the right, a variety of designs and colors is featured in the several objects. The two necklaces have unusually heavy fringes with regular alternations of vari-colored beads; comparable alternations appear in the main part of each necklace. All designs are geometric and include typical motifs. (*Photos by Joseph Muench*)

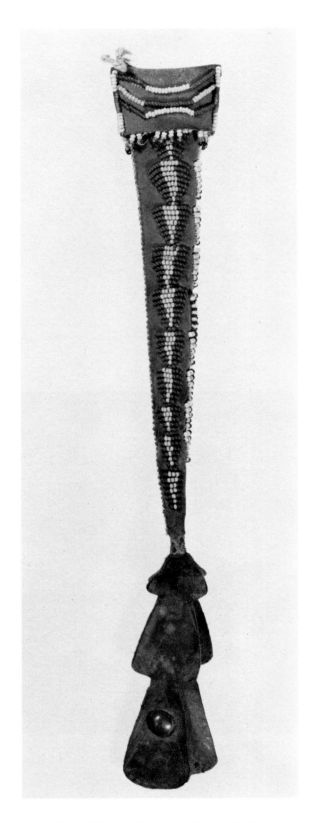

FIGURE 7.14 Western Apache awl case. Basket weavers kept their awls in plain or decorated buckskin cases. This one is ornamented with beads of various colors, an elaborate tassel at the bottom with one metal bead, and a decorated flap. Total length is 11″.

bands of varying widths of beads of several colors, or they added another design on the toe, such as a cross in one or two colors. Sometimes this moccasin type was even more elaborately ornamented with beads.

Bags varied in shape and decoration. The most common shape was a square or rectangle (Fig. 7.13), with or without a flap. Some bags were gently curved along the lower edge; still others had more pointed bottoms with a slight restriction just below the upper border. Like the moccasin, the edge of the bag often had a simple outlining in beads; at the opposite extreme was an allover but not solid treatment. One example of the latter had a single row of diagonal bands at the bottom, two rows along the sides including a continuous line of blue triangles, a second of diagonal and joined pairs of red-blue beads, and over the face of the bag blue, red, yellow, and green zigzags. As the Apache bag was commercialized, it became more ornate in scalloped edges, floral themes, beads of many colors on one piece, and more elaborate designs.

Awl cases (Fig. 7.14), which were not commercialized, remained simple in their decoration. A typical example has vertical bands across the slender piece and red beads alternating with similar rows of tin tinklers. The latter are the same as the ones decorating the Apache burden basket — small cones of tin suspended from short lengths of buckskin, but close enough together to jingle one against the other. Fringes of these tinklers were favored on any type of bag.

If objects were made of beads alone, the woman wove them on a loom. A common loom was made by nailing two short upright pieces of wood at the ends of a horizontal board. Over these end pieces and around the loom were arranged the "warps," usually of size 40 commercial thread. The worker picked up the proper colors of beads on the end of her needle and sewed them into the loom threads. Usually she sewed back through the beads a second time to secure them in position.

Pieces which were made solely of beads, some on the loom, include a T-shaped necklace, other necklaces, medallions, hatbands, and solid bands which were woven and then attached to belts (Fig. 7.15). The most interesting of these pieces is the T-shaped necklace (Fig. 7.16) which more recently has been worn by some of the Apache girls in their Coming Out Ceremony or Puberty Rite. Two bands are woven separately and sewed together to form this unusual piece. On one such T-necklace the horizontal band is 9 inches long and 2½ inches wide; the vertical element is 3 inches wide and 10 inches long. Both bands are solid except for the bottom 2¼ inches of the vertical piece which is made up

FIGURE 7.15 Western Apache bead worker. This woman wears the currently popular medallion on the end of a rolled necklace. She is sewing cloth on the back and ribbon on the ends of the T-necklace. About her are various other bands and necklaces. (*Photo by Charles W. Herbert*)

of many short and loose strings of beads. Colors in this necklace include yellow, red, green, dark blue, and white. Designs include triangles, hexagons, diamonds, and odd geometric forms.

In recent years Apaches have been encouraged to make necklaces more suitable for wear by white women. Some of these are in a style long made by the Apaches, a narrow band 36 inches long, more or less, with simple geometric designs throughout its length. A fringe of loose strings of beads decorates the bottom; just above the fringe is a pendant, often round and designed. Even more wearable are short choker-type necklaces, plain or with scalloped or pointed edges, and done in one or two colors which are less gaudy (Fig. 7.17). Bolo ties are formed of a pencil-thick round of beads with a slide which is circular and decorated with geometric designs.

Other Southwest Indians have not developed as much work in glass beads as the Apaches, nor have they developed pieces which possess any more native flavor than the Apache work. But there are several tribes, the Navajos and Zuñis in particular, which have been encouraged to produce items which can be labeled strictly commercial. One such piece is the rabbit's foot which is made into several figures. Workmanship, comparatively speaking, is often very good on these pieces, but they have no particular artistic value.

Colors vary greatly in this Indian beadwork, but generally they have been on the darker side. For many years this was true of most of the beads in the Southwest, exclusive of the Paiutes who favored lighter colors for this craft. In recent years, however, lighter-colored and more varied beads have been

FIGURE 7.16 Western Apache T-shaped necklace. This kind is usually worn by young girls at their puberty rites. As this is a fairly recent piece, there has been no development of distinctive pattern, and most of it involves familiar geometrics. Colors in this necklace include much yellow and white, with less red, blue, and green. The fringe of beads at the bottom incorporates the same colors.

traded to some of the other Indians. Earlier beads were of the rounder type; today many are faceted, and thus are more shiny. Iridescent beads, clear beads, pearl beads, and other variations have appeared during the past twenty-five or thirty years.

Rabbit's feet may be plain or they may be so worked as to represent figures of men and women. Small figures of the men are generalized but complete with a "feather" headdress done in beads. Women are represented with full skirts: some of them sit at a tiny loom. Although only several inches high, there is much detail; there are individual fingers (too large), eyes, nose, and mouth, and not only colored garments but also some with designs on them! One man wears yellow pants and a flowered shirt. Women's skirts have bands of color in them.

Zuñis have expanded beadwork to include several other all-bead pieces, among them men on horseback and women in full pueblo dress. Some of the former show spotted horses with manes upright and wrapped tails, a saddle blanket, and the man in proper and very colorful dress (Fig. 7.18). Better examples of the beadwork figures of women are remarkable in that they are complete to the last detail of costume — some have pots on their heads

(Fig. 7.19)! One such beaded figure shows the pueblo woman's native black dress with red and green bands, a scalloped-edged petticoat, light blue blouse under the blanket dress, and a white apron with red and green flowers on it. The representation of the silk scarf which this women wears is quite remarkable: it is red with a blue and white border and on the red background are five decorative motifs, one in the center and one in each corner. Other details which make this piece outstanding are black-soled white moccasins; semi-blue, white, and red beads which simulate a turquoise, shell, and coral necklace; the figure-eight hairdo; and a pot on the head. Even the beaded pot has a design on it.

To be sure, many of these pieces, such as the rabbit's foot, miniature drums, moccasins, and others, are out-and-out curio items; they reflect little or no skill but do show imagination. Work of this type is done not only by Zuñis and Navajos but also by Yuman and Apache tribes. More skill is demonstrated in the larger Zuñi figures of women or horses and men.

Both skill and artistry are demonstrated in many of the "Big Bertha" collars (Fig. 7.20) made by the Mohave and Yuma Indians of the Lower Colorado River about the turn of the century and shortly thereafter, with a few made in recent years. Generally they were made of dark blue and white glass beads in an openwork weave. Designs were strictly traditional in the earlier pieces, such as hexagons in outline. Later other themes were woven into these collars — an American flag or an eagle with outspread wings; examples of both of the latter two were observed in pieces made in the 1950's. Many smaller pieces are made today (Fig. 7.17).

Cradle Boards

Baby cradles (Fig. 7.21) represent one of the very old crafts of Southwest Indians, for they are found far back into prehistory. Some tribes still make and use them while a few make occasional cradles for sale. There is variation in cradles, or cradle boards as they are commonly called, with definite differences from tribe to tribe. There is also some variation within a given tribe depending upon the age of the child for whom the cradle is made.

One type of cradle board is based on the bending of a stout withe into an elliptical form which is a little smaller at the base; the greater part of this is then crossed with transverse bars or slats. This type was made by the Havasupais, Walapais, and the Apaches. The latter tribe makes a hood of two bent rods, and this is overlaid with pine lathes.

FIGURE 7.17 Mohave and Yuma beadwork. Although made by these two tribes, these pieces illustrate a type of work done by other Indians; the choker (a) and closed collar (c) styles, for example, also have been made by the Apaches. The short multiple strand necklace (b) is unusual (commercial beads). Small pieces like the cigaret case (d) have been made by other tribes also. Dark blue and white beads predominate in most of the Mohave work. All work here is Mohave except the cigaret case, which is Yuma, possibly.

Formerly buckskin was used for wrappings, hood covers, and other details; today canvas, heavy cordage, and even wire replace the older materials. The Apaches dye the canvas a bright yellow with the root of the crown of thorns (*Canotia halocantha*).[8]

Mohaves and Pimas used a U-shaped foundation which tapered toward the base, and over this were fastened wide-spaced cross bars. Pimas wove a twilled hood. The Navajo cradle is made of two long boards, holes are drilled close to the center edge of each board so that they may be tied together. Holes are also drilled close to the outer edges to accommodate ties for holding the baby on the board. Cochití Pueblo Indians make a cradle like that of the Navajos. The main difference is illustrated in an example in the Laboratory of Anthropology, Santa Fe: the top is carved in stepped "cloud" style. A wicker cradle is woven by the Hopis.

All cradles have a board or some type of foot rest, a hood, and loops or other devices at the sides to aid in securing the baby on the board.

Cradles range in size from about 33 to 40 inches long and from about 8 to 14 inches wide at the top. Thongs, cordage, buckskin, cedar bark, native woods, woven mats — all of these were used natively. Some still are, but more commonly they have been replaced by commercial string, wire, strips of cloth, a great variety of commercial fabrics, and wood from crates, boxes, and other such sources. In most cases, and despite substitution of materials, each tribe adheres to its traditional style even when making a cradle for sale.

Dolls

The women in several Southwest Indian tribes make cloth dolls. In general, the dolls are clothed in the styles of each respective tribe, crude facial features are painted or penciled on white or tan

FIGURE 7.18 Zuñi beaded man on horseback. This one is typical of these gay little figures, with their horses of various colors (this one is red), and the men even brighter in their colorful war bonnets and dress; colors here are white, dark and light blue, orange, yellow, and black. Color is also used to bring out facial and head detail.

cloth, and bits of tin, leather, beads, or other "extras" may be added to make the dolls more realistic. Proper materials are sometimes used, such as velveteen for a Navajo blouse or cotton print or synthetic fabric — even the old-style buckskin costume — for the Apache dress.

Today cloth dolls are made by Navajos, Apaches, and a few are made by Papagos. Navajo dolls range from several inches in height to about 2 feet; occasionally some are larger. Both men and women are represented by the Navajos (Fig. 7.22). Very commonly the man has on red-brown moccasins, white cotton trousers, a velveteen blouse of bright color, and a band about his head. The woman is dressed equally gaily, with moccasins plus white leggings, a long, full, flounced cotton or velveteen skirt, and a velveteen blouse. Men and women alike wear the chongo hairdo tied with bright wool yarns or white string. Usually both dolls are also decorated with concha belts, earrings, and necklaces; red-, white-, and turquoise-colored glass beads simulate the real coral, shell, and turquoise worn by all Navajos. Bits of tin, often with markings on them, suggest the silver original.

Even these dolls reflect the march of time and the changing culture of the Indian. Sequins have appeared in recent years; so too have gay pieces of commercial braid, and silver or gold and white bands used about the waist.

FIGURE 7.19 Zuñi beaded woman. Rather clever bead work is to be noted in the larger figures made by the Zuñis; this woman is 11 1/2″ high. Designs are woven in the pot on her head, on her embroidered apron, petticoat, and shoulder shawl. Turquoise, shell, and coral beads are simulated in the alternating white and blue commercial beads and the red ones about her neck. The high white, black-soled moccasins worn by these women are also represented. Even her hair is done up in figure-eight style and wrapped with a broad band of beads.

Apache dolls (Fig. 7.23) are made in the same general manner. Facial features tend to be a little more Indian but not completely so. The hair is banged in front and hangs loose down the back. Typical Apache women's dress of the past seventy or more years is represented (male dolls are not made by the Apaches). The skirt is long, full, and flounced; it is of cotton, either plain or a print. The dress is often decorated with ricrac braid on the yoked neck of the blouse and at each flounce on the skirt. New synthetic materials have had a great appeal for the Apache, and the dolls reflect this trend in their costumes.

Other Items

An analysis of all the other small miscellaneous crafts cannot be made here, but several of them should be mentioned. Real skill is evidenced in some of the fine lariats made by the Papagos; today a few are still made of braided horsehair or rawhide. Until a few years ago, one man among the Walapais made quirts and lariats of cowhide. Curved rabbit sticks are still made and sometimes decorated by the Hopi Indians; they are effective as weapons but they do not return as does the Australian boomerang. A number of tribes continue to make bows and arrows; some use them ceremonially, but more produce and decorate them for sale.

In recent years another interesting craft expression has developed to a slight degree among a few Navajos. This is the making of sandpaintings on boards. Plyboard forms the base on which is put a neutral color, the latter serving as the ground on which the designs in multi-colored sands are created. Patterns are taken from the sacred sandpaintings used by the Navajos in their curing rites. A complete or nearly complete design or only a part of one may be so used.

One last craft expression, a little known one and one long since abandoned, will be discussed briefly — just out of sheer interest. This is the making of playing cards by the Apaches (Fig. 7.24) and possibly by some other tribes. The probable time that the Apaches made them is "not earlier than 1850 and not later than 1900."[9] Few of these cards exist today; those observed include four decks in the Southwest Museum, Los Angeles, two (one is thought to be Yuma) in the Arizona State Museum, Tucson, and one in the Amerind Foundation Museum, Dragoon, Arizona. Various numbers of cards have survived, although forty are in the complete deck in the Arizona State Museum.

The Indian cards were made on skin "prepared by the rawhide method";[10] this, perhaps, assured durability and rigidity. There is slight variation in size; in one set cards measure 2¼ inches by 3⅝ inches. The cards are not absolutely regular and even. Quite generally the corners are rounded, although they are sometimes squared. They are painted in several colors — yellow, red, black, and blue (orange in place of blue in one set) on the Southwest Museum examples, and red, black, and yellow on the Arizona State Museum Apache cards — with variation in the shades of these colors. Colors of the Yuma deck are odd; they appear to

FIGURE 7.20 "Big Bertha" collar made by the Mohave Indians. This dark blue and white piece has typical Mohave designs in it. Most of these collars were fringed. Formerly these were burned on the funeral pyre.

be inks rather than paints; this is particularly true of a greenish tone. The drawing bears this out, too, for outlines, details, and the execution as a whole are finer than on the other cards. There is variation in painting in the several decks, perhaps reflecting individual ability.

Wayland notes that Spanish decks of cards in 1500 and the Mexican one of 1960 have forty cards of four suits each. Suit symbols include a sword, a club, a coin, and a goblet or cup. Each suit has an ace, numeral cards two through seven, king, knight in place of queen, and page.[11]

On the back of the Apache deck in the Arizona State Museum is a clipping from a newspaper (no name or date) with this note which differs slightly from Wayland's comment. "The spade is a sword . . . ; the club is a veritable club or bludgeon; the heart is a heart enclosed in an urn, and the diamond a gem or jewel represented as set in the center of a dish or brooch of some kind. The spot cards end with the unevens, the eights, nines and tens not being included in the pack. In the Apache cards the queen is represented by a female figure rudely drawn . . . the king is represented by a man and the jack or knight by a man on horseback."

Some interesting expressions came out in the painting of the Apache cards. For example, as the artist moved from one to seven in the unit cards, the drawing became progressively simpler and colors more limited. Lacking experience in painting, the Indian also had difficulty in representing a man on horseback; in some cases he managed to get the rider's legs over the animal, but in others the crude full-front drawing of the man terminated the body in a straight line when it met the horse's back. Interestingly, often the painting in the former is superior to the latter. On one card the rectangular figure of the knight stands on the horse's back! In

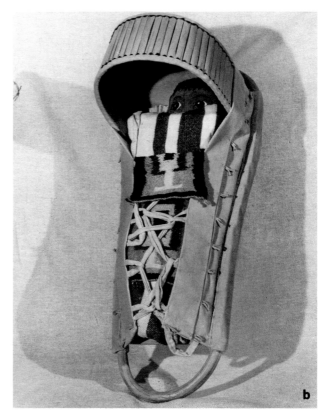
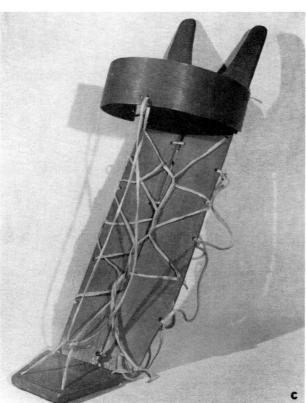
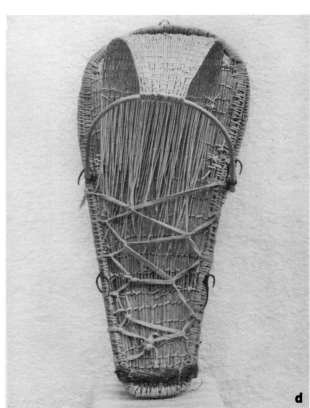

FIGURE 7.21 Hopi, Apache, Navajo, and Paiute cradle boards. A variety of forms and materials was used by Southwest Indians in making these cradle boards. Reeds were woven in wicker fashion by the Hopis (a) and willow in twined weave by the Paiutes (d) for both the board proper and for the hood. Apaches used slats for both parts, while the Navajo used two boards lashed together in the center and double pointed at the top for the main part and a thin sheet of bent wood for the hood. All use cloth for padding, sides, and ties; formerly buckskin was more common and often handwoven ties were used. The Navajo made a footrest of wood, the Paiute from a roll of juniper bark. (*Paiute cradle courtesy Robert Euler*)

FIGURE 7.22 Navajo cloth dolls of a type which has developed recently. These two are fairly elaborate. They are dressed in the traditional velveteen man's shirt and woman's blouse, while the man wears cotton trousers and the woman a full velveteen skirt. Commercial beads are used for the necklaces, rings, and bracelets, and a few sequins are sewed to the blouses. The man's belt, bandolier, and headband are of commercial braid.

one deck at the Southwest Museum several of the male figures have straight lines projecting from the shirt as though the artist were attempting to suggest that the fellow was wearing a fringed buckskin garment.

Inspiration from Spanish-Mexican originals is reflected to a greater or lesser degree in the Indian's painting of his cards. Now and again the Apaches' own cultural background was strongly expressed. For example, the outline of the king on one card is Spanish but the designs within are Apache; swords become arrows; coins become an Indian shield on another card; and on still another a page is much more of an Apache Crown Dancer than a Spanish character.

Summary

Thus, the minor crafts are one more demonstration of the distinct flair of the Indian for projecting many of his skills and his artistic tendencies into new and very different expressions. This, of course, is how art survives and thrives. And it is the ability to convert the old into new forms with freshness, vigor, and spontaneity that is the mark of real art, whether in the crafts or in fine art.

FIGURE 7.23 Western Apache woman and dolls. The dolls are dressed in the gay colors and style popular with Apache women to this day. The gathered yokes and the full skirts are decorated with braid as are their originals. Apache women's hair styles are also represented. (*Photo by Charles W. Herbert*)

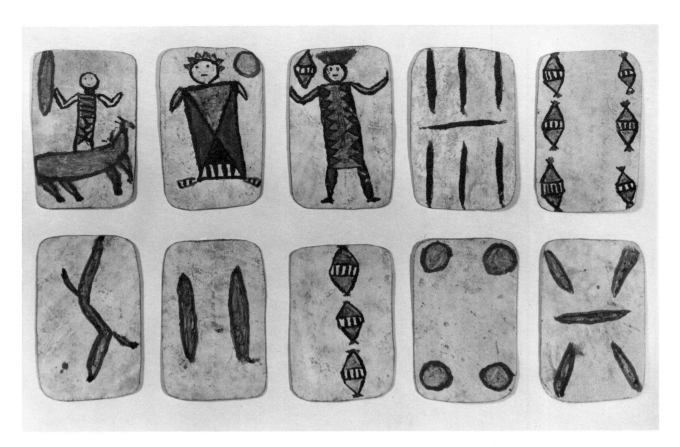

FIGURE 7.24 Western Apache playing cards. Back in the later 1800's playing cards were made by the members of this tribe out of skin prepared by the "rawhide method." Then they were painted; these are done in red, black, and yellow. Note that the cards are not absolutely regular and that the maker resorted to several devices in arranging figures (man on horseback) and numbers — the club lost the additions it had in the one card when the two and five cards were made.

Many crafts of lesser nature, as well as certain new developments in the major arts, have appeared in recent years. In some instances these are the result of experimentation inspired through contact situations, such as the playing cards or the silver chalice described above. Often such expressions reflect an individual's revolt against the traditional, or merely a desire to try something different and, perhaps, more difficult and challenging. Again, the truly artistic nature of the Southwest Indian comes to the fore in the highly esthetic qualities of his endeavor. Thus are created new forms, new decorative ideas, new crafts. Many of these minor crafts were so born.

In Retrospect   *Chapter VIII*

SOUTHWEST Indian craft art is, first and foremost, a tribal art. It is and was produced by members of societies for use within each respective tribe. Extensions of use-value beyond the tribe do not deny this basic premise, for when a clay vessel is made for a white man, the majority of the traditional tribal concepts direct its creation. Too, this art is primitive.

But, primitive does not mean simple and elemental, for it has been demonstrated that much of the native art of the Southwest has progressed far into the realm of sophistication. Primitive applies to the general quality of the culture out of which this art comes, a culture which has not yet reached the state of the more advanced civilizations of the world.

Neither primitive nor tribal implies great age or obsolescence, for this is a craft art that lives today. Some of it thrives and is developing year by year, such as Navajo silversmithing, while other forms have become lost or nearly so, such as Apache basketry.

Moreover, a number of the Southwest Indian groups have not yet lost their tribal identity. The Papago tribe, for example, is a distinct entity with an established roll of membership, functioning as a unit under a council, with a culture peculiarly its own, and with problems which pertain specifically to this group. In the same way, the products of their basket makers are distinctly Papago and not to be confused with the baskets of other tribes. The same statements apply to many other tribes.

Not only are there qualities distinctive of the art of the Southwest Indians as a whole, but also there are traits in the art forms peculiar to each individual tribal group in the Southwest. Douglas characterizes the overall Southwest style in terms of a geometric, stepped pattern; this is to be found in Hopi pots, Apache baskets, kachina masks, and on old Rio Grande textiles. At the same time there are the intimacies of design and form which separate the products of these tribes, making each distinctive. Apaches do not carve kachina masks, Hopi pots differ from all others in color and shape as well as designs, and Rio Grande textiles were woven and ornamented with specific designs in colors and materials not used by any non-puebloan groups.

Of all the Southwest craft arts discussed in the preceding chapters, Navajo silver and rugs are perhaps more widely known than any of the others. This is most interesting in view of the fact that silver is a late historic introduction and rugs present a new form to this tribe in a European-introduced material — wool. Nonetheless, these two crafts, partially or wholly borrowed as they are, have been converted to "Navajo" by virtue of designs and general art styles.

These facts simply point up basic thoughts which are pertinent to the understanding of any art form. Art is a part of culture. All cultures change or they die. So too with art. Whether the trend is advancement or degeneracy, change is as essential as breathing — or the art dies. And in the process of change, there is borrowing, exchange of ideas, and the dropping of old forms and concepts and creation of new ones. This process has been going on for centuries in the Southwest; there has been ample precedent for the acceptance of new materials, such as wool and silver, for new forms, as in choker necklaces, and for completely new designs, as, for example, the squash blossom. Thus, it may be said, the "changed" art of today is still as much Indian as was the Avanu of the past, for the idea of this snake motif probably came to the Southwest from the Mexican cultures to the south.

So when the question is asked, "What is Indian craft art?" the answer is: "The products of these people at any time, the crafts produced by these folk called Indian, Navajo, or Apache, or any other, as the case may be." In 1966 the Indian should not be producing the same forms and designs in silver that he was making in 1880, for his cultural experiences have introduced him to some new equipment and many new ideas.

The history of the craft arts in the Southwest is long and complicated, and the intelligent craftsman takes advantage of what comes his way as would any student of the fine arts. The world would never have known the beauty and grace of a golden cup had not Cellini been an alert student of the advanced technical knowledge of his day and time. The Southwest Indian has not ignored the best of his past, for this has been the firm foundation upon which he has built. Without the ancient and splendid developments in technology, forms, and designs, the Navajo rug in wool could not have developed. Sophisticated design such as is found in contemporary pueblo pottery speaks for centuries of refinement in this craft art.

Thus, history and contacts have been very much a part of the development of Southwest craft arts, and continuing developments are not going to stop now because some sentimental white man would like to have the Navajo perpetuate the bracelet style his forefathers made in the 1880's. Because of the terrific impact of the conqueror, certain drastic changes were bound to occur, changes which have little or no connection with the slow and gradual growth of culture in pre-conquest days.

Quite generally the survival or perpetuation of Southwest crafts has followed one of two patterns. First, certain limited expressions, such as the weaving of kilts and shoulder blankets, have persisted within one group only, for these products have lost all their use-value except for the ritual. Hopis can supply the limited demand, so all other tribes have ceased to produce them.

The second, and the more general sequence of events, has been the following. The white man introduces substitutes for a craft product, so the craft dwindles in production. Then, some white man — or group of them — decides that this should not happen and takes the matter into his own hands. Let us say that the craft in question is pottery. Whites encourage individual women to produce certain wares, then they go out and create a market for the same. In time, the "revival" is a healthy and growing craft, quite naturally taking new directions. Perhaps the native potters are encouraged to change forms, or decrease size, many of these things in keeping with the pocketbook, taste, and use-value of the buyer in mind. This has been one of the most important influences in the perpetuation of Southwest Indian crafts. It is one of those cultural factors which has to be accepted whether one likes the changes or not.

Perhaps the greatest problem in this second situation has been the poor taste of the white man and not the inability or lack of artistry of the craftsworker. Rugs have gone through periods of decline only because too many white men thought that to be Indian a rug had to be garish in color and wild in design. This could discourage the stoutest-hearted artist. Couple this with the barbaric custom of selling all rugs by the pound, and the last ounce of artistry is drained from the weaver. The up-turn from low levels created by such situations resulted from the education of the white man as to what is good in Indian craft and the adjustment of price accompanying the straightforward encouragement of the worker in the direction of better craftsmanship.

Thus, the survival potential has been directly dependent on the white man in many cases. He had no use for a Navajo blanket but he could well use a rug from the same loom. If traders had not been interested in silver work, in many instances to the point of financing the craft one way or another, Zuñi and Navajo silver might well have remained an insignificant craft, or, for that matter, might have died out completely. The latter could well have been the case after the introduction of machine-made jewelry.

Since art is conceptually a part of the total culture of any group, and since it is not to be separated from the everyday life of the Indian, further change is as inevitable as it has been in the past. The environment, both physical and cultural, in which the Indian is growing up today, is rapidly changing. In the past the puebloan weaver was limited to the cotton he could grow or for which he could trade. Today almost any thread is available. Is it surprising, then, that some Two Gray Hills rugs have a bit of nylon thread in them? Is it any the less Indian if the weaver chooses to spin her thread on the sewing machine instead of tediously working with the spindle stick and whorl? Imagine cutting 125 small stones for a Zuñi bracelet without benefit of the lapidary wheel! We accept the latter but feel offended by the former. It is the white man who is changing the Indian's environment; he gave the Indian both the lapidary's wheel and the sewing machine.

An even greater change is going on among the Indians which is turning their crafts into ever-new channels of expression. In his natural environment, before the arrival of the white man and for a surprisingly long time thereafter in some groups, the Indian grew up as an intimate and close part of this native culture. The Navajo baby on the cradle watched its mother weave, or the Apache infant, from a similar vantage point, saw the lovely burden baskets with the freshly dyed yellow thongs filled with foodstuffs for all those present on ceremonial occasions. The spindle stick is picked up or a bit of fluffy wool pulled back and forth by the small and inexperienced hands of a little girl. Or the Apache youngster grabs a sweet out of one of the baskets. Thus the child grows with and into the crafts of his tribe. The design of the rug becomes a part of him, the basket form and ornament he knows intuitively as being that of his own Navajo or Apache tribe. It is thus that the child grows to maturity, and in time weaves the rug or basket and of course it is, accordingly, Navajo or Apache. His tribal craft is a living part of him.

But this picture is changing. The ceremony is abandoned, the baskets are sold to the first white man who comes along. The woman no longer weaves, for her husband is making good wages working on the new highway on the reservation. Or the girl goes to the new public school near her home, and there the teaching is like that of the whites, so there are no craft classes. After graduation, the tribe offers the young lady a scholarship to go on to college. In this way of life there is little or no tribal art, and if a little, it is so fleeting that it leaves no impressions on the young of the art styles of their people.

The only difference in these situations among the varied tribes today is degree and not kind.

The economic level of a tribe bears a certain ratio to the amount and kind of crafts that groups will develop. With rare exceptions, few or no great arts or crafts have come from groups dogged by poverty. Lack of any economic well-being leaves no leisure time, and certainly some freedom is essential to the creative arts. In the Southwest the puebloan, through the higher developments of agriculture and the storage of a surplus against the future, gave himself that leisure so precious to the arts. Slight wonder that he expressed a wide variety of crafts and developed several of them to a high point. Sometimes comparable high developments may come out of less fortunate situations, for example, in the case of the Navajo.

Other aspects of life were significant in the development of the arts; for one, the puebloan sought secrecy in the enactment of certain of his rituals. By no means was the man occupied with ceremonies all of the hours of the many days he spent in the kiva before an afternoon appearance for the public ritual. There was some leisure time, and even gossip could not take up all these hours. Of an industrious nature, many of these men set up the loom in the kiva and pursued weaving. It is quite possible that the religious atmosphere of the setting did not detract from creativity. It is probable, too, that exchange of ideas about various crafts brought new vigor of expression year after year.

Enforced leisure because of seasonal work patterns also may have played a part in the development of the crafts. Certainly in the long winters, when cold and snow prohibited farming (and in the native state there were no domestic food animals), enforced leisure probably contributed a share to higher developments. Surely this was a factor in pueblo religion, and well could it have been in the craft arts.

In a way, it is surprising that the Southwest tribes, and particularly the pueblo groups, did not aboriginally develop something of a guild system. But it was not until late in the historic period — in the 1930's — that such an idea was introduced to the Indians by the national Arts and Crafts Board. Perhaps some of the success of the guilds can be attributed to the fact that the framework already existed in the basic pueblo concept of cooperative thinking, particularly in their religion which expressed a deep and abiding conviction in the necessity of group action and thought.

Guilds have played a part in the appearance of "specialists." Before the guilds, there was little effort in this direction. One of the rare instances of such was the Hopi production of decorated pottery on First Mesa, coiled baskets on Second Mesa, and the wicker basketry on Third Mesa. Undecorated utility pottery, and the common utility basket — the plaited ring bowl — were made on all three mesas. This, of course, was group specialization; individual specialization was related to commercialization — the native-use piece was made by anyone. This trend toward Hopi village specialization began before the turn of the twentieth century. Regional types of Navajo rugs represent a comparable specialization.

The rich material culture of the Southwest Indian gave him a wide and varied opportunity for the development of the decorative arts. Natively his variety of tools, weapons, implements, pots and other vessels, clothing, and jewelry, offered surfaces of many shapes and kinds which invited decoration. A wide variety of materials, including wood, clay, stone, bone, horn, shell, fibers, plus others, added considerable choice of treatment of textures.

Through their own ingenuity and as a result of contacts with other native and higher civilizations, these Indians developed a number of technologies to produce their needs and desires in the great variety of materials which they found in their environment or which they imported. To be sure, certain limitations were imposed on the artist by technology or, for that matter, by materials. But the native went far within these controls, and expressed individual tribal feelings within them. A good example of this is the yucca basket of the Hopis and the Papagos, one developing a large round coil, the other a flat one, one refining the sewing element so that design became greatly diversified and sensitive while the other used coarse sewing splints and seldom got beyond heavy and simple design elements. Wide variety and considerable perfection in the basketry craft as a whole in the Southwest, and among the Apaches, Pimas, old Papagos, and Hopis in particular, stand as a monument to the artistic genius of these folk.

A long familiarity with materials has been no small factor in the perfection of artistry and the establishment of tribal styles, whether in basketry or other crafts. To this day the continued use of native fibers and clays has aided the perpetuation of native styles and designs in baskets and pottery. On the other hand, newly introduced silver, with its specialized technology, brought in its wake new forms and designs. Its recency of acquisition may well be reflected in the many deviations from the first styles which too often are thought of as "traditional." Pawn pieces merely reflect some of the early stages of development of design in this craft art, and there are bad pieces of pawn as well as good ones. Perhaps it is the sustained simplicity and massiveness in a larger number of early pieces which is appealing. Let it not be forgotten, however, that these qualities still prevail in the best of Navajo silver. Changing and developing technologies have contributed to a greater refinement in workmanship which should not detract from the appraisal by the critical eye.

The changing economy of the Indians has played a vital part in the story of their crafts. In the barter phase, one craft object was exchanged for an item not produced by the other group. When the trader came in, crafts were again exchanged, but in this later instance for newly introduced foods, clothing, or yardage goods. The trader created new desires among the natives, then capitalized on these desires. No money was involved, as a rule. Finally came a cash economy, but not until World War II among some of the Southwest tribes.

A cash economy has become one of the greatest motivations to increased production in many of the Southwest Indian craft arts. Although too complicated to elaborate upon here, it may be said that it is intimately tied in with increased "necessities," such as kitchen stoves, other household furnishings, or a new pickup truck, and such personal desires as hair permanents. A certain element of prestige is involved, also. In the old days the crafts were an end in themselves; today they are a means to an end. In the old way of life, there was not time for specialists, for one had to do many things. Now one works for the railroad and earns cash with which to provide for his family. A woman buys her pots and pans in town, then weaves a fine basket to sell.

Thus in the old days prestige was not sought through the craft arts. To be sure, slovenly work did not produce the best and most usable basket, consequently the Hopi had good reason to criticize the poor craftsman — and did. Too, the prevalence of a democratic feeling throughout their society was a leveler which did not contend with prestige-seeking. Other factors were significant too; for example, the Pima girl was not considered marriageable until she could produce a good basket.

Primitive artists are no less aware of tradition and style than the civilized artist, although they do not verbalize on these points. This has been illustrated in the outstanding quality and style of the Apache basket. But the unity of a tribal style (Hopi pottery decoration), or the distinctive art of a given village (Acoma pottery) or part of a tribe (Hopi Second Mesa coiled basket) may be lost with the transfer from art-for-the-Indian to art-for-the-white man (similarities of San Ildefonso, Santa Clara, and San Juan polished wares). The decrease in size of pottery jars and bowls and of baskets is related to this same problem, for in growing smaller, the pieces have lost their distinctions of form. Originally, perhaps, the Indian expressed these ideal forms, these traditional styles as part of his tribal consciousness. Or, perhaps, the attainment was unconscious. It is not in technical specialities alone, nor in form, nor even in design, but in the whole product that the tribal style finds its fullest expression.

Individual production in the Southwest Indian craft arts has been and is the rule. Bench methods practiced by the Zuñi silversmith, where an entire family may be involved in production, represent a recent, white-inspired trend. Limited cooperative production is found, as in some cases where the woman makes the clay pot and the man decorates it — for example, in the Rio Grande pueblos of San Ildefonso and Santa Clara. Communal activity is practiced in some ceremonial situations, but even here each man will decorate his own mask for that same ritual. Native communal art activity is unknown.

Many whites are under the misimpression that all Indians are artists. Certainly most if not all of the women of the village had to make and decorate pottery, and many more, percentage-wise, were capable along these lines than is true in civilized groups. But there was and is individual capability, there was and is individual creativity. The individual produces within his traditional background, often guided by a deep and profound conservatism (pueblo). Yet the greatest artistry within these bonds reflects imagination and the creative, as seen in the silver of the Navajo, Tom Burnsides, or the pottery of María. The artist is not merely a better technician; he is a better *artist* who draws on his tradition with critical discrimination.

There is much variation in all hand crafts, Indian or otherwise. How the native Southwesterner has avoided duplication in the centuries of his production is one of the wonders of his craft activity. There was no out-and-out duplication until the white man asked for two identical bracelets or pieces of pottery. The same elements and units may be repeated over and again, duplicating symmetry may characterize a style, or a limited number of themes may be used by a tribe, but machine duplication is lacking.

Degree and quality of artistry vary from tribe to tribe. A simple style featuring lines and dots characterizes Yuma-Mohave painted decoration. At the other extreme are the creative abstractions so effectively placed in relation to form and space by the Hopi potter.

There is a wide range of art motifs in the Southwest as a whole, but some tribes use only a limited number of them while others employ the whole panoply of design. Many basic elements are the same but they are combined in entirely different ways, thereby creating tribal styles. It may well be repeated that Douglas maintained that the stepped motif was basic to all the Southwest; certainly it is prominent both prehistorically and in historic times. But the range in design is great, from this simple step pattern and other geometric elements to highly conventional patterns and even fully realistic themes.

Formalism characterizes much Southwest Indian art. Some authorities maintain that this trait is typical of agricultural societies. It is to be seen in the radial symmetry of the Hopi wicker basket, in the balanced symmetry of the Pima basket, in the rhythmic repetition of the Navajo bowguard pattern, in the alternating symmetry of Hopi jar-shoulder designs. This formalism may well have grown out of technology-controlled designs of basket and textile weaving, but the Indian carried it far beyond a purely technical quality. He combined color and form in design with variety to reach high peaks in formalism. Many Southwest Indian craftsmen became experts in their feeling for and handling of line and color.

The essentially decorative nature of Indian art contributes heavily to its formal style. The shape of the object not only limits the artist to how much is to be painted or otherwise decorated, but also it may divide the total area into discrete units which invite formal expression within them.

Artistry is often expressed in the shape of the object produced by the craftsman, without bene-

fit of any further "decoration." The exquisite lines of an undecorated María pot are as expressive of the artistic instinct as any painted design. The fine relationship between the low and broad neck and the full, bulbous body of a Santa Clara storage jar bespeak an artistic sensitivity in its maker.

The arts described in this book are the secular forms used in everyday life. It is true that they often express a vitality, a spontaneity and freshness not possible in the more conservative and more rigid sacred arts. Navajo sandpaintings show no designs borrowed from white men, yet the rugs and certainly the silver of the same tribe are replete with white-inspired artistic elements.

Southwest Indian secular arts are not symbolic. Sometimes the same design element or motif may be found in sacred and secular context; in the former, it is symbolic, in the latter it is not, for here it is a design and no more. A yei pattern in a rug is a design, while in a sandpainting it is a sacred symbol of the gods or of the intermediaries between man and the gods. The Hopi kachina dancer is sacred, the kachina doll is not. There is a wide gap between the "story" told by an obliging Indian for the benefit of a gullible white man, or a "sales pitch" story of a trader and the design which is receiving all this attention. Craft arts are not arts of magic, as are primitive religious arts in many instances. Interaction between various aspects of life of the natives may lead to the use of craft pieces in ceremonies, such as an Apache basket which holds pollen in a puberty rite; this does not make the basket nor its designs sacred. Some tribes express a distinct dichotomy in sacred and secular designs, such as the Zuñi who will not use the dragon fly, tadpole, snake, and certain other designs on cooking and eating bowls. These themes are reserved for use on sacred "cloud" bowls or fetish jars.

Southwest Indian craftsmen have a sense of esthetic appreciation. Surely this is reflected in the preservation of the splendid "saddle blanket" weaves of the Navajo for the object he uses and not for the one he sells. The fact that a Papago woman will not use a yucca basket to replace the superior willow style is reflective of the same. The Indian did not live by art alone, but he did not neglect the opportunity to make those objects he used more esthetically appealing. Decoration did not improve utility value, but it satisfied a feeling almost as old as man himself.

Contrary to some opinions relative to primitives, the Southwest Indian not only appreciates but evaluates his art accomplishment. The criticism by Hopi women of poor work is an example of this feeling; so too is the excited chatter of a cluster of women gathered about the superior craft piece made by a tribal sister. Verbalization on a critical esthetic level about such matters in response to a white man's query may be difficult for the Indian, but he can and does express appreciation. His craft pieces are silent but often vivid expressions of his appreciation of beauty.

No one factor is all-important in the development of Southwest Indian craft arts. Historical incident, a strong traditional inheritance, influences from many who crossed their paths — these are but a few of the significant directing factors. So too are the thorough exploitation of their environment, the changing economy, the changing political, religious, and social life of these people. And above all else, the craft art of the Indian is changing, changing each day. World War II seems to have set the stage for a drama of accelerated motion which may lead to the final acculturation of the Indians of the Southwest.

Divested of his traditional background, his crafts will no longer be traditional as viewed at the present moment. Will they emerge into the realm of the pure arts, the fine arts? Will the new form be more white or more Indian? As long as there are *tribes* with a modicum of native blood and traditional culture there will be Indian craft arts.

Chapter Notes

Chapter II

1. Jennings 1957: 285.
2. Morris and Burgh 1941: 22-23.
3. Underhill 1959: 22.
4. Ellis and Walpole 1959: 183.
5. Underhill 1959: 22.
6. Douglas 1940d: 199.
7. Kissell 1916: 138.
8. Shreve 1943: 43.
9. *Ibid*: 44.
10. Colton, M. R. 1951a: 13.
11. Mason 1904: 505.
12. Euler Conference: 3-30-63.
13. *Ibid*.
14. *Ibid*.
15. Lindquist ms. 1962.
16. Euler Conference: 3-30-63.
17. Roberts 1931: 137.
18. *Ibid*: 150.
19. *Ibid*: 146.
20. *Ibid*: 130.
21. Opler 1941: 381.
22. Underhill 1959: 20.
23. Colton, M. R. 1951a: 14.
24. Underhill 1959: 24.
25. Lindquist ms. 1962: 9-10.
26. Douglas 1939b: 152.
27. *Ibid*.
28. *Ibid*.
29. Mason 1904: 231 and Plate 17.
30. Spier 1933: 122-23.
31. *Ibid*.
32. Jeançon and Douglas 1931b.
33. Ellis Conference: 4-27-63.
34. Hester 1961: 194.
35. Adams Conference: 2-17-55.
36. *Ibid*.
37. Tschopik 1940: 444.
38. Cumming Correspondence: 5-28-63.
39. *Ibid*: 5-15-63.
40. Roberts 1931: Figure 18.
41. Kissell 1916: 197.
42. Estrada Conference: 2-1-63.
43. Kissell 1916: 244.
44. Shreve 1943: 6 ff.
45. Kissell 1916: illus. p. 196.
46. Shreve 1943: 59.
47. Mason 1904: 503.
48. *Ibid*: Plate 214, 3, bottom row.
49. Ellis and Walpole 1959: Figs. 1 and 2.
50. *Ibid*: 187-88.
51. Danson Conference: 2-23-63.

Chapter III

1. Amsden 1932: 217.
2. Kidder 1926: 623.
3. Jennings 1957: 277-78.
4. Danson Conference: 2-23-63.
5. Martin, *et al.*, 1952: 207, Fig. 74.
6. Smith 1952: Figs. 24 and 25.
7. Kent 1957: 652.
8. Douglas 1939c: 158.
9. *Ibid*: 159.

10. *Ibid* 1939d: 162.
11. *Ibid*: 163.
12. *Ibid*.
13. *Ibid*. 1939b: illus. p. 153.
14. Parsons 1932: 212.
15. Douglas 1940c: 183.
16. Rummage Correspondence: 4-13-63.
17. Douglas 1940c: 183-84.
18. *Ibid*: 184-85.
19. *Ibid*: 185.
20. Jeançon and Douglas 1931a.
21. Danson Conference: 2-23-63.
22. Kent 1957: 469.
23. Colton, M. R. 1951a: 18.
24. Douglas 1940b: 176.
25. Spier 1955: 6.
26. *Ibid*.
27. Spier 1933: 111.
28. *Ibid*: 115.
29. Amsden 1934: 141-142.
30. Young 1940.
31. Amsden 1934: 63.
32. Kent 1957: 650.
33. *Ibid* 1961: 6.
34. Mera 1949: 76-95.
35. Amsden 1934: Plates 60 and 61.
36. *Ibid*: 140.
37. Mera [1947]: 2.
38. *Ibid*.
39. Dutton 1961: 4.
40. Young 1940.
41. Kent 1961: 9.
42. Mera [1947]: 95-96.
43. *Ibid*: Plate 94.
44. Franciscan Fathers 1910: 244.
45. Kent 1961: 10.
46. Amsden 1934: 179-80.
47. Mera [1947]: 25.
48. Amsden 1934: 89.
49. *Ibid*: Plate 45.
50. Kent 1961: 17.
51. *Ibid*: 23.
52. Mera [1947]: 51, Plate 48.
53. Amsden 1934: Plate 111.
54. Mera [1947]: 29, Plate 27.
55. *Ibid*: 30, Plate 29.
56. Amsden 1934: 195.
57. James 1937: Figs. 203, 217, 228-234.
58. Mera [1947]: 82.
59. Amsden 1934: 194.
60. *Ibid*: 196.
61. Mera [1947]: 87.
62. Dutton 1961: 15.
63. James 1937: Figs. 200, 201, 202.
64. Dutton 1961: 37.
65. Moore 1911: Plate XXVIII.
66. *Ibid*: 21.

Chapter IV

1. Gladwin and others, 1937.
2. Martin 1959: 80.
3. Wormington 1956: 52.
4. Amsden 1936: 44.
5. Danson Conference: 2-23-63.

6. New Mexico Department of Vocational Education 1943: illus. 23-27, 33.
7. Ellis Conference: 4-27-63.
8. Chapman Correspondence: 4-21-54.
9. *Ibid.*
10. Dutton 1963: 91.
11. Marriott 1948.
12. *Ibid*: 217-218.
13. New Mexico Department of Vocation Education 1943.
14. Gunnerson 1959: 150-52.
15. Guthe 1925: 22.
16. Ellis Conference: 4-27-63.
17. *Ibid.*
18. Breazeale 1923: 16-17.
19. Jeançon and Douglas 1930b.
20. Fontana and others, 1962: 46.

Chapter V

1. Woodward 1947: 25.
2. Tanner 1950: 117-133.
3. *Ibid.*
4. Matthews 1897.
5. Kidder 1932: 305-308.
6. Adair 1944: 3-5.
7. *Ibid*: 124.
8. *Ibid*: 15.
9. *Ibid*: 14.
10. *Ibid*: 9.
11. Mera 1959: iv.
12. Adair 1944: 29-30; Woodward 1938: 19-20.
13. Adair 1944: 32.
14. Woodward 1938: 35.
15. Adair 1944: 41-42.
16. Woodward 1938: 36.
17. Mera 1959: 66.
18. Adair 1944: 33.
19. Mera 1959: 90.
20. Adair 1944: 48.
21. Woodward 1938: 30-31.
22. Adair 1944: 41.
23. Woodward 1938: 38.
24. Adair 1944: 51.
25. *Ibid*: 7.
26. *Ibid*: 12.

27. *Ibid*: 202.
28. *Ibid*: 122.
29. *Ibid*: 134.
30. Neuman Conference: 2-10-63.
31. Kirk 1945: 43.
32. Adair 1944: 173.
33. Colton, M. R. 1951: 32.
34. Adair 1944: 176.
35. Kabotie Mimeo sheet 1950: no page.
36. Adair 1944: 178-194.
37. Ellis Conference: 4-27-63.

Chapter VI

1. Haury 1945: 200.
2. *Ibid.*
3. Smith 1952.
4. *Ibid*: 296.
5. Tanner 1957: f. p. 8.
6. Dockstader 1954: 98.
7. *Ibid*: 10.
8. *Ibid*: 101.
9. Fewkes 1903: 3-127.
10. Colton, H. S. 1949: 6.
11. Wright and Roat 1962: 3.
12. Harvey 1963: 4.
13. Hewitt 1943: 4.
14. Dumarest 1919: 141.
15. Lange 1959: 296.
16. Harvey 1963: 5.
17. *Ibid*: 8.

Chapter VII

1. Underhill 1959: 127.
2. Adams Conference: 2-27-55.
3. Densmore 1929: 3.
4. Underhill 1959: 128.
5. Purchase Conference: 7-6-63.
6. Underhill 1959: 117.
7. *Ibid*: 118.
8. Purchase Conference: 7-6-63.
9. Wayland 1961: 7.
10. *Ibid.*
11. *Ibid.*

Bibliography

ADAIR, JOHN
  1944 *The Navajo and Pueblo Silversmiths.* University of Oklahoma Press, Norman, Oklahoma.

AMSDEN, CHARLES AVERY
  1932 "The Loom and Its Prototypes," *American Anthropologist,* Vol. 34, No. 2, N.S. April, June.

  1934 *Navaho Weaving: Its Technic and History.* The Fine Arts Press, Santa Ana, California.

  1936 *An Analysis of Hohokam Pottery Design.* Medallion Papers, No. XXIII, Gila Pueblo, Globe, Arizona.

BREAZEALE, J. F.
  1923 *The Pima and his Basket.* Arizona Archaeological and Historical Society, Tucson.

BUNZEL, RUTH LEAH
  1929 *The Pueblo Potter.* Columbia University Contributions to Anthropology, v. VIII, Columbia University Press, New York.

CHAPMAN, KENNETH MILTON
  1936 *The Pottery of Santo Domingo Pueblo.* Laboratory of Anthropology, Memoirs, v. I, Santa Fe, New Mexico.

COLTON, HAROLD S.
  1949 *Hopi Kachina Dolls.* The University of New Mexico Press, Albuquerque, New Mexico.

COLTON, MARY-RUSSELL F.
  1951a "Arts and Crafts of the Hopi Indians," in *Hopi Indian Arts and Crafts.* Museum of Northern Arizona Reprint Series No. 3, Northern Arizona Society of Science and Art, Flagstaff.

  1951b "Hopi Silversmithing: Its Background and Future," in *Hopi Indian Arts and Crafts.* Museum of Northern Arizona, Reprint Series No. 3, Northern Arizona Society of Science and Art, Flagstaff.

DENSMORE, FRANCES
  1929 *Papago Music.* Bureau of American Ethnology, Bulletin No. 90, Government Printing Office, Washington, D.C.

DOCKSTADER, FREDERICK J.
  1954 *The Kachina and the White Man.* Cranbrook Institute of Science, Bulletin No. 35, Bloomfield Hills, Michigan.

DOUGLAS, F. H.
  1931 *Santa Clara and San Juan Pottery.* Denver Art Museum, Department of Indian Art, Leaflet 35, Denver, Colorado.

  1939a *Types of Southwestern Coiled Basketry.* Denver Art Museum, Department of Indian Art, Leaflet 88, Denver, Colorado.

  1939b *Acoma Pueblo Weaving and Embroidery.* Denver Art Museum, Department of Indian Art, Leaflet 89, Denver, Colorado.

  1939c *Weaving in the Tewa Pueblos.* Denver Art Museum, Department of Indian Art, Leaflet 90, Denver, Colorado.

  1939d *Weaving of the Keres Pueblos. Weaving of the Tiwa Pueblos and Jemez.* Denver Art Museum, Department of Indian Art, Leaflet 91, Denver, Colorado.

  1940a *Main Types of Pueblo Cotton Textiles.* Denver Art Museum, Department of Indian Art, Leaflets 92-93, Denver, Colorado.

  1940b *Main Types of Pueblo Woolen Textiles.* Denver Art Museum, Department of Indian Art, Leaflets 94-95, Denver, Colorado.

  1940c *Weaving at Zuñi Pueblo.* Denver Art Museum, Department of Indian Art, Leaflets 96-97, Denver, Colorado.

  1940d *Southwestern Twined, Wicker and Plaited Basketry.* Denver Art Museum, Department of Indian Art, Leaflets 99-100. Denver, Colorado.

DUMAREST, FATHER NOEL
  1919 *Notes on Cochití, New Mexico.* Memoirs VI, American Anthropological Association.

DUTTON, BERTHA
  1961 *Navajo Weaving Today.* The Museum of New Mexico Press, Santa Fe, New Mexico.

  1963 *Indians of the Southwest.* Southwestern Association on Indian Affairs, Inc., Santa Fe, New Mexico.

ELLIS, FLORENCE H. AND MARY WALPOLE
  1959 "Possible Pueblo, Navajo, and Jicarilla Basketry Relationships," *El Palacio,* Vol. 66, No. 6.

FEWKES, JESSE WALTER
  1903 "Hopi Katcinas," Bureau of American Ethnology, *21st Annual Report,* U. S. Government Printing Office, Washington, D. C.

FONTANA, BERNARD L., AND OTHERS
1962 *Papago Indian Pottery.* The American Ethnological Society, University of Washington Press, Seattle.

FRANCISCAN FATHERS
1910 *Ethnologic Dictionary of the Navajo Language.* St. Michaels, Arizona.

GLADWIN, HAROLD S., AND OTHERS
1937 *Excavations at Snaketown: Material Culture.* Medallion Papers, No. XXV, Gila Pueblo, Globe, Arizona.

GUNNERSON, JAMES H.
1959 "Archaeological Survey in Northeastern New Mexico," *El Palacio,* Vol. 66, No. 5.

GUTHE, CARL E.
1925 *Pueblo Pottery Making.* Phillips Academy, Department of Archaeology, Papers of the Southwestern Expedition, No. 2, Yale University Press, New Haven.

HARVEY, BYRON III
1963 "New Mexican Kachina Dolls," *The Masterkey,* Vol. 37, No. 1.

HAURY, EMIL W.
1945 *The Excavation of Los Muertos and Neighboring Ruins in the Salt River Valley, Southern Arizona.* Papers of the Peabody Museum of American Archaeology and Ethnology, v. XXIV, No. 1, Peabody Museum, Cambridge, Massachusetts.

HESTER, JAMES J.
1961 *Early Navajo Migrations and Acculturation in the Southwest.* Unpublished Ph.D. dissertation, University of Arizona, Tucson.

HEWITT, CHARLES H.
1943 "The Kachina Cult of the Pueblo Indians," *The Kiva,* Arizona Archaeological and Historical Society, Vol. 9, No. 1, Arizona State Museum, University of Arizona, Tucson.

JAMES, GEORGE WHARTON
1937 *Indian Blankets and Their Makers.* Tudor Publishing Company, New York.

JEANÇON, JEAN ALLARD AND F. H. DOUGLAS
1930a *Pueblo Indian Pottery Making.* Denver Art Museum, Department of Indian Art, Leaflet 6, Denver, Colorado.

1930b *The Ute Indians.* Denver Art Museum, Department of Indian Art, Leaflet 10, Denver, Colorado.

1931a *Hopi Indian Weaving.* Denver Art Museum, Department of Indian Art, Leaflet 18, Denver, Colorado.

1931b *The Navaho Indians.* Denver Art Museum, Department of Indian Art, Leaflet 21, Denver, Colorado.

1933 *Navaho Spinning, Dyeing and Weaving.* Denver Art Museum, Department of Indian Art, Leaflet 3 (2nd Edition), Denver, Colorado.

JENNINGS, JESSE D.
1957 *Danger Cave.* Memoirs of the Society for American Archaeology, Vol. XXIII, No. 2, Part 2.

KABOTIE, FRED
1950 (No Title. On Hopi Silver). Mimeo sheet, Oraibi, Arizona.

KENT, KATE PECK
1957 *The Cultivation and Weaving of Cotton in the Prehistoric Southwestern United States.* Transactions of the American Philosophical Society, New Series, Vol. 47, Part 3, Philadelphia, Pennsylvania.

1961 *The Story of Navaho Weaving.* The Heard Museum of Anthropology and Primitive Arts, Phoenix, Arizona.

KIDDER, A. V.
1926 "A Sandal from Northeastern Arizona," *American Anthropologist,* N.S., Vol. 28, No. 4.

1932 *Artifacts of Pecos.* Yale University Press, New Haven, Conn.

KIRK, RUTH FALKENBERG
1945 "Southwestern Indian Jewelry," *El Palacio,* Vol. LII, Nos. 2 and 3.

KISSELL, MARY LOIS
1916 *Basketry of The Papago and Pima.* Anthropological Papers of The American Museum of Natural History. Vol. XVII, Part I, New York.

LANGE, CHARLES H.
1959 *Cochití: A New Mexico Pueblo, Past and Present.* University of Texas Press, Austin, Texas.

LINDQUIST, FREDERICK
1962 *Havasupai Basketry.* Unpublished manuscript.

MARRIOTT, ALICE
1948 *María: The Potter of San Ildefonso.* University of Oklahoma Press, Norman, Oklahoma.

MARTIN, PAUL S.
1959 *Digging Into History.* Popular Series, Anthropology No. 38, Chicago Natural History Museum.

MARTIN, PAUL S. et al.
1952 *Mogollon Cultural Continuity and Change: The Stratigraphic Analysis of Tularosa and Cordova Caves.* Fieldiana, Anthropology Vol. 40. Chicago Natural History Museum.

MASON, OTIS TUFTON
1904 "Aboriginal American Basketry: Studies in a Textile Art Without Machinery," Smithsonian Institution, *Annual Report,* 1902, Part 2, Washington, D.C.

MATTHEWS, WASHINGTON
1897 *Navaho Legends.* Published for American Folklore Society, Houghton, Mifflin & Co., New York.

MAXWELL, GILBERT S.
1963 *Navajo Rugs: Past, Present and Future.* Desert-Southwest Publications, Palm Desert, California.

MERA, H. P.
1939 *Style Trends of Pueblo Pottery in the Rio Grande and Little Colorado Cultural Areas from the 16th to the 19th Century.* Memoirs of the Laboratory of Anthropology, Vol. III, Santa Fe, New Mexico.

[1947] *Navajo Textile Arts.* Laboratory of Anthropology, Santa Fe, New Mexico.

1949 *The Alfred I. Barton Collection of Southwestern Textiles.* San Vicente Foundation, Inc., Santa Fe, New Mexico.

1959 *Indian Silverwork of the Southwest Illustrated.* Vol. 1, Dale Stuart King, Globe, Arizona.

MOORE, J. B.
1911 *The Navajo.* Williamson-Haffner Company, Denver, Colorado.

MORRIS, EARL H. AND ROBERT F. BURGH
1941 *Anasazi Basketry: Basket Maker II through Pueblo III . . . A Study Based on Specimens from the San Juan River Country.* Carnegie Institute of Washington, Publication No. 533, Washington, D.C.

NEW MEXICO DEPT. OF VOCATIONAL EDUCATION.
(Carmen Espinosa, foreword).
1943 *New Mexico Colonial Embroidery.* Santa Fe, New Mexico.

OPLER, MORRIS EDWARD
1941 *An Apache Life Way.* University of Chicago Press, Chicago, Illinois.

PARSONS, ELSIE CLEWS
1932 "Isleta, New Mexico," Bureau of American Ethnology, *47th Annual Report,* U. S. Government Printing Office, Washington, D.C.

ROBERTS, HELEN H.
1931 *The Basketry of the San Carlos Apache.* American Museum of Natural History, Anthropological Papers, Vol. XXXI, New York.

SHREVE, MARGARET B.
1943 *Modern Papago Basketry.* Unpublished M.A. thesis, University of Arizona, Tucson.

SMITH, WATSON
1952 *Kiva Mural Decoration at Awatovi and Kawaika-a.* Papers of the Peabody Museum of American Archaeology and Ethnology. Reports of the Awatovi Expedition, Report 5, Vol. XXXVII, Harvard University, Cambridge, Massachusetts.

SPIER, LESLIE
1933 *Yuman Tribes of the Gila River.* The University of Chicago Press, Chicago, Illinois.

1955 *Mohave Culture Items.* Museum of Northern Arizona, Bulletin 28, Northern Arizona Society of Science and Art, Inc., Flagstaff.

TANNER, CLARA LEE
1950 "Coral Among Southwestern Indians," in *For the Dean.* Hohokam Museums Association, Tucson, and Southwestern Monuments Association, Santa Fe, New Mexico.

1957 *Southwest Indian Painting.* The University of Arizona Press and Arizona Silhouettes, Tucson.

TSCHOPIK, HARRY JR.
1940 "Navaho Basketry: A Study of Cultural Change," *American Anthropologist,* Vol. 42, No. 3, Part 1.

UNDERHILL, RUTH
1959 *Pueblo Crafts.* U.S. Department of the Interior, Bureau of Indian Affairs, Branch of Education, Washington, D.C.

WAYLAND, VIRGINIA
1961 "Apache Playing Cards," *The Masterkey,* Vol. XXXV, No. 3.

WOODWARD, ARTHUR
1938 *A Brief History of Navajo Silversmithing.* Museum of Northern Arizona, Bulletin No. 14, Northern Arizona Society of Science and Art, Flagstaff.

1947 "Notes on Coral in the Southwest," *The Masterkey*, Vol. XVI, No. 1.

WORMINGTON, H. M.
1956 *Prehistoric Indians of the Southwest.* Denver Museum of Natural History, Popular Series No. 7, 3rd Edition, Denver, Colorado.

WRIGHT, BARTON AND EVELYN ROAT
1962 *This is a Hopi Kachina.* Museum of Northern Arizona, Northern Arizona Society of Science and Art, Inc., Flagstaff.

YOUNG, STELLA (Comp.)
1940 *Navajo Native Dyes: Their Preparation and Use.* Education Division, U.S. Office of Indian Affairs, Indian Handcrafts, 2, Chilocco, Oklahoma.

Conferences

Adams, W. Y. 2-17-55, 2-27-55, Tucson, Arizona.
Danson, Edward B. 2-23-63, Flagstaff, Arizona.
Ellis, Florence H. 4-27-63, Santa Fe, New Mexico.
Estrada, Elizabeth 1-30-63, 2-1-63, 3-11-63, 3-15-63, Tucson, Arizona.
Euler, Robert 3-30-63, Tucson, Arizona.
Neuman, David 2-10-63, Tucson, Arizona.
Purchase, Albert 7-6-63, Tucson, Arizona.

Correspondence

Chapman, Kenneth 4-21-54.
Cumming, Dorothy 5-15-63 and 5-28-63.
Rummage, Mahala 4-13-63.

Index